FINNEGANS WAKE: A PLOT SUMMARY

Irish Studies

IRISH STUDIES

Irish Studies presents a wide range of books interpreting important aspects of Irish life and culture to scholarly and general audiences. The richness and complexity of the Irish experience, past and present, deserves broad understanding and careful analysis. For this reason an important purpose of the series is to offer a forum to scholars interested in Ireland, its history, and culture. Irish literature is a special concern in the series, but works from the perspectives of the fine arts, history, and the social sciences are also welcome, as are studies which take multidisciplinary approaches.

Irish Studies is a continuing project of Syracuse University Press and is under the general editorship of Richard Fallis, associate professor of English at Syracuse University.

John Gordon

Finnegans Wake: a plot summary

Syracuse University Press

For my mother

Contents

Acknowledgments

Author and publisher would like to thank the following for their permission to quote copyright material from the works of James Joyce:

The Society of Authors as the literary representative of The Estate of James Joyce, and Jonathan Cape, London for extracts from *Dubliners* and *A Portrait of the Artist as a Young Man*; Faber and Faber, London for extracts from *Finnegans Wake, Letters of James Joyce*, vol. I, edited by Stuart Gilbert, vols. II and III in the same series, both edited by Richard Ellmann, and from *The Selected Letters of James Joyce*, edited by Richard Ellmann, 1975; for extracts from *Ulysses*, reprinted by permission of The Bodley Head Ltd; Oxford University Press for extracts from *James Joyce* by Richard Ellmann, 1982.

From *Dubliners* by James Joyce. Copyright 1916 by B. W. Heubsch. Definitive text copyright © 1967 by The Estate of James Joyce. Reprinted by permission of Viking Penguin, Inc. From *A Portrait of the Artist as a Young Man*, by James Joyce. Copyright 1916 by B. W. Heubsch. Copyright renewed 1944 by Nora Joyce. Definitive text copyright © 1964 by The Estate of James Joyce. Reprinted by permission of Viking Penguin, Inc. From *Finnegans Wake* by James Joyce. Copyright 1939 by James Joyce. Copyright © renewed 1967 by George Joyce and Lucia Joyce. Reprinted by permission of Viking Penguin, Inc. From *Ulysses* by James Joyce, reprinted by permission of Random House, Inc., copyright © 1945. From *Selected Letters of James Joyce*, edited by Richard Ellmann. Copyright © 1975 by the Viking Press, Inc. Copyright © 1975 by F. Lionel Monro, as administrator of The Estate of James Joyce. Reprinted by permission of

Viking Penguin, Inc. 1966. From *Letters of James Joyce*, vol. I, edited by Stuart Gilbert. Copyright © 1957 by The Viking Press, Inc. From *Letters of James Joyce*, vols. II and III, edited by Richard Ellmann. Copyright © 1966 by F. Lionel Monro, as administrator of the Estate of James Joyce. Reprinted by permission of Viking Penguin, Inc. From *Notes on Issy* by John Gordon in A Wake Newslitter Press, 1982.

Lastly, our thanks to George Ulrich for the illustration on p. 33.

'Mimesis'

THIS BOOK aspires to the 'thoroughly reductive' account of *Finnegans Wake* that I wished for in an earlier work, *James Joyce's Metamorphoses*. Its purpose is to recount the events of Joyce's book in their order of occurrence, and to describe as accurately as possible the place and the people involved in the action. I work from the hypothesis that the Joyce of *Finnegans Wake* had not turned his back on the aggressive realism of the earlier books, that in his fashion the author who was reassured by the thought that his 'Anna Livia Plurabelle' chapter really *sounded* like a river (he walked down to the Seine to check out this particular correspondence of fact and artifact[1]) was of a piece with the young man who insisted that the characters of *Dubliners* be allowed to sound like real Dubliners. I can find little evidence in Joyce's letters or recorded remarks for the about-face in aesthetic principles that the opposite hypothesis assumes, much to confirm my own uniformitarian view. 'He has reduced the veil between literature and life, which is what every writer tries to do':[2] so Joyce in praise of Hemingway, not in 1905 but in 1923, already at work on *Work in Progress*.

From beginning to end, Joyce remained a mimic in the root sense of the word. What changed, and deepened, between 1905 and the years that produced *Finnegans Wake* was not his mimetic intention but his understanding of the world he wished to render and the resourcefulness which he brought to the task. In particular he became, over these years, increasingly conscious of the paradox at the heart of the mimetic enterprise — that since the objective world must be represented, as it is experienced, through the prism of some individual consciousness, the artist seeking fidelity to fact must represent both simultaneously, must turn inward as well as outward. The quest for objectivity becomes the study of subjectivity, or rather the study of how the two interact. The author listening to the Seine must also attend to himself, listening, and indeed 'Anna Livia Plurabelle' is a *tour de force* not only for its rivering cadences but also for the voices of the women hearing it, making of it a symbol for their old lives, mingling their memories with its reality — and we can hear, if *we* listen, the purblind, ageing author doing the same thing, listening to a river in exile and remembering the river of his homeland: "Tis endless now senne eye or erewone last saw Waterhouse's clogh. They took it asunder, I hurd them sigh. When will they reassemble it?' (213.15-17).* The acutely sensitive presence of the earlier work becomes 'reminiscensitive' (230.26).

So in tracing the events and characters of the *Wake*, even its furniture, we will be tracing as well what the mind in question makes of them. This book about people and things is also necessarily about the manufacture of symbols. Now, there are many who feel that the last thing the world needs is another book about Joyce's symbols, and I understand their feeling. It is hard not to sympathise with the irritation of Clive Hart when he says, 'Our lives are full of fucking symbols: we don't need them in our reading matter as well.'[3] The natural reaction — exemplified in Joyce studies by Robert M. Adams and, before him, by Joyce's brother Stanislaus — is to echo Freud and insist that sometimes a cigar is just a cigar.

Well, yes and no. That a cigar is not necessarily a phallic symbol I agree. But which cigar are we talking about? I don't smoke, so if I had one on my desk here it would represent something unusual — probably the person who gave it to me, let us say to commemorate a recent birth. Behind that gesture would lie a slightly archaic custom towards which any American male of my generation is liable to feel ambivalent, and which I for one associate with movies of the 1930s and comic strips popular in the same period, movies and comic

---

*All such numbers in parentheses refer to the Faber: Viking Press edition of *Finnegans Wake* (paperback). Numbers before the point refer to page, numbers after the point to line. A Roman numeral and Arabic numeral separated by a diagonal (e.g. I/1) indicate book and chapter number, respectively.

strips in which beaming males wearing vests and spats, released from the waiting room in which their pacing has worn a circular rut, present one another with blimp-shaped 'stogies' while slapping one another on the back and announcing 'It's A Boy!' (Joyce saw the same cartoons. See 53.21-26.) Or it could be a cigar being smoked by a friend, either male (symbolising various things about him), or female, (symbolising various things about her plus, I suppose, liberation), or even child (symbolising stunted growth, etc). The cigar in the best-known picture of Freud symbolises, for me, cancer, needless suffering, and a pathetic infirmity in a great man who knew better.

That is the world of which *Finnegans Wake* is made, a world not of 'cigars' but of this cigar or that cigar. The objects surrounding its characters turn into symbols because that is what the objects we live with do. Man, said Aristotle, is the symbol-making animal, and *Finnegans Wake* is in that sense man-like: it is a vast symbol-making conjurer, replicating more faithfully than anything else ever written the process by which each individual generates, as opposed to receives, the meanings around him.[4] Generates, not receives: that, it seems to me, is the distinction behind Joyce's objection to Freud — that he was not so much wrong as simplistic, fixedly translating certain things into certain other 'symbolic' things: house into womb, fire into phallus.[5]

Being creatures of characters imagined by a man who was exceptionally sensitive to verbal and especially etymological nuance, a man who once made a point of hanging a picture of Cork in a cork frame, the symbols formed may have more to do with word-associations than we would normally expect: it matters, for instance, that the 'Argentine' in the sleeper's room is phonically close to both a kind of silvery fish and a South American country. In general, words are taken more literally than we're used to: it helps to be the kind of person who instinctively cringes on hearing an expression like 'pay through the nose' or 'peel your eyes'. But the essential process is identical to that discoverable by anyone who will look around and look within. All places we inhabit become middens of symbols. That is the reason that a book whose events virtually all occur in one room can be an autobiography and, because the life recounted has been lived in the world outside, over many days each 'dense as a decade' (292.26), a (highly eccentric) universal history. In fact the history evoked can be dauntingly far-ranging and esoteric, because Joycean characters since *Ulysses* are permitted at times to plug into the intellectual resources of their erudite author. Leopold Bloom conjures up the hallucination of a figure, Virag, who gives utterance to his preoccupation with morbid sexual arcana through allusions unfamiliar to Bloom himself; the male principal of *Finnegans Wake*, reminded of Waterloo, refers readily to military *minutiae* beyond his ken.

That modification understood, the essential dramatic premise of the *Wake* is a familiar one in the annals of dream literature and its analogues in other arts. It is the premise of, for instance, Ravel's '*L'enfant et les sortilèges*', of the various 'Transformation Scene' effects in Buñuel and Dali's '*L'âge d'or*' or Fritz Lang's *Metropolis*, of similar effects in children's classics such as Disney's *Dumbo* or Maurice Sendak's *Where the Wild Things are*: under the influence of night or intoxication or imagination, familiar figures change into symbols generated from the interaction of their physical selves, the memories and conventions connected with them, and the state of the observer. The process is always to a certain extent one of projection, as in these two *Rashomon*-like set-pieces recording different characters' perceptions of, first, a stick with some sort of protuberance at one end, second the plink-plunking of water drops:

> Batty believes a baton while Hogan hears a hod yet Heer prefers a punsil shapner and Cope and Bull go cup and ball. (98.29-31)

> The rushes by the grey nuns' pond: ah eh oh let me sigh too. Coalmansbell: behoves you handmake of the load. Jenny Wren: pick, peck. Johnny Post: pack, puck. (278. 09-13)

Most Wakean mutations are more elaborate than these examples because of their capacity for coming to life, for taking command of the text and making its story their story. The phenomenon itself begins as a familiar one in literature, essentially identical in origin with the common practice —

variously called *'erlebte Rede'*, *'le style indirect libre'*, or
'narrated monologue'[6] — of letting a given character's idiom
either take over or influence the narrator's style for as long
as that character is the centre of attention. In Joyce's work
this practice is often compounded by characters who are
themselves, as it were, readers, their idioms infected by something recently read or heard. Here is a double-barrelled, and
quite Joycean, example from Max Beerbohm's *Zuleika
Dobson:*

> But, just as he set pen to paper, his hand faltered, and he
> sprang up, victim of another and yet more violent fit of
> sneezing.
>   Dibuskined, dangerous. The spirit of Juvenal woke in
> him. He would flay. He would make Woman (as he called
> Zuleika) writhe.[7] (Compare *Finnegans Wake*, 228.02-12.)

Like Beerbohm's character here, a Wakean figure who contemplates another symbol — a book of Juvenal, a calendar
picture — will simultaneously revive, bring to life, its appropriate voice, and the narrative will record the process.

In the later Joyce particularly, both will go still further.
They will, to a great extent, adopt the story or other set of
conventions associated with that symbol — as if the young
man of Beerbohm's book were for a page or ten to become
Juvenal, and the events of the book thereafter were to be to
some extent determined by the known pattern of Juvenal's
life as well as by the requirements of the original Oxford
fable. The practice is implicit in Joyce's work almost from
the beginning. Florence L. Walzl has pointed out that the
Eveline of *Dubliners* winds up acting out the story of a picture
on her wall,[8] that in effect 'Eveline' turns out to be the story
of that picture, transmuted through Eveline's consciousness.
A more complicated version of the same thing occurs in the
last story of *Dubliners*, 'The Dead'. Early on, Gabriel Conroy
takes in two pictures:

> A picture of the balcony scene in *Romeo and Juliet* hung
> there and beside it was a picture of the two murdered
> princes in the Tower which Aunt Julia had worked in red,
> blue and brown wools when she was a girl (*Dubliners* 186).

It seems an idle enough observation, and yet consider: Gabriel is a professor of literature, attuned to the literary, and especially Shakespearian, ramifications of those pictures. The story of that balcony scene will return to him at the end of this night, when his wife tells him of her farewell to the young star-crossed lover who stood calling to her window from the back garden, under her window. Mingled with it will be the story of those two princes, murdered by Richard III in the play Gabriel knows well, whose ghosts return in the last act of that play to tell their assassin what the imagined ghost of the young Michael Furey tells Gabriel, at the end of *his* story: 'Despair and die!' ('. . . some impalpable and vindictive being was coming against him, gathering forces against him in its vague world'. — *Dubliners* 220) Those two Shakespearian stories have entered into Gabriel through his eyes and memory, and after a spell of subterranean ferment their working-out comes to control his own story — comes in a way to write it, in fact, to determine its events as well as its style: the picture of the 'vindictive' haunter may be laid solely to Gabriel's literary imagination, but who or what has determined that his wife shall tell him her Romeo-and-Juliet story on this night? Who if not a narrator whose account of what is done and said is, in some strange way, conditioned by what occurs to the mind of his central character?

In fact the further along we get in Joyce's work the more it can seem as if the books are being improvised by the characters, the events related the product of fancies generated in the characters' minds by earlier events. There is an early, rudimentary version of the phenomenon in the first chapter of *A Portrait of the Artist as a Young Man*, where Stephen Dedalus reads about heroic Horatio-types in his book of Roman history and is immediately called on to stand fast against Father Dolan, the barbarian from without with his washerwoman's name. By the middle of *Ulysses* it is possible to find entire chapters being generated out of previous chapters by way of the central character's mediating sensibility: Leopold Bloom, for instance, leaves a bunch of men boozily singing an inflammatory patriotic song, 'The Croppy Boy', about a martyr being betrayed and hanged, and walks into a personification of such sentiments in a chapter, 'Cyclops', which is all about hanging and martyrdom, especially his.

By *Finnegans Wake* the improvisation is near-absolute. The character sees or hears things, or remembers or imagines seeing or hearing them, and the patterns and stories evoked in that act come to life and take command, become the patterns and stories of the text. He goes, or imagines going, to a privy containing a picture of a Waterloo battle scene, and the text is given over to rendering a notably faecal account of that battle. He hears, or imagines hearing, his daughter whisper to him from another room, and immediately the forbidden temptress of his desires appears, front and centre, casting everything else into background. To be sure in these as in other cases we cannot easily distinguish what is being imagined from what is being experienced, just as we may have trouble at times distinguishing what Stephen Dedalus is doing and what he is thinking of doing. All the events of *Finnegans Wake* occur in double focus at least: emanations depart from their dreaming original to go about their business, responding to stimuli in the way he would envision himself doing were he awake, and beget other emanations in turn, and so on; as we will see, it is the commonest thing in the Wakean world for a figure to be in two or more places at once. But the very difficulty in separating these multiple projections from one another, in distinguishing what is happening from what is imagined as happening, testifies to the extent to which they behave according to the same rules. All respond to the cues of their environment with improvisations compounded of public and private associations which immediately become the matter of the text. Imagination and experience are difficult to tell apart because the ways of the former follow the laws of the latter.

I have written this book with Roland McHugh's *Annotations to Finnegans Wake* on one end of my desk and Clive Hart's *A Concordance to Finnegans Wake* at the other, and wish here to acknowledge the debt which must often go unnoted in the pages to follow. Adaline Glasheen's *Census*, J. S. Atherton's *The Books at the Wake*, and Clive Hart's *Structure and Motif in Finnegans Wake* have been as valuable to me as they have to virtually every *Wake* critic over the last twenty years. The glossaries by Brendán Ó hEithir, Helmut Bonheim, Dounia Christiani, and many others have from the beginning of this project been transcribed into my margins and my notes; please don't think that I'm really pretending to know all those languages. Richard Ellmann's biography of Joyce has been my main source for comments on the connection between life and work. The recent *Understanding Finnegans Wake* by Danis Rose and John O'Hanlon, though presenting an utterly different and I suppose in some way rival approach from that urged by this book, has been a useful, often illuminating help as I have sought to extract a coherent narrative from this least reducible of masterpieces.

This book was begun on a summer stipend from the National Endowment for the Humanities and completed on a grant from the American Council of Learned Societies. My sincere thanks to them and to Connecticut College, which offered help in various forms. Special thanks go to Mr Peter Costello of Dublin, who found out valuable things not easily found out by someone on this side of the Atlantic, to Mrs Keenan, present owner of the Mullingar House, who kindly responded to requests for information about her establishment, and to Dr John Garvin.

CHAPTER ONE

'Place'

Finnegans Wake is set in Chapelizod, the hamlet which Mr Duffy of 'A Painful Case' considered to be as far away as he could get from Dublin while still considering himself a citizen, the neighbourhood compared to which all others were 'mean, modern, and pretentious'. Visiting there, you can see what he liked about the place. It is a gentle, leafy settlement, like almost all the settlements of *Finnegans Wake* following a river, the Liffey, which at this point, three miles from Dublin bay, appears to be free of pollution. Swans are frequent. Adding to the sense of pastoral is the Phoenix Park, which borders on the north and east, and the Arthurian associations preserved in the town's name, recalling the legendary Irish princess, la belle Isolde, supposed to have stayed there.

So much is known about the place James Joyce chose as the setting for his most ambitious book. As for his reasons — doubtless they were manifold, but certainly one must have been that his profligate father once had part ownership in the distillery (long 'disused', Mr Duffy tells us) which sits on an island in the middle of the river.[1] As recorded at 299.30, John Joyce once suggested that his son follow in his footsteps by taking a job in a distillery, thus no doubt further confirming James's conviction that the elders of Ireland were, in Stephen Dedalus's words (*Ulysses* 572), out to break his spirit. The young Joyce was not about to follow in anyone's footsteps, but there is a sense in which *Finnegans Wake* represents a return, even a submission, to the land once spurned: the first sentence takes us 'back to Howth Castle and Environs', and the end tells us, bitterly, what that means: 'And it's old and old it's sad and old it's sad and weary I go back to you, my cold father. . .'

The centre of action is a building called the Mullingar House, so named because in coaching days it was the setting-out point for travellers to Mullingar.[2] It still stands. Like the inn of *Finnegans Wake*, it is a three-storey structure, painted white (139.30), sharing a 'party wall' with a building to the (approximate) 'South' (559.05), with a backyard large enough to contain chickens (see 10.32ff.) and, in earlier times, a privy.[3] Because the construction is irregular — there is an addition to the front whose floors, due to the slant of the ground, do not exactly match those of the older structure — and because modifications have been made since Joyce's time, it is probably futile to look for exact correspondences between the layout of the present structure and that of the *Wake*'s inn. Generally, we may note that the Mullingar lies northwest by southeast in the shape of a stunted L — a rectangle with an extension backward from the northwest end — facing onto the Dublin Road and away from the Phoenix Park. (There is a second party wall at the northeast end of this extension, joining the Mullingar with a building called 'Rose Cottage'.) Both the bridge and Bridge Inn, with which it is sometimes paired,[4] are a short distance to the west. In coaching days a yard and stables occupied the area now taken up by the front addition.[5]

The *Finnegans Wake* version of this building is a three-storey structure whose floors divide its population along Viconian lines: the second floor contains the room of the parents, the third floor the rooms of the children, the first floor the two servants, who, as the 'downstairs' part of the establishment, are typically represented hanging around the ground floor fireplace with the twelve customers, pretty clearly identified with the people of Vico's third age. There is also a cellar in which ale and porter are stored ('We rescue thee, O Baass, from the damp earth . . .' (311.17-18)), therefore the manservant's province. Hence (remembering the children on the top floor) we get a passage like this, from the house's owner: '. . . in morgenattics litt I hope, in seralcellars louched I bleakmealers' (545.27). Or this, from a catalogue describing the father and his house: 'has come through all the eras of livsadventure from moonshine and shampaying down to clouts and pottled porter' (138.30-2).

(Kate the cleaner wears a clout; the manservant is the inn's porter.)

The 'moonshine' and 'morning' of the above passages are cues for the children on the third floor, especially HCE's daughter Issy. The boys sleep in the northwestern room — the Shem-figure who reports on HCE in I/3 is called a 'north-roomer' (69.32) — and Issy at the southeast end. We are told a good deal about Issy's room. It has blue wallpaper (396.11-12) with white stars decorating the ceiling (see 148.13-14, where Issy recalls the 'twinkly way' over her bed. See also 627.09, 238.29-30.) In consequence Issy is connected with stars (at 8.32 she is an astrologer, studying her 'book of stralegy'; at 340.30 she is remembered raising her legs to the constellations), at times becoming a type of blessed damozel, for instance at 157.09 looking down over the 'bannistars'. The role is reinforced by the fact that her window faces northeast onto the yard, and beyond that the park, the city, and the bay. She is the benign watcher on high, by turns star of the sea, beacon (267.12) and (327.22-3) faithful lookout. Her view also takes in the backyard privy (362.34-5), of which more later, and an elm, which brushes against her windowpane: at 267.25-6 she is pictured 'under the branches of the elms' (and the light from her window, shining through the leaves, is green (267.13)). So she is connected with trees as with the sky — which helps explain, for example, why HCE should deny 'unlifting upfallen girls . . . out of unadulterous bowery' (363.33-4).

Most of the rest of her room's furnishings are quite standard: a bed with a 'crazyquilt' (556.16) and a mirror hanging above it (327.13-14), a chamberpot and washstand, a dresser with yet another mirror (561.16), a journal of some kind containing fashion news and serialised sentimental fiction (28.20-7) and a counter containing make-up, tissue paper, and a jar of Pond's vanishing cream (144.02-3, 486.33, 526.28-36) — 'Pond's' because Issy is at times Narcissus, vanishing into the pond (see, for instance, 526.34-6). There also seems to be a sofa next to which she keeps her sewing equipment (268.07-14) and a cat, which is given a number of names but which Issy most frequently addresses simply as 'pet', and which she both cuddles and curses (504.28-31).

461.19-20 tells us that the cat matches the wallpaper in colour, which would make it, I suppose, a Persian or Abyssinian (the phrase 'pershan of cates' at 280.15-16 may be a clue). 461.20 also tells us that the room contains 'priceless pearlogs' and lilac curtains. 'Pearlogs' may be a scrambling of 'pierglass', indicating yet a third mirror; in any case she is in the habit of addressing one mirror or other as 'precious', a short jump from 'priceless'.

Finally, there is one other feature, of the utmost importance for the whole of *Finnegans Wake*, also mentioned on page 461: Issy's room contains a fireplace. It is this fireplace down which Issy tries to call birds on behalf of her cat, 'decoying more nesters to fall down the flue' (28.09), presumably with the bird calls re-enacted at 359.31-360.16. A 'nester' is also a Nestor, HCE in his old-man incarnation, who falls for Issy every time, and to whom Issy's voice repeatedly calls from above by virtue of one simple crucial fact: his room is directly below hers, so that their fireplaces share a common chimney.[6] The chimney which passes from the second-storey bedroom of HCE and ALP to Issy's room has its origin in the downstairs kitchen, location of the servants. The route which brings a voice from above can also carry noises from below, and so for instance at 346.14-8 the sound of pots being banged together in the kitchen is remembered to have awakened HCE. Inevitably, the chimney becomes at times, in the dreamer's imagination, an axis with Dantean overtones: a Beatrice-like Issy above (with the sky over her), the grumbling voices of the lower orders in the vicinity of kitchen's fires below (with 'Baass' underneath), mankind in between, aspiring to one but too often sinking to the other.

Less detail is available for the ground floor. There is a bellpull (245.25) operating a doorbell which, on the evidence of 245.25-6, 262.26-7, and 560.13-15, is a source for the 'Zinzin' sound echoing through the book. The front door is dark, perhaps black (139.30). Before it are staple-ring and stepping stone (262.20-1), and there is probably a patch of flowers or hedges on one or both sides of it. Over it is a fanlight bearing the image of a white horse (262.22-3, 535.09-10), a Unionist symbol which may contribute to the Protestant owner's troubles with his Catholic neighbours. The kitchen

appointments are what we would expect from the period —
a fireplace, of course, along with the usual fire irons, implements including a rolling-pin, a ladle, a kettle, pots and pans,
a steam iron and ironing board, housebells for calling the
servants, a meatsafe and a set of blue pattern china (213.04-5),
a relic of the wife's genteel pretensions. The bar-room itself
features a bar with bar-stools, a radio which sometimes,
through a process to be described later, doubles as a television, a piano or pianola, a slate with chalk for keeping
accounts (a subject of some anxiety, since the pub has its
share of deadbeats; see 542.32-4, 589.31, and the p's and
q's — pints and quarts — of 319.23-30 and elsewhere), the
usual mugs, bottles, and barrels, a basin behind the bar for
washing glasses and bottles, a cash register, and one or more
of those oversized beer-pulls that look like tillers. The floor
is covered with sawdust.

It also features one item which surfaces often in the
dreamer's memory: the illustrated calendar sent last Christmas
by Alexander Findlater and Company, suppliers to HCE's
pub. Some relatively clear references to it, too lengthy and
numerous to quote, may be found at 191.05-8, 194.06-9,
245.35-6, 334.24-7, 334.32-6, 512.04-6, 561.12-16, and
622.21-31. Anyone familiar with the popular art of the last
century and much of this one who reads over these passages
will recognise the scene. It is a standard racing print tableau,
usually the first in a series of four or six. Called something
like 'The Parting Cup' or 'The Stirrup Cup', it routinely features a huntsman in regalia ('To the pink, man, like an
allmanox'), surrounded by hunting dogs ('canins to ride with
em') and usually flanked by fellow riders (622.26-7), sitting
on horse-back in the front yard of a tavern, in or before the
door of which stands a pleased-looking innkeeper in leather
apron. The picture's centre of focus is a cup, which is being
lifted the rider by a comely lass, clearly the taverner's
daughter. In some versions he has the cup already to his lips,
but in this one he has yet to taste it. Other details, less standard, seem inferable. The horse is probably white; the girl is
probably blonde; the rider probably has a moustache. ALP's
account (622.22-31) says that there are two female figures,
doubling as members of the hunt (Lady Pagets)[7] and servers

(lady pages), and that testimony, along with various *Finnegans Wake* episodes evidently influenced by the picture, indicates that the innkeeper's wife is also in the composition, standing by her husband in the doorway. Finally, one non-typical detail is especially prominent, the peculiar device which in *Finnegans Wake* as a whole becomes a symbol of HCE, and which in the above-cited passages is described as 'the flowerpot on the pole', a 'stickup', and a 'capapole'.

That a minor detail in this conventional piece of calendar art should emerge as an heraldic emblem of *Finnegans Wake*'s hero ought not to surprise readers of Joyce, remembering if they will how the roses of Stephen's wallpaper mutated into the 'rose and ardent light' of his dream and thence into the 'roseway' leading to the temptress of his villanelle, or how the *Titbits* print above Bloom's bed became, in 'Circe', his vision of heaven. 'The memories framed from walls are minding', *Finnegans Wake* tells us (266.20-1), explaining in part why by 496.01-14 we should be seeing the almanac picture everywhere, 'in debt and doom, on hill and haven'. The whole story of HCE's 'nomengentilisation' (31.33-4), for instance, which occupies the beginning of I/2, seems to be mainly a dramatisation based on the picture.

Certainly the central scene evokes HCE's forbidden yearning for his daughter, which is why the cup is (in Shem's words), a 'gracecup fulled of bitterness'. To wish for consummation with the daughter is at least on one level to wish to abandon the mother, to divorce her in order to make (see 545.27, cited above) a morganatic marriage. ALP is certainly aware of that possibility, even to some extent complicit: at 200.17-28 she is remembered by the washerwoman as 'stand[ing] in her douro', teaching 'every shirvant siligirl or wensum farmerette' the art of 'holding up a silliver shiner' to her lord (so the cup is probably silver).

So like all the artifacts encountered frequently or pondered on for long by the characters of *Finnegans Wake*, the picture has become an emblem for the family and its history. The two major male figures, resplendent horseman and humble innkeeper, have become symbols of what HCE considers his two sides, that of romance (the rider) and reality (the innkeeper); throughout the book the dreamer will concentrate on those two aspects of himself — the one who stayed and tended shop versus the glamorous outsider arriving or re-arriving at the door. The two attendants become his sons, the servant girl Issy (or his younger wife, remembered as sailor's bride), the housekeeper in the door his wife today as ball-and-chain, the pub's sign his symbol. In most instances the picture has come to represent the authority of the father in his zenith. The hunting outfit becomes a symbol of royalty, recalling that for a maiden to hand a cup to a man can be a ritual of coronation as well as marriage.[8] At other times, like the white horse in the fanlight, the almanac picture seems an exposed and vulnerable symbol of parental authority, all the more so because of the feelings about his daughter which it evokes. It is no accident that everyone's attention is drawn to it immediately before the book's most extended parricidal episode.

The enemy within notwithstanding, HCE generally feels most threatened from the area immediately outside his house, especially from the backyard. That is due in part to the gusty March weather, blowing in from the bay to the northeast to beat against the window in the rear. It is also due to the presence in the backyard of a privy, a 'greenhouse in prospect' (362.34) overlooked by the bedrooms. It is located 'on his brach premises where he can purge his contempt' (422.07-8) — probably at the northwest corner: 447.15-16 appears to situate it in that area, and the twins, who occupy the northern end of the third floor, are its most frequent spectators. Hence one reason for HCE's anxiety about it; we recall that in *Ulysses* Bloom was concerned that nobody from the 'nextdoor window' see him at stool. One other reason for the anxiety is that Joyce has contrived to make the privy a centre of erotic as well as scatological associations. Like Bloom, HCE supplies his privy with reading matter, convincingly identified by H. Burrell[9] as a reproduction of Aubrey Beardsley's illustrated edition of *Lysistrata*. This is the book of which HCE reports that he has been 'turmbing over the loose looves leaflefts jaggled casuallty on the lamatory' (357.21-2) — that is, in the lavatory of love.

Beardsley's edition is a piece of classy porn, peopled by steatopygous women and ithyphallic men. HCE's statement that he pays it his 'warmest venerections' (356.33) suggests why the privy should be the place reserved for its perusal: where else can a middle-aged married man go to masturbate? Hence such innuendoes as 'Gricks [pricks] may rise and Troysirs [trousers] fall' (11.35-6), shortly after HCE's first visit to the privy, or the description of him with 'his alpenstuck in his redhand . . . on the brink (beware to baulk a man at his will!) of taking place upon a public seat, to what, bare by Butt's' (85.11-15), not to mention the first page, which describes him (3.06) as wielding an isolated penis.[10] Hence, I think, the source of HCE's mysterious, much-bruited sin, which seems so busy, involving as it does voyeurism (looking at the pictures in the book), exhibitionism (and being watched by the boys), sexual indiscretion (while masturbating) and scatology (in the privy). The notorious girls in the park, spied on indiscreetly, probably have their origin in those pictures on HCE's lap. Later recounting his time in the privy reading the Beardsley book, HCE reports that they were 'liggen gobelimned theirs before me', and goes on to imagine himself peeking at them, outside in the park, through a kind of porthole, a 'shylight window' (357.27-358.05).

But more about that later. As 294.17-20 indicates, the privy is also a place for smoking. And two other features should be mentioned. First, it has a lock, evidently to keep out deadbeats (see 520.04-7), which is why on entering it in I/1 we have to ask for the key from the 'janitrix' Kate, who likes to extort a 'tip' for the favour. (Please note: if it takes a key, it has a keyhole.) Second, like Gerty MacDowell's it has, or had within recent memory, a picture hung up inside, an 'outwashed engravure that we used to be blurring on the blotchwall of his innkempt house . . . where used to be blurried the Ptollmens of the Incabus . . . By the mausolime wall'. (13.06-15; 'lime', as in 'limewash', was a feature of privies: see *Ulysses* 68, 355.) The overtone of 'Ptolemy' indicates that the picture has a regal or lordly subject, of 'tall man' and 'incubus' that it features a formidable father-figure in an aspect of sexual menace. It is in fact a battle scene from Waterloo, with Wellington, on horseback, in the foreground, and its presence will be enough to transform the privy, when we enter it, into a museum, a 'museyroom'.

About the yard which HCE crosses to reach it nothing is very surprising: there is lawn, at least one chicken (as in the Blooms' yard) and hence presumably a henhouse, the elm mentioned previously, and a gravel path. Kate, who has the job of emptying the chamberpots, understandably and typically describes both privy ('Pat's Purge') and adjoining yard and path as she usually sees it, a repellent heap of 'droppings of biddies, stinkend pusshies, moggies' duggies, rotten witchawubbles, festering rubbages and beggars' bullets [stones]' (79.27-80.12).

We may now look at the second floor, using as the main source the description of the sleeper's bedroom given at 558.35-559.16. A four-poster bed lies with its headboard to the south-east ('party') wall. A small bed table is on its right-hand side. It holds a 'gazette' and a lamp, with no globe. The 'ticker' beside it is the watch which at 52.06 is a 'repeater' and at 516.18 merges with a gun (which can also be a 'repeater') as HCE's 'pocket browning'. 497.35-6, where it is a 'German selver geyser and he polished up, protemptible, tintanambulating to himsilf so silfrich', tells us that it is silver and either German or Swiss. Its being called a 'ticker' indicates, of course, that it is still ticking, and according to 36.14, which remembers it as a 'chronometrum drumdrum', that ticking can be quite loud. 257.08-9, which transmutes it to 'that Boorman's clock', gives a version of its sound: 'nin nin nin nin . . . a winny on the tinny side.' Tinny or not, the Shem-type who challenges HCE's version of the time by telling him that 'his granfather's was all taxis and that it was only after ten o'connell' (70.28-9) indicates that it is a family heirloom, the Joyces having been distantly but proudly related to Daniel O'Connell. For this and other reasons it is a symbol of authority (e.g. at 516.17-19); in a sense HCE's authority is being challenged by the cad who, beginning with the account of I/2, asks him for the time.

The bed has a 'strawberry bedspread', a 'Spare' and a 'Flagpatch quilt' of 'Yverdown [eiderdown] design'. 'Flagpatch' seems to be a Wakeism for a patchwork with the patches either made of or resembling tiny flags; if you envision the rotund HCE with such an article draped over his middle, you can understand why he is sometimes represented as a map of the globe. The apparently incongruous 'Limes' (559.13) describing it reinforces earlier suggestions that its dominant colour is green: 380.26 describes HCE as having gone 'under the grass quilt', and later that conceit is the basis for HCE's proud claim (553.04-11) that in taking ALP to bed he gave her first the life of the lawn party set, then (with those flagpatches) the wonders of the earth. HCE and ALP sleep under an emblematic League of Nations, bordered in Ireland's own green — a neat epitome of the book's microcosmic vision.

The strawberry bedspread cues the Strawberry Beds, a Chapelizod landmark, and Issy (64.22-8, 265.06-8), who is connected in the dreamer's mind with fruit of all kind, a connection probably established by HCE's memory of the time he and the young ALP (generally identical with Issy) went 'berrying', apparently in the Strawberry Beds themselves. The spare blanket is probably folded or rolled up at the foot (that's how you can tell it's a spare) so that the bed has something like a pillow at each end — and in fact the first sleeper we meet, Finn, is discernible in the landscape by virtue of a mound at each end, and the second, the Napoleon of *Les Invalides* (8.06), rests in a tomb which resembles a marble bed bordered with two scrolled bolsters. The male sleeper lies nearest the northeast wall (next to the bed table), the female nearest the southwest wall.

The most prominent feature of the bed is the bedposts, each aligned with one cardinal point of the compass (as they would be, in a bedroom lying northwest by southeast), each therefore identified with one of the four provinces of Ireland. The northern bedpost turns out to be the one over which the 'Man's trousers with crossbelt braces, collar' are draped, a detail which helps account for the authority maintained by Ulster over the other three during the investigation of Shaun in III/3 (especially at 521.21-522.04). Also, its position apparently makes it the most visible of the posts: 533.21 tells us of 'Gregorio at front with Johannes far in in back'. The 'crossbelt braces', viewed from the opposite end of the bed, emerge in Ulster's proclaimed 'crusade' (480.07). The collar is separate and comes accompanied by a stock (619.35), indicative of stiff, old-fashioned notions of rectitude ('You can ken that

they come of a rarely old family by their costumance'
(560.32-3)) which in Joyce's day were rapidly yielding to
the soft-collar generation (and here manifest in the proverbial rigidity of the Protestant north); in America, for instance,
the last president to wear the old style, Herbert Hoover,
was supplanted in 1933 by what *Finnegans Wake*, during a
similar turnover, calls 'the bright young chaps of the brandnew braintrust' (529.05). Still, a pair of pants is a dubious
symbol of authority, particularly when they are notably
'*speckled*' (383.06) with 'spots' (302, fn.1), and made, as
these are, of mohair — an identification hinted redundantly
at 276.12-3, where there are multilingual goats aplenty as
a shepherd prepares to 'sate with Becchus', and lying behind
Shaun's repudiation of '*Rere* Uncle Remus, the Baas of
Eboracum and Old Father Ulissabon Knicker*bock*er'(442.08-9;
my italics, and cf. 98.20-22 and 177.04-7). Goats are traditionally hairy and lecherous; and Shaun warns Issy not to let him
find 'corsehairs on your river-frock' (444.27-8).

The four posts are most often identified with the four
apostles, north, south, east and west as Matthew, Mark, Luke
and John respectively, an identification traceable to the
sleeper's remembrance of the old childhood prayer 'Matthew,
Mark, Luke and John/Bless the bed that I lie on./Four cor-
ners to my bed/Four angels overhead.'[11] What is more natural
than that a child with a four-poster bed should imagine its
knobby finials as those four watchers, named nightly as he
drifts off to sleep? Or that when grown up, lying in a similar
four-poster, reliving his childhood, he should look up at the
posts and see the same four figures?

Three other items in the room, a chamberpot, a hat, and
bell-pull or buzzer, are omitted from the survey of 558.35-
559.16. The last of these is used to summon the servants.
The hat — generally described as a bucket-shaped affair[12] — is
whisked before our eyes in one of the book's teases when an
actress is described as speaking 'while recoopering her cart-
wheel chapot (ahat! — and we now know what thimbles a
baquets on lallance a talls mean)' (59.06-7). If this means
anything it means that the 'tombles a'buckets' of 5.03, 'clot-
tering down' the bauble-topped tower there is the same thing
as the thimble-shaped *baquet* on the tall lance here — that is,

a hat. As such it is perhaps the primary source of the pot-on-pole insignia already mentioned, and the readiest way of accounting for it is to conclude that HCE, like many men, has hung his hat on the handiest vertical, one of his knob-topped bedposts; as one of Issy's notes puts it, 'the night-cap's on nigh' (306.fn.2), on high.

Which bedpost that might be is indicated when HCE describes himself as a 'sleeping giant' lying 'From the hold of my capt in altitude till the mortification that's my fate' (540.17-18). This tells us once again that the hat — or, here, cap — is perched up somewhere, with 'mortification' under-neath. As for the 'mortification' at the feet, that particular combination has appeared earlier, when HCE is pictured as simultaneously dead, enthroned, and at stool, being hailed in a series of salutations which largely by virtue of the sonic closeness of '*mort*' and '*merde*' begin by mourning his death and end by calling him a shit. Death and dung go together in *Finnegans Wake* as surely as in introductory biology, so consistently, in fact, that we may suspect that the phrase 'the mortification that's my fate' is just HCE's grandiloquent way of telling us that like most people of the not-distant past — like Molly and Leopold Bloom, for instance — he sleeps with a chamberpot at his feet, beneath or next to the end of his bed. And those feet, remember, are said to point west (in fact the sleeper's feet should be pointing northwest), the direction of death. Hence the book's insistent melding of two words, 'west' and 'waste' (19.32, 35.31, 58.35, 64.01, 153.23, 158.10, 235.07, 320.17, 494.14, 523.25, 578.30). The hat is probably atop the bedpost above the sleeper's head, the chamberpot at the bed's foot.

'Clubsessel' (559.06), the peculiar misspelling of German *klubsessel* — 'easychair' — puts it within echoing distance of 'closestool', a term (current in Bloom's day — *Ulysses* 179, 709) for a commode; though dubious, the innuendo seems supported by 'wickerworker', which combines 'wickerwork' with *Ulysses*' carminative gadget named 'Wonderworker'. If so, and the 'wickerworker clubsessel' is identical with the bedroom 'chair' by the bed, it must be galling to the woman that it is her own 'woman's garments' which are on that 'klubsessel'. (Compare Molly Bloom, whose 'lady's black straw hat' sits atop her 'commode'.) Just what those garments are is unclear, but since ALP's gown is described separately they are probably, as they say, intimate, and an early testimony about HCE's sin, in which a pair of girls give 'silkinlaine testimonies' about what went on in a 'rushy hollow' where they had gone to answer the call of 'dame nature' (34.19-22), leads me to believe they are made of silk. 621.11-20 also indicates that they include an 'owld Finvara' shawl — a reminder of Nora Barnacle's Galway origins — and a girdle.

To recapitulate: moving northeast to southwest along the party wall, we encounter first the table, then a chamberpot and/or easychair near the far end of the bed, then the bed itself. The next items, occupying the room's southern corner and the lower region of the southwest wall, are the 'bookshrine without, facetowel upon' of the catalogue and, very near it (the facetowel is a clue), a water basin.

The basin is a sink-and-faucet affair, set into the wall. It is mentioned explicitly in I/5, where we hear that HCE 'takes a szumbath for his weekend and a wassarnap [German, 'water basin'] for his refreskment' (129.29), a practice recommended on 525.02-3. At 207.19-20 it joins with the Bassein River as the source of the riverine ALP — naturally enough, since what comes out of the faucet is, after all, a stream, with a source in the Wicklow Mountains not far from the Liffey's. That elevated origin is one reason that when the spigot is turned in IV the water is said to be 'minnyhahing here from hiarwather' — higher water, 'her' water, Hiawatha, Gaelic for 'remote' water; another is that the pipes descend from above, that is from the room of the cloud-girl, Issy. Those pipes, which tend to be noisy — at 23.16-24.02 the sound of 'moaning pipers' mixes with the faucet's dripping — are therefore a second link between father and daughter.

We hear of the basin juxtaposed with the next article on our circuit, the fireplace, when HCE boasts of how in making a home for his woman he included 'a shallow laver to slub out her hellfire' (552.26-7). The fireplace, set in the southwest wall, is described thus: 'empty Irish grate, Adam's mantel, with wilting elopement fan, soot and tinsel, condemned . . . Over mantelpiece picture of Michael, lance, slaying Satan, dragon with smoke.'

'Condemned' it may be, but the 'soot and tinsel' show that
there has been a fire in it during the night just past, since
'tinsel' derives from the French *etincelle* or *etincelles* for
'spark' or 'sparks', here turned into tinsel, perhaps, by the
same 'grey streaks' of morning 'silvering by' (580.21) that
have turned the coins in the casement into 'argentine'. (See
also 551.09, where 'tinsel and glitter' consort with 'cindery
yellows'.) What an 'Irish' grate is I don't know, unless perhaps
one in which turf is burnt; various passages (4.14-15, 347.34-
348-01, 382.14-16, 404.05-6) indicate that both turf and
wood are used as fuel.

I have already noted the fireplace's role as a conduit to
Issy's room upstairs. Inevitably, Issy is envisioned as Cinderella
(224.30, 280.21, 440.27, 551.09), as 'Mades of ashens'
(436.32), as 'our fiery quean' (328.31), as a pranquean who
'lit up and fireland was ablaze' (21.16-17). In at least one
passage she is herself the tinselly sparks, 'tarnished' and
'glooming' as they fade to ashes, waiting for their lover's
'wind' to blow them to life (226.04-8), a conceit developed
in her companions' demand that Shaun 'bellows up the tom-
bucky in his tumtum argan and give us a gust of his gushy
old. Goof!' (234.32-3), and which explains why ALP's gift
to Issy of a 'bellows, bellow me blow me', should be described
as not only 'golden' but 'guilty' (211.34-5). That the official
bellows-wielder is not HCE but his manservant has a lot to
do with the friction between them.

Other fire-furnishings are mentioned throughout the text
— broom, scuttle, fireguard or fender, tongs. By far the most
prominent of them is the three-pronged firefork with which
HCE takes an inordinate delight in poking and stirring the
fire, in language which leaves little doubt that the act symbolises his desires towards Issy, on the other end of the flue:

> Elevating, to give peint to his blick, his jewelled pederect
> to the allmysty cielung, he luckystruck blueild out of a
> few should-be santillants, a cloister of starabouts over
> Maples, a lucciolys in Teresa street and a stopsign before
> Sophy Barratt's . . . (155.23-6).

('Peint' includes the German for 'pain', 'blueild' the Norwegian
for 'fire'; the scintillant sparks are sainted while on their way

to becoming the stars of Issy's blue bedroom, their cluster a cloister; 'lucciolys' contains 'Lucia'.) Versions of the firefork are everywhere, usually with overtones of phallic menace. It is behind the (three-pointed) pike taken up by HCE-as-rebel (134.15-6), the 'tritan stock' brandished by him as lord of the seas (547.23-4), the 'dungfork' he carries as a faction-fighting bumpkin (87.14), the 'fork lance of lightning' with which the Jarl chases the pranquean (22.31), the 'piercing' for which he is held 'respunchable' (29.35) and which con-tributes to his nickname of Persse/Pierce O'Reilly, and above all the three-pronged prowess he is said to enjoy as a lover, a 'threelegged man' with his 'tulipied dewydress' (331.08-9), a 'big treeskooner' with his 'lil trip trap' (332.01-2), who 'with three plunges of my ruddertail . . . vanced imperial standard by weaponright . . . under starrymisty' (539.18-21; cf. quot-ation from 155.23-6 cited above). There is a weird kind of Wakean logic to the idea that a man who has begotten three children should be envisioned as having three penises, and to the idea that from this oddity should derive what is variously called his 'mark' (135.01), his 'brand' (566.24) and 'miss-brand' (68.19), the three horizontal lines of the capital E which is his siglum. That brand (it is, after all, a fire-iron) is what he used to to mark ALP as his own (547.33-5), and branded she is (512.23-5), as registered by their children, variously numbered as (in Roman numerals) III and (in Arabic) 111 — which number, in turn, may give her her name, since as Fritz Senn points out,[13] three parallel vertical strokes mean 'plurality' (as in 'Plurability') in Egyptian hiero-glyphics. Small wonder that her feelings about the implement should be mixed: at 370.11-12 she can be heard telling HCE 'I do so much now thank you so very much as you introduced me to fourks', but she reverts to a scared child at the very end when, heading out to sea, she begs, 'Save me from those therrble prongs!' (628.05).

Situated near the fireplace, on the floor, the three-pronged firefork counterpoints a feature of the mantel picture on high, the single shaft of the 'lance' with which St Michael is represented 'slaying Satan, dragon with smoke'. The basic tableau would seem to be easily recognisable: righteous warrior in shining armour goring fire-breathing dragon. But we may have problems when we try to visualise it. How does a painter demonstrate that a dragon is not just evil but identical with Satan? Does he give it horns? Or are there supposed to be two villains — and if so, how can Michael be slaying them both with one lance? By skewering both, as on a shishkebab?

The evidence suggests this answer: that the picture is of St George and the dragon, that for a number of reasons the most important of which is probably that Joyce's son was named 'Giorgio' it becomes in the sleeper's imagination a paradigm for the triumph of new over old, light over our reptilian heritage, Shaun over Shem, that during the night, when these two forces are in seemingly equal combat, the typologically similar struggle of Michael and Satan (Mick and Nick) as it were takes it over. We can occasionally find traces of the original peeping through the book's Mick-Nick oppositions, as for example when the two are called 'too male pooles, the one the pictor of the other and the omber the *Skotia* of the one' (164.04-5) — Pict and Scot, of course, but 'pictor' also sounds like 'picador', a mounted lancer stabbing a beast — or when Butt grows terrified at the sight of the Russian general as a 'Saur', swingeing the scaly horror of 'that tourrible tall' (344.12-345.03). There is oblique evidence that this creature, conventionally enough, is breathing a forked flame: on p. 281 an Issyan note about the scene is prompted by the phrase 'trifid tongues', an allusion to Ovid's *trifida flamma* (three-forked flame). This feature helps account for one of the book's pervasive oppositions, between three-pronged and one-pronged implement, firefork and the hat-on-pole insignia. The lance-vs.-forked-flame opposition of the mantel picture seems to function as a kind of step-up transformer, augmenting and focusing the association impulses of firefork and post. Hence, for instance, 'Mickmichael's soords shrieking shrecks through the wilkinses and neckanicholas' toastingforks pricking prongs up the tunnybladders' (90.10-2), or the later equation of the twins with a fork and knife (561.02).[14] The Mick-Nick George-dragon fight is an alembic through which HCE's particular furnishings become symbolic in a particular way, and from which all manner of congruent oppositions exfoliate, for example Napoleon's assault (a 'three-pronged attack', according to historians) against the Wellington symbolised by a monolithic obelisk, or the 'three of clubs' (222.29) which Nick-Shem brandishes against the monotheistic Mick-Shaun, or the shamrock, used in the Patrick-Druid contest of 611.04-612.30 to assert polytheism (the Trinity) against the oneness which the high priest sees behind all appearances.

That the painting in question is described as 'Over mantelpiece' tells us that the mantelpiece is itself something else, almost certainly not another painting; that the mantel is also called an 'Adam's mantel' after the Adam style tells us that it most likely features a round or oval mirror. Book I seems to hint to that effect in two accounts of HCE's confrontation with the figure who is clearly in some ways his double (70.15 calls him a *h*ikely *e*xcellent *c*rude man'; my italics), first when this figure stands on the Brocken ('swobbing broguen eeriesh myth brockendootsch') to make 'his reporterage on Der Fall Adams' (70.04-5), second when HCE is presented with his 'glasstone honophreum' including 'a stone slab with the usual Mac Pelah address of velediction, a very fairworded instance of falsemeaning adamelegy' (77.24-34). (See also 112.36-113.09.) As these passages suggest, the Joyce of *Finnegans Wake* is not one to overlook the possibilities offered by a mirror — *Ecce Homo* — named 'Adam', especially when it is accompanied by a picture of two figures who are among other things Cain and Abel, and who are in turn repeatedly shown to be mirror images of one another, plus shifting reflections of the father whose image must be hovering under theirs whenever HCE looks at the mantelpiece head-on.

Before the mantelpiece mirror is a 'wilting elopement fan', which strange as it sounds is exactly that: the fan which ALP carried when eloping with the young HCE, apparently in place of the traditional bridal bouquet, now preserved — albeit 'wilting' — as a sentimental memento. It can be said to wilt because it is either painted in a flower pattern (probably on feathers; cf. the 'old feather fans' preserved by Mrs Dedalus: *Ulysses* 9) or brightly coloured enough to resemble a floral bouquet, those 'curtsey flowers' with which HCE once 'profused . . . allover' his bride (301 fn.3). At 220.03-6, for instance, it is a source of 'The Floras', 'a month's bunch of pretty maidens' who, coming as they do from 'St. Bride's', are the flower girls for Issy's elopement-marriage. (At 143.01 they are reminders of 'elope year'.) The fan accordingly has associations of flight, romantic ocean voyages, wedding-night memories: at 147.33-4, for instance, ALP-Issy taunts HCE with a recollection of the night 'I coloured beneath my fan, *pipetta mia*, when you learned me the linguo to melt' (HCE has a somewhat different version: '. . . me to she her shy-blumes lifted: and I pudd a name and wedlock boltoned round her' (548.04-5)). Clearly James and Nora Joyce's elopement by sea without benefit of clergy (described, for instance, at 230.13-14) is behind these accounts.

As with the painting, the fan's corona of associations often merges with other stories stimulated by other cues. It blends most often with the fireplace, probably because the fireplace carries Issy's voice and thus recalls ALP from the elopement days. So for example ALP, in the passage cited above, stirs up the fire at the same time that she flutters her fan, 'with Sparks' pirryphlickathims funkling her fan, anner frostivying tresses dasht with virevlies' (199.35-6); see also 538.26-7. The two come together most compactly in certain occurrences of the word 'flu' which combine the sense of the English 'flue' with Latin *flubellum* for 'fan', as in this account of Issy luring her hot lover (here also a louver) through the chimney: 'while her fresh racy turf is kindly kindling up the lovver with the flu, with a roaryboaryellas would set an Eriweddyng on fire' (327.31-33).

This passage also depends on the fireplace connection, between Issy and her father, through which her voice can reach him. Although for her part Issy evidently does little more than call birds on behalf of her cat, to the guilt-ridden Earwicker, listening in, her voice becomes taunt and tease, at times an incitement to sin and die. (See, for instance, 360.23-361.17.) To be sure not all the symbolic permutations from this 'Secret Hookup' (360.16) are so sinister: at 583.32-3 ALP's orgasmic cry is imagined going 'jessup the smooky shiminey', a conceit which helps enable the lovely concluding account (627.02-13) of Issy's birth from above, as if through the same channel.

The hearth is of course a traditional symbol of the family, and we have seen enough by now to appreciate how thoroughly the fireplace of HCE's bedroom fills the bill. There is the firefork (the father), the elopement fan (the mother), the picture (the twins), and the voice from the flue (the daughter). There is even a cricket on the hearth (138.26-7; cf. 404.05-6), and a three-legged stool, the 'caneseated millikinstool' of 559.07, elsewhere remembered as the 'tripos' on which HCE in his domestic Shaun-incarnation likes to sit, staring into the fire and idealising the Issy whose voice comes to him from above, until he is 'transported' (452.08-14). There is also a bearskin rug stretched out facing the fireplace. We get an oblique glance at it, next to the fire, in a passage cited already, where ALP fans the fire, scattering 'virevlies', and 'the prom beauties sreeked nith their bearers' skins!' — hiding beneath the nearest cover (199.34-200.01). The same juxtaposition is behind HCE's demand that his son 'take the coocomb to his grizzlies' and tell him 'who done that foxy freak of his bear's hairs like fire bursting out of the Ump pyre' (516.13-15), and of course the often-quoted account of the animals of the Phoenix Park Zoo becoming 'rugs' stretched out by the hissing fireplace as night falls and they go to sleep (244.15-18). The rug's presence is natural enough in a cold room with a linoleum floor (391.21) so unpleasant to the step that HCE — 'Flannelfeet', he's called (422.09) — goes to bed wearing two pairs of socks (578.08-9).

About that rug we should note the following: that bears hibernate until the beginning of spring, when they emerge to eat voraciously, mate, and, according to legend, purge themselves and stop up their innards with what the *Larousse Encyclopedia of Animal Life*[15] terms a 'faecal plug' of leaves and grass, that they are known to like honey and hence often represented as liking flowers, that in the Finnish *Kalevala* the bear is a sacred animal who rises again after being sacrificed and eaten,[16] that as exemplars of brute strength they are natural symbols of our primitive inheritance ('as urs now, so yous then!' (535.03-4)), and that the most famous bears of fiction are the three who have the adventure with Goldilocks.

The northwest wall, opposite the bed, is the one with the

door going out to the hall and the 'chequered staircase' (560.09) leading up to the children's rooms. Accordingly it has come to be associated with petitions, encroachments, sometimes attacks from the younger generation — a connection tracing back to the prediction in Joyce's 'The Day of the Rabblement' that Ibsen's successor 'may be standing by the door', itself an allusion to the prophesy in *The Master Builder* that 'the younger generation will one day come and thunder at my door'.[17] The nineteen-year-old Joyce who wrote that essay wrote as much to Ibsen himself: 'Your work on earth draws to a close and you are near the silence. It is growing dark for you'.[18] However reverentially put, that is a hell of a thing for a youngster to say to an old man. By the time of *Finnegans Wake* it has become Joyce's turn to sink into a darkness more literal than any that afflicted Ibsen, and so HCE spends almost all of *Finnegans Wake* in a dark or dimly-lit room feeling anxious about being 'moidhered by the rattle of the doppeldoorknockers' (445.31), of becoming a 'bland old Isaac' — blind old eye-sick — 'buttended' by a 'kidscad' (3.11). That this usurper is at one point accused of 'Ibscenest nansence' (535.19) confirms that the tables have been metempsychotically turned.

The door is also a focus of anxiety for a reason familiar to many couples — the fear that the kids will hear or, since there is a keyhole, see the marital love-making in the bed opposite. Just such an event (which Margot Norris, drawing on Freud, has called the 'primal scene'[19] of the *Wake*) has occurred under circumstances which have much to do with the 'Woman's gown on ditto' of 559.10-11, 'ditto' referring to, first, 'gown' — there are in fact two — and, second, the 'nail' on which the 'Man's corduroy surcoat' is said to hang.

The two gowns are an old one and a new one, apparently identical in design. The new one is HCE's birthday present to ALP, acknowledged at the end: 'I am so exquisitely pleased about the loveleavest dress I have. You will always call me Leafiest, won't you dowling?' (624.21-3) The fact that she has been called 'leafy' suggests two things, first that her old gown resembles the new, second that they are both green. Both inferences are confirmed by Issy's note at 271.fn.5: 'Tho I have one just like that to home, deadleaf brown with quicksilver appliques, would whollymost applisiate a nice shiny sleekysilk out of that slippering snake charmeuse'. In other words the leafy green of the silk (produced by the charming silkworm, among its leaves) is going brown with age; time to get a replacement. So the women *in excelsis* are richly green, leafy: the washerwomen are impressed by ALP's 'period gown of changeable jade that would robe the wood of two cardinals' chairs' (200.02-3) — that is, would appear to have robbed the woods of two trees — and the distinction no doubt contributes to both females' identification with Daphne's laurel and such peculiar blessings on ALP as 'May all have mossyhonours!' (552.30), moss on her. As Jacques Mercanton learned from the author, the 'leaves' which 'have drifted' from ALP on the last page of her monologue are the last vestiges of the gown given by her lover, now in disintegration.[20] The 'quicksilver appliques' are two in number, crescent-shaped (as ALP has requested: 276.fn.3) on each side of the bodice, a position which gives them a certain lunar allure (e.g. at 245.06-9). Both Issy and ALP are accordingly cast now and then as moon goddesses 'in their halfmoon haemicycles' (375.12-13), Dianas (e.g. 261.10-11) or Selenes (192.30; compare 245.06-9).

Gift or not, the gown is a cause of contention with ALP, whose greatest grievance is that she doesn't have a thing to wear. In I/8 (208.20) she is forced to wear her husband's 'cordroy coat', apparently loaned to her in accordance with the law, cited elsewhere in the *Wake*, that a husband's obligation to keep his wife clothed may be satisfied with such lendings,[21] and even at the end she can't resist imagining the contrast people may draw between her husband's expensive clothes and her own modest wardrobe (620.03-6). The present seems to be one side of a trade-off: according to ALP her husband pays her 'his duty on my annaversary [the anniversary of Anna's birth] to the parroteyes list in my nil ensemble' and then, as the continuation of this passage makes clear, requires that she pay her duty in return, by yielding to him sexually (493.04-15). (She does, in III/4, where the narrator informs us this happens 'every ephemeral anniversary' (583.23).) Probably some such awareness of the gown's ulterior purpose, augmented by the usual oedipal tensions, is behind the ambush by a Shem-like assailant, said to be 'jealous', of HCE when returning home and 'humping a suspicious parcel' (62.27-34), which parcel later re-emerges as 'the christmas under his clutcharm', a present for 'his [the assailant's] murder [mother]' (186.19-187.14), and still later as 'the new satin atlas [Norwegian: satin] onder his uxter' (324.03) being brought home by the soon-to-be-ambushed Norwegian captain making for his beckoning lover. One of the charges against the Russian general is that 'he'll be buying buys and go gulling gells with his flossim and jessim of carm, silk and honey' (354.30-2), and there is especially strong resentment of 'the Setanik stuff that slimed soft Siranouche' (338.23-4), with 'Setanik' including Italian *seta*, silk.[22]

The location of the nail from which both gowns hang is indicated by the following lyrical address to Issy:

> Ding dong! Where's your pal in silks alustre? Think of a maiden, Presentacion. Double her, Annupciacion. Take your first thoughts away from her, Immacolacion. Knock and it shall appall unto you! Who shone yet shimmers will be e'er scheining. (528.18-22).

With the lamp turned on (as we have just learned at 528.04), the two silk gowns, one dark and one pale, shimmer in the light, against — 'Knock and it shall appall unto you!' — the door. Which is to say that there is a green 'dianaphanous' garment over the keyhole, through which anyone who peeps in must look. The 'surcoat' also hangs on the door, but evidently does not reach to the keyhole, although one description of HCE says that it occupies a good deal of doorspace along with the silken 'leafscreen': '. . . the false hood of a spindler web chokes the cavemouth of his unsightliness but the nestlings that liven his leafscreen sing him a lover of arbuties' (131.18-20). (The coat is made of corduroy which is made of cotton which is spun on a spindle; the gown is made of silk from worms cultivated on mulberry leaves.)

Noting, again, those silkworms, and remembering that Issy seems to think of them as snakes, slithering around the green garden of her gown (271.fn.5), we can consider now ALP's thoughts about that 'leafscreen' on the door of the 'cave' she shares with her husband: 'What those slimes up the cavern

door around you, keenin . . . had the shames to suggest can
we ever? Never!' (615.34-6). (For the watcher's version of
this event, see 297.06-16). This is one of her attacks on the
libeller, variously sneaky and snaky, singular and plural, who
has been slandering her husband. With it, we are ready to
return to the subject of the 'primal scene' associated with
the door and its keyhole. As we will see later, Joyce has
incorporated the details of his own sufferings from glaucoma
into his book, particularly into the stories of the father's
fall and Shem's shame. Shem — like Noah's son, like Actaeon,
like Peeping Tom — has been cursed for witnessing a forbidden sight, and his punishment has been glaucoma, the initial
stage of which, according to Joyce, the Germans call 'green
blindness'.[23] So in *Finnegans Wake* both Shem ('greeneyed
mister' — 88.15-16) and HCE when playing the accused rather
than the accuser ('grand old greeneyed lobster' — 249.03)
suffer accordingly for the sin which the prosecutorial Shaun
makes clear: 'Just a little judas tonic, my ghem of all jokes,
to make you go green in the gazer. Do you hear what I'm
seeing, hammet? And remember that golden silence gives
consent, Mr Anklegazer!' (193.09-12) Incorporating as it
does 'dammit', Hamlet, and probably Shakespeare's son
Hamnet, 'hammet' reminds us of the oedipal component to
all this. As for 'judas tonic', it is probably just that flattering
betrayer alcohol, which Joyce could never stay away from
in spite of the knowledge that it was bad for his sight,[24] and
which Shem has been ruining himself with, becoming 'a drug
and drunkery addict, growing megalomane of a loose past'
(179.20-1), ever since he saw something through a keyhole.
(So the peeping 'Thom' of 507.01-5 winds up drinking 'at the
Green Man', with its intimation of glaucoma.) It is also, the
context shows, an allusion to a 'judas', which in the words of
the *Oxford English Dictionary* is 'A small lattice or aperture
in a door . . . through which a person can look without being
noticed from the other side; a peep-hole'. And here we may
remark that a gauzy screen covering the keyhole of a door
one side of which is lighted (because of the lamp by the bed)
and one side of which is dark (ALP has to take the lamp with
her when she enters the hall and ascends the stairs, where it
casts a moving 'Spotlight' (560.04)) makes for a perfect judas

for those on the dark side, in the hall, and that because of the gown anyone looking through this peephole is going to see everything within as green, for instance the father, the 'Caesar' of this book's Roman rebellion, engaging in some vigorous and apparently violent activity in the bed opposite: 'what is seizer can hack in the old wold a sawyer may hew in the green' (549.25-6).

Considering the capacity of the room's elements to inter-penetrate and influence one another in the dreamer's mind, it seems to me a good bet that the transformation of the door's keyhole into a 'judas' is partly enabled by a feature of the adjacent northeast wall: 'Argentine in casement' — that is, a pile of silver in something whose name cannot but remind us of the most conspicuous Irish martyr of Joyce's adult years, a latter-day version of the Parnell (both victims, so it was believed, of forgeries) who was for Joyce a latter-day Christ. Just as the keyhole can become a 'judas', so too can that 'Man's corduroy surcoat with tabrets and taces, seapan nacre buttons on nail', hanging on the door, become a hanged martyr, a Christ or Christ-type, as in this account of it juxta-posed with the coins (doubling as wafers): 'figure right, he is hoisted by the scurve of his shaggy neck, figure left, he is rationed in isobaric patties among the crew' (133.03-5). In fact throughout the *Wake* the sight of that hanging coat is liable to set off HCE's persecution mania.

The 'taces' on that coat are almost certainly 'taches', the clasps of the coat's belt (see 208.20-1, where the coat, worn for the nonce by ALP, has a 'twobarred tunnel belt') with a secondary meaning of 'spot, blotch, blot' (*Oxford English Dictionary*). This last meaning is much in evidence when the surcoat shows up on Festy King, who looks like 'Kersse's Korduroy Karikature, wearing . . . stains, rents and patches' (85.33-4). The incongruous juxtaposition of King's regal name with his downtrodden appearance is implicit in the coat's 'corduroy', a word meaning *corde du roi* but designat-ing (the *OED* again) 'A kind of thick-ribbed cotton stuff, worn chiefly by labourers or persons engaged in rough work'. So HCE, wearing it, can be either royal or common, or, as at the beginning of I/2, both. The colour is red.

Last on the itinerary is the northeast wall, with the window looking out into the backyard, toward Phoenix Park and Dublin bay beyond. That the coins piled or stacked in the window's casement are 'Argentine' in the 'silvering' light of dawn tells us, probably, that all or some of them are silver. 'Argentine' are small silvery fish (thus 524.18-525.05, where the submerged Shaun looks 'windwarrd' and sees a dozen 'dirty little gillybrighteners' shining 'by yon socialist sun') and also, of course, Argentina, home of the Buenos Aires of 'good air' which for the Eveline of *Dubliners* symbolises freedom from dusty Dublin. As in the case of Shaun's 'windwarrd' gaze, it makes sense that the 'argentine' of the northeast should be associated with windiness, airiness; as the 'Welter focussed' of 324.26-34 confirms, the winds of *Finnegans Wake* come from the northeast.

The northeast is also the historic source of Viking invasions, and indeed the window, like the door, is often a focus of the dreamer's anxieties about assaults from the outer world, anxieties amplified by the hailstones which early beat against his window and windowboards. Those boards, mentioned at 316.04 for their effectiveness in 'aerian insulation resistance', go through a number of changes. 583.14-15 indicates that they are 'Persian blinds', a kind of sturdy outdoor version of Venetian blinds, consisting of horizontal slats or planks set in a frame. They are two in number, hinged on either side of the window and fastened by a clasp. Three things to bear in mind about them are, first, that tending them is the manservant's responsibility (at 23.05, for instance, he is ordered to close them); second, that like the window, a camera has a shutter, and that HCE fears cameras as threats to expose him; third, that according to P. W. Joyce's *English As We Speak It* the expression 'under-board' means 'the state of a corpse between death and interment',[25] a usage which may owe something to the 'grave-boards' of the defunct poor. When HCE senses himself as locked behind his windowboards, 'sure behind the shutter' (513.01), it is not arbitrarily that he also envisions himself as a body at a wake.

Above the window is a permit featuring the seal of the city: two maidens on either side of a shield displaying three burning castles, with the city motto 'Obedientia Civium Urbis Felicitas' spelled out beneath. Bernard Benstock has pointed out that HCE's sin in the park, featuring as it does two girls and three watching soldiers, is at times associated with this seal,[26] and I would propose further that the connection is causal, that the dreamer's memory of his sin, already situated for him in the direction of Phoenix Park (because that's where the privy is, with its forbidden reading matter) is shaped and filled out by the emblem which overlooks his view of that area: the maidens become the girls, the castles the soldiers (a connection probably aided by memories of 'The Castle', from which British soldiers took their orders), the authoritarian Latin the voice of civic censure — one reason the four old judges who condemn HCE for his Phoenix Park transgression are pompously latinate in their speech. See, for instance, 523.21-524.07, where the four old men's standard idiom introduces the soldiers, who testify alternately about HCE's sin in the park and his fitness to maintain his 'epscene licence'.

So much for the window, except to say that just because it has 'No curtains' at 559.05 doesn't necessarily mean that it didn't have any at some earlier point.

The influence of the 'Salmonpapered walls' (559.02) on the dreamer's dream is too ubiquitous to need detailing.

To recapitulate, the room looks like this:

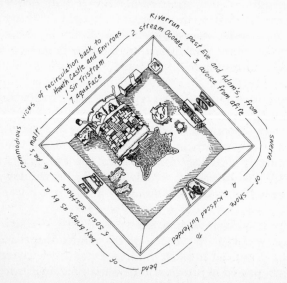

As surveyed clockwise in the book's opening sentence: 'riverrun [the faucet and basin], past Eve and Adam's [the Adam mantle], from swerve of shore [this one doesn't fit as nicely as the rest, but both shore and door are borders, separating one region from another] to bend of bay [as in 'bay window': at 626.34-5 ALP says of the light of dawn coming through the window, 'this baylight's growing'] brings us by a commodious vicus of recirculation [circling past the commode; with 'swerve', 'bend', and 'recirculation' we are traveling in a circle] back to Howth Castle and Environs [HCE, in his bed] '. And then once more, in the seven-clause sentence which, as we will see later, epitomises the *Wake*'s story:

1. 'Sir Tristram . . .': Beginning where we just left off, with HCE in bed;

2. 'nor had topsawyer's rocks by the stream Oconee . . .': and back again to the faucet's 'stream';

3. 'nor avoice from afire': on to the fireplace, with Issy's voice coming from it;

4. 'a kidscad buttended a bland old isaac': the door, as usual, is the locus of caddish challenges from HCE's sons;

5. 'sosie sesthers wroth with twone nathandjoe': the two girls on the seal on the permit over the window, evoking HCE's imagined sin in the park;

6. 'Rot a peck of pa's malt had Jhem or Shen brewed by arclight': the 'arclight' is from a lamp on the bedside table; the chamberpot is probably the origin of pa's rotten malt;

7. 'and rory end to the regginbrow was to be seen ringsome on the aquaface': coming to the end of this ring, we once again confront HCE's face, looking forward to yet another watery re-beginning.

Excessively neat as this may seem, its rationale is firmly based on the author's understanding of psychology, and it has a precedent in the ancient art of memory:

It consisted in memorising a series of places in a building, and attaching to these memorised places, images to remind of the points of the speech. The orator when delivering his speech, passed in imagination along the order of memorised places, plucking from them the images which were to re-mind him of his notions.[27]

Such a system, which Joyce would have encountered through his readings in Giordano Bruno, might have first taught him to consider the extent to which a person's environing circumstances may be both palimpsest of past associations and prompting of future mental acts, the extent to which 'memories [are] framed from walls', as conjured by a 're-miniscensitive' observer. In making of the furniture of his own little room an everywhere, our dreamer simply follows suit. Like everything Joyce wrote, *Finnegans Wake* begins in a richly particular here and now.

TWO

'Time'

THE DATE of *Finnegans Wake* is Monday, the twenty-first of March, 1938, and the early morning of Tuesday the twenty-second. I have argued this earlier, in *James Joyce's Metamorphoses*,[1] and will here review and amplify my reasons.

1. Up until the beginning of Book III, when the clock strikes midnight, the day is a Monday. The washerwomen are doing the laundry (in I/8), and as the mention of 'a tubtail of mondayne clothes' (333.23-4) reminds us, Monday is wash-day. Sure enough, at the dawn of the next day, ALP tells HCE, 'Here is your shirt, the day one, come back.' When an announcer on the pub's radio advertises the week's pro-grammes, he begins with Tuesday, tomorrow (325.06-11); when, the next morning, a newspaperman sends off a dis-patch, his dateline is 'Deemsday', German *Dienstag*, Tuesday (602.20); when ALP announces McGrath's funeral, it is on 'by creeps o'clock toosday', Tuesday, today (617.20-1). Similarly the calamitous events at the beginning of I/1 are later remembered as having occurred ('along about', please note, 'the first equinarx in the cholonder') on a 'moist moon-ful date' — a wet Monday (347.01-7).

2. The month is March. At 211.30-1 Shaun receives 'a sunless map of the month, including the sword and stamps', and we would expect a sword in any picture of Mars' month. At 603.15 someone is overheard remarking of the sunny morning that it's beautiful weather for this time of March. At 347.01 'Butt' remembers the calamitous event of the day as having occurred on 'a white horsday', and although he is obviously referring to the 'big white harse' of Waterloo (I/1), it is also pertinent that the Welsh for horse is *'march'*.[2] And

the weather is indeed typical of this proverbially inconstant month – cold, wet, and blustery on Monday, with fog and mixed precipitation, fine on Tuesday. The wind is from the northeast – the right direction for the month.

Mars' month is also known as the time for the commencement of military campaigns and for fertilisation, both animal and vegetable – and we may note that a child conceived in March, for instance during the love-making recorded in III/4, would be born in December, around the time of Christmas and St Lucy's Day, for which Joyce named his daughter. Hence: 'When otter [daughter] leaps in outer parts then Yul [July, of course – Lucia Joyce's actual birth month – but also Yule, in December] remembers Mei [not only May but Norwegian for 'Mars': the daughter's birth in December will recall the mother's, in March]' (245.05-6).[3]

3. The date is 21 March and the morning of 22 March – set, that is, on Nora Barnacle's birthday, and the day after. As I have noted, the event is behind the new gown, her present, hanging on the wall. It is also probably behind the marital love-making in III/4, since 583.22-5 seems to say that this occurs once a year, 'every ephemeral anniversary'; thus behind Issy-Lucia's birth at or around the time of a festival of light in the dark dead of winter, nine months later.

Just as oblique references to the *Wake* Monday and Tuesday are planted here and there, so too for 21 and 22 March: at 438.23-5, shortly after the clock has struck midnight, Shaun complains of the state of the marriage market, 'newlaids bellow *mar* for the *twenty two*toosent time *thwealthy took* thousands in the slack *march* of civilization' (my italics); a little later we encounter '*marsh*alsea' (my italics), 'calendar', 'twenty', and 'two' within a few lines of one another (456.31-457.04). Still later, Shaun testifies that the incident with his father and the subsequent brother battle, which the *Wake* places in Book I, occurred on 'The uneven day of the unleventh month of the unevented year. At mart in mass' (517.33-4) – Armistice Day, falling on Martinmas, the eleventh day of the eleventh month, but 21 March is also an uneven day in a Lenten month of unleavened bread, and 'mart' sounds a lot like both Mars (a war is ending) and March.

Although like HCE *Finnegans Wake* goes 'Dawncing . . .

round the colander' (513.11-12), the weight of evidence indicates that the central or base time is 21 March, the date which Shem recalls as 'along about the first equinarx in the cholonder' (347.02-3), in relation to which the other dates (especially Christmas) take significance. 21 March was once, and in some places still is, New Year's, a time for ringing out the old and ringing in the new (213.19-20). As a moment in time for a book extending to eternity, it therefore makes an ideal vantage point. In America, anyway, producers of greeting cards like to symbolise New Year' with pictures of old men yielding the stage to babies; in *Finnegans Wake*, at the stroke of midnight and with choruses of *Auld Lang Syne* in the background, the cherubic Shaun supplants the Shem who embodies all the buried sins of his father's past. It has at one time or other been the date of two ancient festivals especially prominent in the *Wake*, *Sechselauten* (whose bells we hear at 213.18-19),[4] and *Bealtaine*.[5] It occurs within a few days of two national events much in the minds of the *Wake* characters, St Patrick's Day and the Irish Sweepstakes draw. As the usual end of winter and beginning of spring — 'But receive me, my frensheets, from the emerald dark winterlong!' (603.08-9) — it is a perfect choice for 'waking', in both main senses of the word. It is the time for 'thon rising germinal' (354.34-5), the rising seed plus the beginning of *Germinal*, on 21 March, for '*early spring dabbles*' (342.25), for gusts of spring wind (321.31), for fashionable people to discard their furs and don macintoshes (346.01-2). It is also the traditional day for that bear whose presence we noted on the floor of HCE's room to end its hibernation and start foraging, and as we will see in III/4 the bear does just that, fusing with the 'hibernating' (79.05) HCE. Finally, it is the day of leaving Pisces the fish and entering Aries the ram, and so in I/1, immediately after telling Finnegan to lie down and 'Finn no more', his watchers add, 'For, be that samesake sibsubstitute of a hooky salmon, there's already a big rody ram lad at random on the premises' (28.35-6): Tris*tram* supplanting Finn is also ram supplanting finny fish.

4. The date is 21 and 22 March 1938. The allusions to radios, automobiles, airplanes, talking movies, Prohibition bootleggers, the Irish Free State, the milk truck which has

replaced the horse-drawn wagon remembered by 'our elderens' (604.12-17), Hitler's autobahn (410.08) and FDR's braintrust (529.05) narrow the choice to the mid or late thirties.

In fact there is one year which fits all the requirements and fulfils one other set of indications: 1938. It is consistent with all the references to the recent history of the time. It is sixteen years after the publication of *Ulysses*, the same talismanic period which in that book had separated Joyce's young and middle-aged incarnations, Stephen and Bloom. Then there is this fact: the period between Nora's birthday on 21 March 1938 and Lucia's on 26 July 1938 was the only time when the ages of the four members of Joyce's family coincided with the ages which emerge behind all the reversions of the *Wake*'s main characters. James Joyce became fifty-six on 2 February 1938; HCE is fifty-six (443.22, 495.31, 497.26-7).[6] Nora Joyce became fifty-four on 21 March 1938; ALP, it has long been noted, is 'LIV', Roman fifty-four, and of her hen-incarnation it is said, 'if you can spot fifty I spy four more' (10.31). Lucia was thirty; Issy, though she is forever fracturing into various earlier childish and adolescent selves, is, we know, a leap-year girl of seven one-year-in-four birthdays,[7] thus 7 x 4 + 1 → 3 years old. Giorgio was thirty-two up until his birthday on 27 July; Shem and Shaun, like Issy, vary widely in their levels of maturity, but 497.09 tells us explicitly that HCE's male attendants equal 'in their aggregate ages two and thirty plus undecimmed centries' (see also 494.33, 581.23), as indeed we might expect, at one point anyway, from a couple who (3.08-9) are doubling their number all the time; throughout the book they are invariably accompanied by the numbers three and two, in either order.

There are a few more fairly definite things we can say about this night and day. *Finnegans Wake* ends, and possibly begins, on or about the hour when Joyce, as he knew, was born, 6:00 a.m.[8] The current is going out at the very end, taking ALP out to sea, as it has been through at least most of Book III, where Shaun is at times a barrel floating down the Liffey. Since Book III begins as a clock strikes twelve, the tide's approximately twelve-hour cycles must at least roughly match the day's two halves, with high tides around noon and midnight. Other evidence seems to confirm this schedule. At about eleven o'clock the servant tells the customers, 'Tids, genmen, plays, she been goin shoother off almaynoother onawares' (371.25-7), a call which, considering that 'Tids' was originally 'tide',[9] seems to warn that the tide is about to turn and that they had better catch it. About an hour later, Shaun will be about to begin a journey which Joyce described as 'a barrel rolling down the river Liffey'[10]; at 409.33-410.19 he complains that because of 'a power coming over me that is put upon me from on high' (the moon, probably, controlling the tides) he must be off 'circulating'; sixteen pages later he looks up from 'his tide shackled wrists through the ghost of an ocean's' (426.20-1) to find out the 'were and will be' of his course, and shortly after that he is off. The 'ghost of an ocean's' is not a bad way of describing the oceanic tides as sensed, dimly, on the river upstream. This information fits with what we know about the moon's course: as McHugh notes, the moon rises a little after sunset (244.03-4) and, apparently, sets sometime after sunrise (623.27-8),[11] so it should be directly overhead shortly after midnight, exerting maximum pull.

The testimony on the weather is quite consistent. There is even a report on it, a 'Welter focussed' (324.24-33) which repeats the previous day's forecast and takes credit for having been right about its prediction for 'Mandig', Monday. That prediction was of a storm from the northeast – wind from the north, its cause a depression originating in Scandinavia which has made its way westward through St George's Channel, heralded by fog signals and thus presumably fog as well, characterised by mixed precipitation and dense storm clouds, currently being dissipated in local drizzles.

The account accords with other testimony about the day's weather, especially in Book I, where we hear many times that 'the wetter is pest, the renns are overt' (39.14-15), that there are clouds and dense fog everywhere (48.01-5). As we would expect for an Irish March, these conditions are changeable, and by six in the evening seem to have cleared up enough for the washerwomen to do their laundry outside, though even then one of them prays to avert the showers in an invocation immediately followed by news that 'Der went is rising'

(213.23-4). As indeed it is: although things seem calm enough during the next chapter, which begins with the twilight ritual of lighting-up time (7:09, on 21 March 1938), there is lightning and rain in the air by 250.23-33, and by around 10:30 that evening it is blustery enough outside to influence the Russian General story being told within; throughout II/4, which takes place between 11:00 and shortly before midnight, we can hear the wind and rain outside the shutters. At twelve the rain has stopped and left a mist prismatically refracting the lights in a 'fogbow' (403.06), and by 449.35-6 Shaun is apparently able to catch intermittent glimpses of the moon through the clouds. The dawn which follows breaks on a beautifully clear day, as promised, and everyone is reminded of summer just as during the storm of II/3 they were reminded of winter (One of the *Wake*'s subordinate points is that an average Irish day in March, that proverbial lion-and-lamb month, is a microcosm of a year's weather.) The report of 'veirying precipitation' (324.28) means just what it says. There is plenty of rain on Monday and possibly some snow, but what makes the biggest impression is a shower of hailstones, rattling against the dreamer's window and walls early in the day and thereafter reverberating through his dream, almost always as stones thrown by rebels, though stones which, strangely, can melt and evaporate; at 73.29-35 they are 'chambered cairns' left by the attacker, but also a 'cloudletlitter' of 'skatterlings' soon to be gathered together 'as nubilettes to cumule'. That property of hailstones is behind one of Shem's most peculiar signatures, the trail of alternately solid and liquid leavings which invariably mark the path of his retreat from the attack on his father, most clearly, perhaps, as the 'trail of Gill . . . rocksdrops, up benn, down dell' which Joyce identified to Jacques Mercanton as stones left by HCE's attacker (244.22-4).[12]

From the usurper's point of view, the hailstone barrage accompanying the encounter can symbolise authoritarian reprisal; although in his attack on the czar-like Russian General he is the one to 'fetch along within hail' of his enemy, it is the Ondt, for instance, who 'loftet hails' (415.34) at the Gracehoper from the 'affront of the icinglass of his windhame', which sounds like a kind of Winter Palace specialising in the production of ice-storms, and the earlier account of

Shem's retreat into his Inkbottle House definitely casts the mixed precipitation of rain and hail with his clerical assaulters:

> One hailcannon night (for his departure was attended by a heavy downpour) as very recently as some thousand rains ago he was therefore treated with what resembled parsonal violence . . . (174.22-5).

The weather report of II/3 mingles with a re-broadcast of 'last mount's chattiry sermon', probably taken from the text of I Corinthians xiii, which in 1938 would have been read last month — on Quinquagesima, which fell in February that year. The day before the narrative begins has been the third Sunday in Lent, 'Occuli Sunday'. The appointed Gospel is Luke xi, an account of Jesus' casting out of devils. Probably its best-known lines are, 'And it came to pass, when the devil was gone out, the dumb spake', 'Every kingdom divided against itself, is brought to desolation; and a house divided against a house, falleth', and 'He that is not with me, is against me'. The Epistle, from Ephesians v, exhorts the congregation to forgo their 'works of darkness' and 'walk as children of light', and concludes, 'Wherefore he saith, Awake, thou that sleepest, and arise from the dead, and Christ shall give thee light.' If the sleeper went to the church near his inn (and 89.14 says that he attends more or less regularly) he should remember these words. Monday is the feast day of St Benedict, Tuesday of St Basil and St Lea. Sunday was the anniversary of Napoleon's escape from Elba and the births of Ibsen and Ovid. Last Thursday was St Patrick's Day. Monday is a likely day (as it happened, in 1938 it was the exact day) for the Irish Sweepstake draw. Migratory geese should be leaving for their northern breeding grounds, salmon spawning, skylark, blackbird, wren, missel thrush, robin in song, crocus, tulip, hyacinth, narcissus, daffodil, cowslip, primrose, polyanthus, and daisy in bloom. The elm by Issy's window should be leafing. It is the time to finish sowing oats and barley, to plant dahlias, hardy annuals, and early potatoes, and to transplant cabbages sown in autumn.

THREE

'Males'

OF ALL the characters in the *Wake*, the one conventionally known as HCE is the hardest to pin down. Every male character in the book may to some extent be derived from him — as is for that matter the book itself, since he or some version of him is the one doing the dreaming. The first difficulty is in trying to name him. I hold to the traditional view that his last name is 'Porter', a view supported by Patrick McCarthy's recent reading of I/1's prankquean riddle. McCarthy interprets this as a name-guessing challenge, similar to that of 'Rumpelstiltzkin', in which the father is asked by the daughter, 'Why do I look like I could pass as a Porter, please?', and slams the door in her face because acknowledging their common name would mean acknowledging the incestuous nature of his desire for her.[1] (Shutting the door, he becomes a 'porter': Wakean dream-language reveals what the speaker seeks to conceal.) We may also note that all the book's reporters — re-Porters — are derivatives of the sons.

The more common name 'Earwicker' is what I/2 calls an 'agnomen', derived from two facts of the dreamer's anatomy. First, he has unusually big ears, a feature which accounts for his quondam incarnation as a bat (148.04-5) and ass. That is why at 361.11 he combines the Victorian travel guide John Eustace with the ears' eustachian tubes to become 'Mr Eustache', and why his house is 'equipped with supershielded umbrella antennas for distance getting' (309.17-18). Second, he is a fat man who habitually tries to minimise his girth by cinching in his belt ('the greater the patrarc the griefer the pinch' (269.24-5)), as revealed by the 'black and blue marks' around his naked middle which 'indicate the presence of sylvious beltings' (564.23-5). Envision a malicious cartoonist's picture of such a figure pulling in his belt, and you can see how someone might have decided he resembled an earwig, and why the name stuck.

About HCE's clothes the book is similarly definite. In bed he wears a nightcap (559.20) which resembles a doge's cap (or, less grandly, a tea cosy (578.13, 578.07)), a woollen nightshirt, and socks (578.05-10). When dressed he wears a shirt with stock and collar, assuming the antiquated dignity ridiculed and resented throughout the book, his scarf (ALP calls it a 'comforter'), the mohair pants hanging on the bedpost, and the belted red corduroy jacket hanging on the nail. He wears brogues and the hat that has been perched on his bedpost, and carries an umbrella (619.34-620.02) which can double as cane. Like Joyce he wears an ornamental ring, perhaps several (138.09) — an 'Imperial Catchering' (498.12-13). There is indirect evidence that this is a Claddagh ring, with its design of two hands joining beneath a crowned heart (the crown may account for the 'Imperial' note), a design with traditional links to the Joyce family, and which *Finnegans Wake* associates with the two-in-one nature of HCE's sons. He is often seen smoking, either a pipe or a cigar.

Physically, HCE is a fat fifty-six year old man in terrible condition, white-haired, red-nosed, toothless, purblind and be-spectacled, once tall and straight, now stooped — he leans on a cane — and gross. We get a poignant glimpse of what he once was when ALP bucks him up at the end, telling him she still recalls the tall, straight 'wonderdecker' of his youth. He has gone from the exemplary straightness of 'the giganteous Wellingtonia Sequoia' (126.12) to the 'orerotundity of that once grand old elrington bawl' (55.36-56.01). He is 'our heavyweight heathen Humpharey' (42.26) who is a 'lot stoutlier than of formerly' (570.17-18), his belly spreading in 'rollpins of gansyfett' (531.07). Humiliatingly enough, to many his distinguishing feature has come to be his enormous backside, the 'big white harse' which awes the watchers of I/1's Waterloo scene[2] and III/4's bedroom scene alike, and which intermittently becomes a subject for witticisms on the order of 'walked as far as the Head where he sat in state as the Rump' (127.32-3).[3] As with his figure, so the other signs of age's decay are seen by contrast with his former state. Having (like

Joyce) lost his teeth (270. fn.2, 467.01), he is prone to remember the days of his flaming youth in dentatious imagery; in II/1 one such memory, of the days '*Whereof in youth-food port I preyed*', prompts another memory of the early toothaches which forecast today's dentures (231.05-22)). In her turn ALP proudly remembers him from the days when he was 'The only man was ever known could eat the crushts of lobsters. (624.35-6). As a young man he was clean-shaven — a 'rawshorn generand' (335.20) — and 'blackhaired' (147.35); today he is an 'icepolled globetopper' (435.12) whose 'hair grows wheater' (26.08) all the time, with a 'frothwhiskered' (558.15) moustache that, along with his grey hair, makes one of III/4's watchers think of 'some king of the yeast, in his chrismy greyed brunzewig, with the snow in his mouth' (578.03-5). His afflicted eyes are a story in themselves, better taken up when we review the subject of Joyce's own eye troubles; here we will simply note that like his creator he wears a black patch (thus contributing to his sometime role as buccaneer),[4] that his vision is so sensitive that daylight is experienced as a shattering assault against which the blinds must be closed, and that his present glaucous state is, once again, cruelly at odds with ALP's thrilled recollection of his piercing stare: 'I'm sure he squirted juice in his eyes to make them flash for flightening me' (626.15-16), she remembers at the end, and has earlier boasted of him, '*The Flash that Flies from Vuggy's Eyes has Set Me Hair on Fire*' (106.26-7). Indeed this Svengali-like stare may have won ALP over: the washerwomen remember her wedding as containing the lines 'And by my wildgaze I thee gander' (197.13-14), and later we hear of 'The must of his glancefull coaxing the beam in her eye' (512.08-9).

Anyway, that is all past. Like the middle-aged Joyce, HCE has a hectic flush (30.21, 582.28-9) and red nose (403.07-13), signs of a history of excessive drinking. In fact he is a Falstaffian ruin, going to pieces in the literal sense that portions of him are constantly leaking, flaking, rotting, or blowing away as he defecates, urinates, ejaculates, vomits, bleeds, spits, drools, smokes, coughs, belches, weeps, breaks wind, sweats, and sneezes. We can understand why he is a compulsive overeater, throwing sandbags of bulk against the rising tide of decay (a reciprocation manifested in the twins: Shem sheds, Shaun stuffs himself).

Not surprisingly, he spends a lot of his time in ill health. Aside from his eye troubles, he is suspected of suffering from a 'vile disease' (33.17-18), obviously venereal — which may explain why an obliquely reported urination should be experienced as 'panickburns' (9.25) — and, at least during the first half of the *Wake*, has terrible problems with his digestion, both in keeping things down (97.29-30) and holding them in (467.19-20). For obvious reasons, his chronic flatulence is especially noticeable, and noticed: the four old men wax Homeric on the subject of 'the gush off the mon like Ballybock manure works on a tradewinds day' (95.02-3), his mourners tactlessly keen him with 'Eheu, for gassies!' (58.18), and even ALP, weighting her pockets to keep from being swept away by his 'blowaway windrush', puts a clothespin on her nose (208.21-3).

His bad health may explain why the book's dreamer stays in bed all day and evening. When not prostrate he sits like a Beckett protagonist propped against the pillow, muffled in bedclothes, contemplating his failing sight and listening to Issy's whispers from the chimney (57.25-29). No wonder he dreams of himself as a corpse or a buried giant. The book gives frequent, if not always coherent, testimony about his condition and its causes. He has a stomach-ache — a gripe ('gripins' — 193.08) or 'coald on my bauck' (German '*bauch*', belly — 365.13). The cause of his latest collapse seems, neatly enough, to be an apple, in some form or other — the 'bad crab' said by the four old men of II/4 to have rendered their variously-named former friend 'seasickabed' (392.06), the 'windigut diodying applejack' with which Shem is said to have become 'sick of life' (171.15-17), the 'fruit' which, says ALP, he was 'forbidden' (492.31-2). Almost certainly a major source of this incident is Jonathan Swift's 'lifelong fear of eating fruit' resulting from his conviction that his fits of giddiness were owing to an apple-eating binge,[5] a conviction which carries over into an early account of HCE's own giddy fall: 'So sore did abe ite ivvy holired abbles . . . wan warning Phill filt tippling full. His howd feeled heavy, his hoddit did shake . . . Dimb! He stottered from the latter. Damb! He was

dud.' (5.29-6.10). HCE's complaint evidently stems from the
apple's supposed laxative properties, which hark back to *A
Portrait of the Artist as a Young Man*, where (p. 61) Uncle
Charles tells Stephen that apples are 'good for your bowels'.
(*Finnegans Wake* concurs: '*A Nibble at Eve Will that Bowal
Relieve*' (106.29-30).) Ironically, HCE's condition may have
been worsened by the medicine he has recently taken for it.
References to this part of the story are among the murkiest
in the book, but 492.13-493.15 seems to implicate a mixture
— both the physician's milk of magnesia and the alchemist's
magnesium — fixed (184.11-185.08) by the alchemist Shem
and administered by the mother.

Aside from the fainting spell brought on by his stomach
problems,[6] HCE is subject to trances: ALP remembers him
'looking at us yet as if to pass away in a cloud' when he first
saw her (615.21-2). Issy tells us that he talks to himself,
loudly, imitating everybody (460.11-12), a predeliction
which, we find at 571.27-34, continues in his sleep (and hers:
at 327.21 she is 'sleepytalking'). 199.02-3, where we learn
that he sleeps with his mouth wide open, would suggest that
he snores as well. Also, of course, he stutters. An amateur
psychologist would deduce that he was as troubled in spirit
as in body, seeking surreptitious outlets for the urge to con-
fess which, as a Protestant surrounded by Catholics, he is
singularly denied.

A major cause of unease is in fact his Protestantism: his
wife is Catholic, and the children have been raised in the
church. One of Issy's footnotes in II/2, prompted by a reference to the local C. of E. church, is a sneering comment on
her father as 'Porphyrious Olbion, redcoatliar' (264. fn.3).
The children's Catholicism makes them, in HCE's mind,
natural allies of the proletarian customers below, who are
ever liable to become a mob, a 'Religious Sullivence' (602.25-6)
following him. The evidence is that the only issues to really
exercise this lot are the availability of credit and drink, but
for the self-consciously non-Catholic HCE their grumbling
takes on sectarian overtones. In his imagination children and
mob alike are especially aroused by his use of prophylactics,
which frightens the children (567.06-7) and of course outrages
the mob, who at 45.14 accuse him of peddling 'immaculate

contraceptives' and who later preside over two pages of trial testimony concerning his use of them (573.35-576.09).

'Mob' is a word he might use. He has an innkeeper's concern for appearances and class distinctions, at times combined with obsequiousness: one of his main fantasies (the so-called 'King's House', nearby, may have something to do with this) is that royalty might stop at his establishment. In general he is as sensitive and overly reactive to slights, real or imagined, as he is to light. ALP speaks truer than she knows when she calls him an 'exsogerraider' (619.30). He is obviously an exaggerator in such instances as the encounter with the cad, where an innocuous question sets him to gesturing and babbling in a self-defeating attempt to avoid appearing out of place, and in a more general sense as well which justifies his being identified throughout with Michael Gunn, manager of the Gaiety Theatre and thus master of pantomime: just as his reaction to the cad is a pantomime of camaraderie ('Shsh shake, co-comeraid!' (36.20)), so the conflicts and reconciliations, rises and falls of the book originate in his pantomimic imagination, his habit of exaggerating the events of his life, as brought out by the events of this day and night.

Our friend the amateur psychologist, attending to the stories told in these exaggerated pantomimes, might conclude that HCE is 'conflicted', and would again be right. He is literally divided by the 'pinchgut' (568.22) belt squeezing him in two, and is sometimes accused of being the most obvious kind of divided personality, a hypocrite. II/2, for instance, characterises him as a drunkard lecturing others on temperance (263.01-6). But he is as hard on himself as on others: at 539.15 he confesses 'I abhor myself vastly', and the washerwomen describe him 'holding doomsdag over hunselv' (199.04-5). The four censorious old judges personify this habit of self-judgment, in a latinate idiom similar to that projected by the guilt-ridden Stephen Dedalus (*Portrait* 136) after being scared by Father Arnall's sermon.

Like Leopold Bloom — another semi-alien — he can envision himself as either triumphant coloniser or spurned invader, Patrick or Sitric Silkenbeard. He is seen by others, and sometimes sees himself, as an oppressive father-figure, particularly as represented by the *Wake*'s quintet of Williams — William the Conqueror, William of the Boyne, William Shakespeare (lord of language, as Stephen calls him in *Ulysses*, symbol of his language's hegemony), the Duke of 'Willingdone', and William IV, HCE's namer — but is also prone to think of himself as oppressed, on the side of the rebels: ALP recalls him 'recitating war exploits and pearse orations' (620.23-4) to the twins, who have picked up their recurring jacobinism at his knee, and according to Shem-Butt he has repeated his message of 'upleave the fallener as is greatly to be petted' (352.03-4) to the point of tedium.

At the heart of these divisions is a contest between licence (drinker, gourmand, lover, rebel, writer) and control (abstainer, belt-tightener, impotent celibate, conqueror, censor). Our dreamer identifies this conflict with what for him is the most significant division, that between his memories of his young slim healthy hot-blooded self and the bloated, ashen-haired form he now inhabits, between past and present. In contemplating this conflict, he is, once again, divided. He can see it as a miserable contrast between past glory and decline-and-fall, between for instance the virile 'big rody ram lad' introduced at the end of I/1 (28.36) and the 'tiresome old milkless a ram' despised by ALP (396.15). Or he can see it as growth from bodily lusts to spiritual wisdom, as onward-and-upward, as conversion from things below to things above. (Or as an uneasy combination of the two: 'time liquescing into state, pitiless age grows angelhood' (251.09-10).) Shaun is being his father's son when he boasts of his toothlessness as 'gumpower' (410.25).

'Shem and Shaun'

In fact both Shaun and Shem speak for their father in different phases — in effect *are* their father's two divisions. Strictly speaking, they do not exist. They are figments, and nothing else — though to be sure in *Finnegans Wake* that is a great deal. Speaking in the language of theology, they are processions, not persons. They can claim at most half a body each, the bottom and top halves respectively of the young male asleep upstairs (3.08 and 562.29 hint he may be named 'Giorgio') who we glimpse in III/4 as forehead and liver, bugle-blowing mouth and 'foundingpen' penis (562.16-563.36) — and even this figure is described mainly in terms of the father's own sense of himself.

This last point, suggested in my *James Joyce's Metamorphoses*, has been independently arrived at, and thoroughly demonstrated, by E. L. Epstein.[7] And there has been another critical contribution which illuminates the pair — Kimberly Devlin's demonstration that both the brother-battles between Shem and Shaun and the oedipal conflicts between father and sons have as their source an individual's internal struggle between 'self' and 'other', that in his sense of his own personal integrity as being in conflict with the encroachments of the outside world, a conflict often represented as one of liberty versus repression.[8]

In other words they reflect the divided father, pinched, earwig-like, between top half and bottom, surveying a life-span divided between riotous past and a future which must extend his necessarily straitened present, with bloated white-topped body (the body, that is, of a Shaun) at the mutinous centre of which sits his snaky penis — the only part of him, such is the gods' perversity, not to have put on weight — amid a still-black pubic bush (the reminder, that is, of a Shem). The Shem-Shaun, rebel-authority, self-other dichotomies of the *Wake* trace to this one division, between the dreamer's remembered past and his projected future, and his body is their major source-book of images, from which they take a local habitation and a name. Like his sometime double Sackerson, who is 'insides man outsiders angell' (141.10-11), he has 'his soilday site out on his moulday side in' (338.18-19), Sunday suit (though soiled) over mouldy inside, Shaun exterior and Shem interior. Shem, who as Butt in II/3 has 'a boodle full of maimeries in me buzzim' (348.07), is the incarnation of the early years, reaching back to HCE's 'very first debouch at the very dawn of protohistory' (169.20-1), when he was a stripling compared to his later Shaun-incarnation: 'Though his net intrants wight weighed nought but a flyblow to his gross and ganz afterduepoise' (407.05-6). Perhaps drawing on the tradition of the fat friar, the narrator of II/2 tells us that HCE-Shaun's devoutness increased in direct proportion to his poundage: 'the dimpler he weighed the fonder

fell he of his null four lovedroyd curdinals' (282.18-20).
Similarly, the white hair of age is tame Shaun (later HCE),
the dark hair of youth wild Shem (earlier HCE): 'passed for
baabaa blacksheep till he grew white woo woo woolly' (133.25).
When the father is a globe, white-haired Shaun plays the frigid
arctic ice-cap, phallic Shem the tropical speak-carrying 'hunter'
(435.12) by whom HCE is 'haunted'.

'Sackerson'

The 'icepolled globetopper' is 'haunted' here because for all
his resolutions he cannot repudiate the past; he is still 'in his
bardic memory low' (172.28), with a 'Nick in his past' (307
fn.6), still living a 'doublin existents' (578.14). *Finnegans
Wake* often depicts him as a secluded revenant rehearsing his
past, attempting to 'pay himself off in kind remembrances'
(589.34-5), 'the spectrem of his prisent mocking the candie-
dights of his dadtid' (498.31-2), and out of that past Shem
is the symbol of everything that needs to be confronted and
subdued. The young man asleep upstairs is one focus of this
projection. But he is upstairs, and if there is one thing we
know for sure about Shem it is that he is 'low'. There is at
least one other person behind Shem, someone literally 'low'
and 'beneath' HCE, on whom he can project his own most
disgraceful memories — Sackerson, his manservant, down on
the ground floor by the fire, under HCE's room.[9] In fact he
bulks larger in the *Wake* than has been realised; as the narrator
tells us, 'we are recurrently meeting em . . . in various poses
of sepulture' (254.24-8). Sackerson is the mystery man of the
Wake, the 'summonorother' (255.05-6) and 'Watsy Lyke'
(245.33) whom we are indeed constantly meeting, in various
guises. He is encountered in the book, for the most part, as
HCE's 'nighboor' (585.34), 'fatherlow' (141.24), the lower
part to suppress or keep suppressed: 'Well down, good other!'
(598.11). As ALP tells her husband at the end, Sackerson is
for HCE what Kate is for her (620.33), a lower self.

His most distinctive features are his black beard and blonde
hair, a striking combination which may chime with HCE's
own features of dark pubic bush and white head, and which
is probably behind his introduction (with a nudge from Pope

Gregory I's 'not Angles but angels', cited at 526.11) as 'insides man outsiders angell' (141.10-11). The hair — 'butterblond', it's called at 429.18 — is, along with his blue eyes (534.18), a sign of his Scandinavian origins, one of many points of similarity with HCE. He is a 'jublander or northquain' (141.22), therefore often thought of in connection with Scandinavian invaders, thence pirates in general. However imposing his beard, he has the look of the downtrodden supernumerary — 'supperaape' (221.07) — he has become. His voice throughout the book has a catarrhal drunkard's 'slops hospodch' (620.32) sound, as if he were underwater: '*Dotter dead bedstead mean diggy smuggy flasky*' (430.15-6). Like the submerged Shaun, he is probably 'bronxitic' (536.13), maybe the source of the coughings (26.26-7) we hear in the first chapter, when he is up and around. The initial description on 141.08-26 seems to say that he is a large, 'bigger' man, but as Mrs Glasheen notes, this is also a reference to the hunchbacked Joe Biggar.

In fact I am convinced that he is the book's hunchback. (It isn't HCE, although the weight he has put on makes him feel like it at times, and his 'imitations' of Sackerson can be misleading — perhaps his hiker's rucksack (621.06-7) contributes to the identification. His first name, after all, designates him as hump-free.) He dresses in blue serge — a material associated with the lower orders, although the homonym 'surge' ought to give his employers pause. He is often compared to a black slave, an identification most likely tracing not only to his subjugation but also to the fact that fire-tenders tend to be sooty. (With suit and soot, *sans* hat, he becomes 'hatless darky in blued suit' (515.33-4).)

Black beard notwithstanding, he is apparently an old man who, like Eliot's Tiresias, has an old man's breasts. This hint of androgyny pairs him with his fellow servant Kate, who as we will see is distinguished by her facial hair. Together, as '*femme a barbe ou homme-nourrice*' (81.29), they illustrate a recurring *Wake* theme: 'when older links lock older hearts then he'll resemble she' (135.32-3). So the Sackersonian 'Magnus Spadebeard' recalled by Shaun 'Laid bare his breast-paps to give suck, to suckle me' (480.13-14). His attendant emblems are fire — he is the 'torchbearing supperaape' (221.07)

— a bottle, the knives which it is his job to grind (141.15-6), and, since he is the pub's handyman, various tools, especially a hammer.

Handyman though he may be, he is anything but handy. He is a 'Chump' who has to be ordered, 'Do your ephort' (560.16), a 'pigheaded Swede' (517.05), often drunk, a lazy 'lizzyboy' (530.21) always needing to be roused. No wonder the paragraph which introduces him in I/6 (141.08-27) is intermittently àn advertisement for his replacement. In fact there are indications that his employment is coming to an end: the Shaun of III/2 promises to 'sack that sick server' (432.33-4), the trial testimony of 572.21-576.11 calls him a 'resigned civil servant', and ALP, to whom he is the source of the odious McGrath, claims that he has been fired for giving guff (616.21-2), that he is 'a Nollwelshian who has been ox-belled out of crispianity' (618.33-4).

ALP's accusation of paganism is borne out by other accounts. Although 'under the inflounce' (221.11) of the piously superstitious Kate, who hopes to convert him, Sackerson remains true to the old Norse faith; he is under Kate's influence only by virtue of being under her flounces, and in the same passage is 'unconcerned in the mystery' and associated with Odin and Loki. Partly for this reason he is sometimes suspected of having rebellious thoughts. These suspicions are heightened by his inarticulateness. His name has apparently become proverbial for substandard language: when Shaun takes his inquisitor's expression 'In epexegesis or on a point of order' as 'pigs of cheesus' and 'pint of porter', he is told, 'You are a suckersome!' (511.16-20).

Perhaps as a consequence of his linguistic isolation he is generally considered as an indrawn, private person, etymologically an 'idiot', therefore a mysterious 'Watsy Lyke' (245.33). HCE, envisaging him down in the 'foyer', speaks of his 'innersence' (538.26-30), and the account of him in I/6 calls him a 'soundigged inmoodmined' ('sinfully introspective') person. So the suspicion arises that as 'insides man outsiders angell' he harbours unvoiced desires: in II/1 when he arrives with his torch he is 'a burning would' (250.16), a phrase which brilliantly describes the id in language evoking Macduff's uprising against the tyrant Macbeth.

He is 'outsiders angell' mainly because as the pub's bouncer, the one who has to shut up shop and throw out stragglers, he is the inn's official super-ego, 'petty constable Sistersen' (186.19), 'Wachtman Havelook seequeerscenes' (556.23-4). That is, he embodies both Shemian instinct and inner vision and Shaunian repressiveness, either of which the sleeper can in different moods find menacing. Menace: that is the constant. Whatever else he may be, he is what the dreamer fears.

HCE's greatest fear is of usurpation, especially of the kind that Leopold Bloom seems to fear when he speculates that his daughter's blonde hair may have to do with his wife's first lover, the blonde Mulvagh.[10] Sackerson is blonde, and so is Issy, the 'bewitching blonde' Izod (220.07-8), the 'Icis' (Isis) of 'the golden falls' (214.31). It is not conceivable in the world of the *Wake* that such a coincidence not be noticed by the dreamer, that certain inferences not be entertained at least — for instance by the Professor Jones of I/6, who in the midst of his attack on the Shem-Caseous wooing Issy's alter ego Marge, starts worrying, it would seem unaccountably, about the provenance of her blonde hair (164.25-31). A good deal of the private mythology coursing through the dreamer's dream has grown out of his lurking suspicion that (forgive me) the bottler did it, that the cuckolder he suspects (and almost the first thing we learn about HCE is that in his coat of arms he is 'horned' (5.07)) is under his nose. This suspicion is behind, for instance, the outburst of the domestic tailor against the 'bugganeering wanderducken' and 'pushkalsson' for whom Issy pines (323.01-16), and who at 530.20 is again identified with Sackerson.

The implications are grave enough to figure in the dreamer's apprehension and fantasies of divorce: the four old men recall an HCE type feeling suicidal and receiving a parliamentary bill of divorce (in other words, a divorce granted on grounds of adultery) 'all on account of the smell of Shakeletin' (392.30-393.01), presumably detected on his wife's person. HCE's suspicion of his servant explains why his presence should be feared as a scandal, 'the depredations of Scandalknivery' (510.27-8; he is the pub's knife-grinder), why the seducer whom Shaun warns the girls against should — like Sackerson, unlike HCE — be bearded (435.03-4), should be described as a *'sukinsin* of a vitch' (437.29-30; my italics), a 'goattanned saxopeeler' (441.33), the disturber/exposer/reincarnation of 'our past lives' (438.10-12), should be identified with 'rebellious northers' being lasciviously enticed (437.04-5), why the domestic ship's husband of II/3 should address the invading wife-stealing Norwegian captain as 'sonnur mine, Shackleton Sulten' (317.15-16), and why ALP herself, whose daughter's vision of Liberty Hall is a place where 'every Klitty of a scolderymeid shall hold every yardscullion's right to stimm her uprecht' (239.18-19), should be remembered as having told the courting HCE that 'the park is gracer than the hole', the life of the landed gentry pleasanter than that of the submerged classes, 'but shekleton's my fortune' (512.28-9).

In the last passage, ALP is also talking about winding up with her husband, a shackler who 'wegschicked Duke Wellinghof to reshockle Roy Shackleton' (541.21-2), bottled up his lower self. Like Bertha at the end of *Exiles* ('O, my strange wild lover, come back to me again!') ALP regrets the repression, wants her old lover, the 'wonderdecker I once', back (620.07). That 'bugganeering wanderducken' turns out to be ALP's vision of her husband in the youthful days of their courtship, when (in his words) 'I abridged with domfine norsemanship till I had done abate her maidan race' (547.26-7). That is, Sackerson has come to be identified with the wild romantic of HCE's youth, long since shackled by the weight of years and the responsibilities of HCE's adulthood. In this capacity he has genealogical affinities with Shem and the mysterious McGrath, who are the repudiated youth of HCE as remembered with loathing and unacknowledged desire by, respectively, the dreamer and the dreamer's version of his wife.

To take these two correspondences, Shem and McGrath, one at a time: First, Shem is Sackerson — Sacker*son* — as he exists in the world of the dreamer's hothouse fantasies, derived from memories of his own past. He is, to the dreamer, a torchbearing, knife-sharpening, grumbling, unmanly yet disturbingly sexual dependent who has some mysterious and menacing affinity with Issy, in turn the young ALP, and who in this connection has seen something or knows something to HCE's discredit which he threatens to publicise. As torchbearer he is behind the Shemish cad, the 'luciferant' (35.11)

HCE meets in the park (he sleeps by the fire (37.24), gets drunk and cherishes the bottles (38.04-8), speaks in (37.15) 'secondmouth language', spills the beans to his consort, a Kate-incarnation, is an 'Abelbody in a butcherblue blouse from One Life One Suit . . . with a most decisive bottle of single in his possession' (63.15-18); all these are Sackerson signs), an identification confirmed at the beginning of III/2, when the leap-year girls are described approaching the 'butterblond' Sackerson: 'attracted to the rarerust sight of the first human yellowstone landmark (the bear, the boer, the king of all boors, sir Humphrey his knave we met on the moors!)' (430.06-8). ('Knave': traditionally a male servant, a Sackerson, contemporarily a cad, a Shem.) As lover he is the piano-playing 'sukinsin of a vitch' stigmatised by Shaun as 'Mistro Melosiosus MacShine MacShane' (437.33); as fire-tender he is, like the Shem addressed by Shaun, 'old sooty' (193.05); as petitioner for his salary he becomes like Shem a beggar. As the one who visits the cellar to fetch beer (and, presumably, coal) he is the Shemian inhabitant of an 'obscene coalhole' (194.18), 'Lowest basemeant in hystry' (535.18). His 'innersence', introspection, is also a Shem quality.

Most distressingly, Shem-Sackerson is a 'seequeerscenes' (556.24), the 'patrolman Seekersenn' (586.28), peering (583.24) at the window behind which ALP and HCE make love, the representative of the 'Sigurd Sigerson Sphygmomanometer Society' which has 'surprised [the couple] in an indecorous position' (608.09-10). It is in this capacity that to HCE he becomes Shem at his most odious, and that to ALP he becomes the hated McGrath: as we will see Shem is punished for his voyeurism by being struck in the eye; Sackerson is found near the end 'rincing his eye' (624.19); both are described as 'Envyeyes . . . when they binocular us from their embrassured windows in our garden rare' (235.24-6). The connection explains, for instance, why Sackerson, 'the boots about the swan', comes running down 'with homp, shtemp and jumphet' (63.36-64.01) when summoned by his master.

'McGrath'

What Shem is to the dreamer, McGrath is to the version of

the dreamer's wife whom we call ALP. He is, first of all, identified with the wild rover she left behind, a Heathcliff to HCE's Edgar.[11] (Which rover was, as noted earlier, in turn a role of the young HCE, 'the gran Phenician rover' (197.32).) The intensity of her reiterated attacks on him is, in its way, evidence of her ambivalence: the lady doth protest too much, and it should not surprise us to find that when coupling with her husband she fantasises about being in the arms of a forbidden other: 'Magrath he's my pegger, he is, for bricking up all my old kent road' (584.05-6). At times her resentment sounds like that of a spurned lover. She is described as 'wronged by Hwemwednoget (magrathmagreeth . . .' (243.03), a portmanteau name conveying 'He no get wed', a charge confirmed by the identification (511.02) of McGrath with the Norwegian, a.k.a. 'nowedding' (325.27) captain.

Her main grievance against him is that he is an outsider looking in. 'Hwemwednoget', Christiani tells us, comes from Danish *hvem ved noget*, 'who knows something'. In the trial testimony of 572.21-573.32, for instance, he is the 'Magravius', double of 'Mauritius' (Sackerson), who 'knows from spies' of ALP's indiscretions with Father Michael. So in addition to being a sneak and spy he is a blackmailer, one of the 'bleak-mealers' in HCE's 'seralcellars' (545.27). ALP agrees that the cellar is the right place for the blackmailing Sackerson-McGrath: 'Well, I beg to traverse same above statement by saxy luters in their back haul of Coalcutter . . .' (492.14-15: 'saxy' as slang for 'Saxon' or 'Sacksoun', which is Mrs Glasheen's favoured name for Sackerson, 'luters' because as both raider and blackmailer Sackerson is a thief, with his 'haul' — even as the pub's constabular bouncer he becomes, in her eyes, the larcenous sergeant 'Laraseny' of 618.31 — with a twinge of sentiment for the lost lover's 'lute' as well; together they recall Sechselauten, the Zurich festival which the book associates with young love and its supplanting of the old.)

So like the twins, McGrath does not exist apart from the dreamer's imagination. He is rooted in the manservant, as perceived and imagined by the dreamer — or rather by the ALP who is herself a function of the dreamer's dream-version of his wife. McGrath is what the dreamer imagines his wife imagines their servant to be. Put another way, McGrath is the dreamer's version of his wife's version of his own Shem. We might accordingly expect to detect some occasional congruence between McGrath and Shem, and I think we can. Of all ALP's epithets for McGrath, the most frequent is that he is a 'sneaks', a sneaking snake. As ALP's former seducer he recalls the serpent of 'Genesis', who because of his seduction of Eve was cursed to crawl and be forever hated by her. Or, as the *Wake* has it:

> Such was a bitte too thikke for the Muster of the hoose so as he called down on the Grand Precurser who coiled him a crawler of the dupest dye and thundered at him to flatch down off that erection and be aslimed of himself for the bellance of hissch leif. (506.04-8)

Just who is the 'Grand Precurser' here? In one sense God, coming before Adam. But Adam has another precursor in the world of *Finnegans Wake*: 'riverrun, past Eve and Adam's . . .' In the *Wake* version Eve is the one who curses her enemy, condemning him to crawl on his belly. In fact, 'Crawl!' seems to have been close to what her curse was, the word buried in her marriage-bed cry of 'Magrath he's my pegger' — or, as it is remembered earlier, 'Up the slanger! [Danish for 'serpents'] Three cheers and a heva heva for the name Dan Magraw!' (494.25-6) 'Crawler', 'Magrath', 'Magraw' . . . and at 615.30 it is 'me craws'. Eden was where the animals got their names, and it seems that our resident Eve has coined the name of her special enemy. Which is to say that she has attached two identities to what the dreamer understands by 'Shem', whose first incarnation is as the cad wearing 'leaky sneakers' (34.01), and who for the dreamer is, though not a crawler, a cawer, a crow — the raven which is one of his main symbols for the bad boy banished from the parents' realm.[12] The original naming has developed thus:

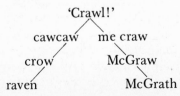

'Crawl!'
cawcaw   me craw
crow   McGraw
raven   McGrath

(ALP is Shem/McGrath's 'McGrath' creator in another way: 'McGrath' means 'Son of Grace' in Gaelic; 'Anna' is Hebrew for 'Grace'.)[13]

'S'

The ground of all these blending projections is, again, the manservant, whose assigned siglum is the letter 'S', 'that strange exotic serpentine, since so properly banished from our scripture' (121.20-1). He is a pathetic old man whose ambitions do not seem to extend beyond getting paid and getting drunk, but who once had brave days: early in the book the dreamer imagines being reincarnated in 'a physical body Cornelius Magrath's (badoldkarakter . . .', that bad old character McGrath in turn being alternately a 'Turk of the theater' scattering piastres and a street arab 'at the streetdoor', begging alms (98.04-14).

His story is one which I believe emerges in the last chapters of *Ulysses*, centred on the sailor Murphy, who was at one point in the book's composition identical with the old beggar who stands under Molly's window[14] — the story of a once-vibrant lover who returns, aged and beaten down beyond recognition, to stare into the window of his old beloved and his replacement, former Turk of the palace, now forgotten street arab at the door, 'romantic in rags' (151.17): 'He stanth theirs mun in his natural, oblious autamnesically . . . the wont to be wanton maid a will to be wise. Thrust from the light, apophotorejected, he spoors loves from her heats.' (251.04-7). At times it recalls 'The Dead', where a resurrected lover is imagined waiting outside the window, threatening to supplant his supplanter. That is Sackerson's story, imagined by the dreamer — the story of a 'pretender' who may yet hope to be master where now he is abused, after the method of a fairy-tale tailor, by marrying the king's daughter and inheriting the kingdom. (In the trial testimony, 'Magravius' is expected to be the one to deflower 'Felicia' — Issy.)

Again, this story is very largely a version of the dreamer's own fantasy, accommodated to the Sackersonian substratum. It betrays, especially toward Issy, the 'burning would', the 'wont to be wanton' (250.16, 251.06) assigned Sackerson and Shem respectively, which are signs of the dreamer's wish to resurrect his youth and recover the love of that time.

The story is mirrored in the dreamer's attitude towards the young man asleep upstairs, the one who alternates between choir-fire brigade (555.17; cf. Sackerson as fire-tender, as organ-player) and scullion (555.21; cf. Sackerson as kitchen-dweller). As Shem-half he is a vindictive blackmailer, whose proper home is the celler which is but a further stage in Sackerson's direction, downwards. But as Shaun-half he is a successful once and future rival, wooing Issy and her companions from their old ways and promising to return, '*sack on back*' (428.22; my italics) after his journey to the heaven which is but a further stage in the son's direction, upwards. To a Wakean father a son is a double threat: he represents a repetition of the father's past, with its remembered sins and follies, and also the future — death, usurpation. In enacting the second of these threats Shaun blends with the mysterious Father Michael, who is suspected by the dreamer of having had a forbidden liaison with Issy and/or the very young ALP. Shem-Sackerson is what the dreamer fears/desires from the past, Shaun-Michael what he fears/desires from the future.

To sum up: Our dreamer lies between son, above him, and servant, below, with his wife (usually) by his side. Contemplating his history, he begets HCE. Contemplating HCE, the earwig squeezed into upper and lower, he begets Shaun and Shem. Contemplating the servant as 'other', a brooding presence threatening revenge, rebellion, and usurpation, the rising-up of suppressed impulses, he finds as it were a psychic place to put Shem. Hearing of the recent death of the pious Father Michael, he likewise finds a place to put Shaun — the fat incarnation of his later and future years, of piety *faute de mieux* and the priest's proverbial unfair advantage with the ladies. Contemplating his wife, he begets ALP, who begins the process again from her perspective as imagined by the dreamer: contemplating the son in her equivalent for the dreamer's Sackerson-Shem aspect, she begets McGrath; Father Michael stays himself. Contemplating her husband, she begets, first the remembered young lover of Vanderdecken vintage, and secondly a figure whose obscurity is at the heart of the book, a corpse whose last initial is definitely M, whose first initial is probably F: Father Michael, Something-or-other McGrath, and, of course, Finn McCool. In a sense, what would seem to be the one-way projection which the dreamer practises on her and others is reciprocated utterly: she is the one by virtue of whose vision the dreamer becomes a giant's corpse, being waked and hoping for resurrection; hers is the letter which tells of the day's only piece of substantial news, the death of a Father, and thus to a great extent sets the whole gazebo in motion. For all that *Finnegans Wake* is the book of one male dreamer, the reiterated equation between it and the wife's words — her letter — has its justification in a matter of fact.

FOUR

'Females'

THE DREAMER'S women make up a continuum symbolised by the River Liffey, with Issy as its source, Kate (as the washerwomen) as its mouth, and ALP the stream in between. At times we can witness one turning into the other, as when in return for HCE's promise to settle down, the female promises to stop being a temptress (that is, an Issy), to become domestic (that is, an ALP), and eventually to turn into a devoutly Catholic widow (that is, a Kate) (243.20-36), or 550.18-23, where HCE's gifts to his bride include a broom and other Kate implements. Kate is what ALP is heading towards, and she knows it — that is why at the end she embraces the 'seahags' as her own people (627.24-32).

In many ways, in fact, the book's females are the same person, at different ages. Issy is the blonde girl whose hair becomes 'deepdark . . . like this red bog' when she has her first sexual encounter (203.25-6); ALP's hair, having been set aflame by her lover's 'flightening' eyes (and singed by her recent 'permanent'), is a fire-coloured 'auburnt' (139.23); Kate's hair is ashen grey. All show signs of lameness (181.17-19, 199.21-2, 333.06-7, 334.29, 548.30, 580.25-6); all talk to themselves. Issy is a temptress with a 'gift of seek on site' (5.25); ALP is an enchantress; Kate is a witch. At least two of the three seem concerned with facial hair: Kate, as I mentioned before, is bearded (evidence follows below), and Issy draws moustaches on her looking-glass reflection (459.05-7) and mentions her own 'shaving water' (146.29); all three are, probably in consequence, given to excessive powdering (ALP: 200.06, 550.18-19; Issy: 440.26-7; Kate: 538.04). All are of course watery, with a high number of 'liquids' in their speech (and ALP, 'with a choicey voicey like waterglucks' (200.08-9), commonly begins sentences with the word 'well'; of Kate we are told 'She's deep, that one' (530.35)). Issy is often represented as having just experienced her menarche; ALP is having her last menstrual period[1] (at fifty-four, she is forty years older than the age at which Milly Bloom had her first menstrual period; like the prankquean she has had a forty years' 'rain'); Kate is stuck with the job of washing away stains, 'the sales of Cloth' (141.30). Small wonder ALP feels herself to be a transitional figure, 'between two ages' (207.36).

The III/4 account of ALP describes her as 'Woman, with curlpins . . . haggish expression, peaky nose, trekant mouth, fithery wight . . . Welshrabbit teint, Nubian shine, nasal fossette, turfy tuft, undersized, free kirk, no age' (559.20-9). Those curlpins are evidence of the permanent 'wave' of ALP-as-river; the curlpins themselves are the 'curlicornies' of her 'headdress', of her 'holden heirheaps' (102.11-2, 24); their curl-papers show up as 'tramtokens in her hair' (194.30-2), the bits of paper floating down the river. The recent singeing of her fire-coloured auburn hair has evidently combined in the dreamer's memory with recollections of his wife's admiring comments on the 'flashing' eyes and 'burning' gaze of his courtship days to generate a surreal vision of his young self, as they say, setting the Liffey on fire,[2] an image which is for example behind the indignant charge of (old HCE) Shaun that (young HCE) Shem is an 'incendiarist' threatening 'to set ever annyma roner moother of mine on fire' (426.01-4), and probably accounts for the 'fireman's helmet' ALP is wearing when her husband visits her at 530.14.[3] Louis Mink observes of such passages that on 9 August 1833 the Liffey, coated with burning rum and molasses, was in fact on fire;[4] and we may add that to Joyce the Liffey was auburn — 'quite brown'[5] — until it passes the Dublin dye-houses which give it 'reddish water'.[6]

The ungallant word 'haggish' of course looks forward to ALP's terminus in Kate; the insulting comparison of ALP's complexion to the cheesy sauce of a welsh rarebit ironically recalls Issy's peaches-and-cream skin, her 'Three creamings a day' (144.02-3), and confirms that (in contrast to her 'ruddy' husband) like the other two women ALP is a blood-letter, growing ever paler: Issy, at her menarche, is frequently represented as 'paling' off, rose becoming lily; Kate is a 'wan warmwooed woman scrubs' (579.33-4); ALP herself says she is becoming 'faint' (626.01). The description of her 'peaky nose', accordingly, probably contains the sense of 'peaked', meaning 'worn'. This is no amply upholstered Molly Bloom; ALP's childbearing (two or three children in reality, but to the washerwomen it seems like a hundred and eleven) has taken a lot out of her, leaving her feeling at times like a 'noughty . . . zeroine' (261.24); rivers, after all, are skinny. The curious triangularity of her mouth ('trekant' is Danish for 'triangle'), useful I suppose when she wants to 'vistule a hymn' (199.27), is along with her pubic delta a determinant of her △ siglum, thence of the book's riverine deltas; perhaps the geometrical congruence of mouth and pubis has to do with the *Wake*'s occasional equation of genital and oral sex.

Despite her thinness ALP customarily wears the girdle we noted in our survey of the room, imagined as the 'stout stays' of the river's banks by the washerwomen (208.14), who also tell us of her extravagant, 'gaudy' hat with streamers, hairpin, and veil — the last contributing both to her status as a veiled harem wife (HCE is sometimes Mohammed) and to the hazy vision which she shares with her creator: 'Illas! I wisht I had better glances to peer to you through this bay-light's growing' (626.34-5). The 'glances' are also glasses, the 'owlglassy bicycles' which according to the washerwomen 'boggled her eyes' (208.09-10). Her perfume is a slightly marshy-smelling *eau de Cologne* (624.24).

Like the other two women she habitually talks or sings to herself, revealing a contradictoriness of which her conflicted attitude towards McGrath is an example. Being between two ages, she is between two voices as well, two ways of seeing the world and describing it; in fact her voice may be recognised by the way it sometimes alternates between innocence and cynicism, between Issy (although Issy knows more than she lets on) and Kate (although Kate can show vestiges of the dreaming girl she once was). Michael H. Begnal is right when he describes her final monologue as having a 'realistic, slangy lilt',[7] and yet this same realistic passage tells us about her that her head is full of the cinematograph (623.19).

In fact she is a master fantasist, her daydreams compounded

largely of memory and popular culture (a large percentage of her 'mamafesta's' titles, for instance (104.05-107.07), sound like *Titbits* articles or previews-of-coming-attractions), who is able to impress her fantasies on others. We get an example of this knack at the end (625.17-25) when she uses the unpromising material of a scent of turf, a mushroom, a pea and a seed to improvise a pantomime for her husband's distraction. It is through this talent that she becomes the source of the dreamer's two main images of himself, as sleeping giant and as Vanderdecken-type. Like Issy in one sense, like Kate in another, she is a 'charmer': 132.16 goes so far as to call her a 'snake charmer'. The main point of her section in I/6 (139.15-28) is that she can make you believe anything she wants you to, and in III/4 she easily replaces her son's nightmare with a substitute fantasy. The very end of her monologue, where cinematic and pantomimic fantasy finally succumbs to reality's oceanic blankness, is as moving as it is partly because it depicts a powerful mind's final overthrow, the collapse of an empire of fancy.

Many of ALP's contradictions are traceable to this uneasy suspension of pantomimic romance and cold fact. There is something of a parallel to the ruined HCE's wish 'to pay himself off in kind remembrances' (589.35) in the way this ageing and increasingly hobbled woman likes to envision herself as a dancer whose favourite number, apparently (200.23-4, 436.35-6, 415.09-11), is the athletic can-can. An account of her letter tells us what we know from other sources, that she is prone to 'fansaties', and then gives us an example which also exposes the facts:

> But how many of her readers realise that she is not out to dizzledazzle with a graith uncouthrement of postmantuam glasseries from the lapins and the grigs. Nuttings on her wilelife! Grabar gooden grandy for old almeanium adamologists like Dariaumaurius and Zovotrimaserovmeravmerouvian; (dmzn!); she feel plain plate one flat fact thing . . . (112.36-113.05)

This is a variant on a daydream Joyce knew well — the famous author fantasy, the scenario here being that some adoring reviewer is saying that if she wanted she could dazzle us with her great accoutrement of sesquipedalian vocabulary, her erudite familiarity with authors whose names most of us can't even pronounce, but that she has goes beyond that: she is just going to tell us the plain truth. But 'uncouthrement', with its obvious 'uncouth', gives the game away. That word 'plate', used in the sense of 'truth on a platter', is a signature of the thoroughly unrefined Kate (e.g. 142.07), into whose argot this passage quickly descends (113.11-18). Like Nora Barnacle, whom some considered too simple-minded for her partner, ALP can remember the courtship days with her future mate when 'the lewdy' were calling her 'his analectual pygmyhop' (268.27-29), an intellectual pygmy compared to him; evidently the words stung. 'Graith uncouthrement' also suggests, of course, a great and graceful accoutrement, regal wardrobe and appointments fit for the 'queenoveire' (28.01) as imagined by a woman who complains to her husband, apparently with justice, that she hardly has a thing to wear.

In examining the fireplace in the dreamer's room, we noted that Issy is something of a Cinderella. The same is true of her mother. Not surprisingly, the testimony about her ancestry conflicts: many times she is a mere tailor's daughter; at other times she is a queen or princess, a 'midget madgetcy' (112.28) who at the end declares regally, 'My people were not their sort' (627.24). Both fathers, king and tailor – also Prince Hamlet[8] – are fused in 'Papyroy of Pepinregn', 'poking out with his canule into the arras of what brilliant bridge-cloths and joking up with his tonguespitz to the crimosing balkonladies' (568.36-569.02).

The washerwomen recount ALP's youthful departure from the 'garden of Erin' into the married life that will make of her a Kate as a pollution of her blond hair, her 'golden lifey' (202.35-203.08), and in her final monologue ALP remembers how just being called 'goldylocks' by her husband was enough to put her 'back in paladays last' (615.22-5) – Paradise Lost, of course, but also a lost palace, the golden realm of her remembered-fantasised girlhood. She loved that, and wishes he would do it more often: 'I am leafy, your goolden, so you called me, may me life, yea your goolden, silve me solve, exsogerraider! You did so drool. I was so sharm' (619.29-31). The charmer, who 'will tell you all sorts of makeup things, strangerous' (625.05), wants to be charmed in turn: 'You will always call me Leafiest, won't you, dowling?' (624.22-3) If, as we have noted, HCE is an accomplished mimic, always 'immutating aperybally' — a fact which more than any other accounts for the pantomime that is *Finnegans Wake* — then we should note as well that ALP is the one who taught him how. She is the one who taught the dreamer how to dream, and who supplied his stock of characters with many of its major parts. A great 'exsogerraider', he is *her* exaggerator, and if we seek an example of just how this habit was taught to him, we need look no further than her letter which, as Mrs Glasheen notes, generally addresses him as 'majesty'.

There is evidence that this kind of bucking-up make-believe especially characterises her love-making, during which she is in the habit of letting out a piercing orgasmic shriek which makes her husband feel majestic indeed: '. . . upping her at king's count, her aldritch cry oloss unheading . . . I pierced her beak with order of the Danabrog . . . what was trembling sod quaked no more, what were frozen loins were stirred and lived . . .' (548.34-549.09) (That eldritch cry takes on a life of its own, for instance 'lickering jessup the smooky shiminey' (583.33), to beget Issy upstairs.) The fervour is almost certainly faked to some extent; as we have seen, she is really thinking of McGrath. In any case it works — allows her husband to feel, against all the obdurate evidence, like her young fancy, sweeping her off her feet.

The reality which overwhelms them both at the end is doubly bitter for revealing her man as a 'bumpkin' and herself as a hag. When she says of Issy 'let her rain now if she likes' (627.11-12), she is in effect saying two other things: 1. Let me die now; 2. Let me become Kate now, the queen's servant. And sure enough, when her last sentence comes round again at the start of the book and re-begins the narrative, the first recognisable voice we hear is Kate's, showing us the museum of the pre-menopausal life of coupling and begetting which she has just left behind, and the female figure we meet next is a 'turfwoman' (12.11), 'steal[ing] our historic presents from the past postpropheticals' (11.30-1).

'*Kate*'

If we seek a lesson in what it means to become a Kate, we can turn to the 'reversed rainbow' interlude of II/1, in which Issy refracts into seven girls/colours each of whom, as if looking into a magic mirror, foresees her destiny. One is to become a 'grocer's bawd', another a bibulous 'lady in waiting', another a 'Mrs Wildhare Quickdoctor' (probably a crone practising folk medicine), another a widow (grieving, incidentally, for McGrath), another a bellowing horsewoman/actress, another a pietistic gossiper, the last a rickety fortuneteller (227.03-11). The very predictability of the catalogue has to do with the note of resignation, of here-we-go-again, in ALP's last words: time for yesterday's Juliet, once the company's 'princeable girl' (626.27), to start playing Juliet's nurse.

Or worse: Kate, with her broom, her curses, her cook's cauldron, is the Mullingar's resident witch, implacably bitter to those younger than herself, a terminal moraine of all those impulses unacknowledged or swept from view in ALP's dutiful wife's progress. (Take a close look, for example, at some of ALP's 'gifts' (209.31-212.19) or, remembering 'Hansel and Gretel', at 563.28-30.) The first sign of this is the feature mentioned earlier, the facial hair which, as *Macbeth* reminds us (I, iii, 46), is a mark of witches. The evidence on this point, the cross-sexual implications of which Joyce first explored in the figure of Bella/Bello Cohen, with the 'superfluous hairs' of her/his 'sprouting moustache', is indirect but overall, I think, compelling: the echo of that phrase, 'superfluous hairs', in describing Kate as 'a rawkneepudsfrowse [German '*Putzfrau*': charwoman] . . . with superflowvius heirs' (526.25-6), the pairing of Kate with the buckpapped Sackerson as '*femme à barbe ou homme-nourrice*' (81.28-9), and the fusing of the two as 'man Shee', male *sidhe* and mannish banshee (409.02), the crone's 'wickered' Kish of 13.36-14.01 ('wickered' joins 'whiskered' and 'Wicca'; a capital 'K' is Kate's siglum). There is also the apparently incidental expression 'beard on prophet' (33.32-3), which may remind us that those bearded witches in *Macbeth* were prophets, and that Kate is a fortuneteller. As washer, carrier of chamberpots, manager of middens, she is the book's foremost authority on the past, on 'dumplan as she nosed it' (79.29), and in this book of 'Doublends Jined' (20.16) it follows that she should therefore be the one who knows about the future too. (To ALP, she *is* the future.)

In fact her necromantic practices are very much of the druidical past, whether remembered censoriously (520.13-14) or nostalgically (79.14-26). She is variously associated with banshees and Bathsheba (468.35-6), with nature religions and magic, and in this sense as in others the other two women of the Mullingar are her true descendants: as 'my ould nourse Asa' she has taught Issy 'all the runes', 'heartswise and four-words', to the point that Issy is prepared to take her place as a pagan priestess 'in Skokholme ... uppum their Drewitt's altar' (279.20-7). (The lesson has been learned — Issy is a 'sourceress' singing 'a song of a witch' (251.11-12), a 'Holy moon priestess' (360.25).)

For Kate, as for the other women of the book, the temptation is toward recidivism, atavism, back to old lovers (McGrath) practices (witchcraft) and ages (Issy's manifest resistance to growing up). The temptation is resisted out of prudence: for all the appeal of the old days and ways, Kate advises Issy to settle on a church wedding with the milk-livered 'Jr', for 'its the surplice money ... what buys the bed' (279.11-12, 32-7). (Compare ALP's similar advice at 268.16-272.08.)

Such passages say much about the nature of Kate's Catholicism, her devotion to the 'surplice'. The deflected sexuality which in the *Wake* characterises the relation of females to priests combines with opportunism: the priest distributes cakes as well as wafers to his female congregation; the multitude drinking communion wine from his spigot are not only women practising mass fellatio but also piglets at a sow's dugs; penitents in the confessional are also informers. When Kate is summoned to try out her powers of conversion, it is in the telling phrase, 'Let succuba succumb, the improvable his wealth made possible' (530.33-4), and in she comes like a demented inquisitor, spouting about paternosters and papal indulgences and the Council of Trent and getting everything wrong. Converted or not, she is still seeing ghosts (136.13-15, 557.04-12), and is still 'everlapsing' (333.06-7).

However badly she may have learned her catechism, she is

a soldier of the Church in the way which, from the *Wake*'s anticlerical perspective, counts most. The trial testimony of III/4 records that as 'Fortissa' she is the one who reported on HCE's confession (572.26-31), and as a rule the chains of anti-HCE rumours feature a link between a pious old woman and her priest.

She is probably named 'Fortissa' in the trial scene because she is so loud. Her speech contains an unusually high percentage of expletives and sudden interjections, as if she were constantly carrying on a high-pitched argument with some inaudible other or, rather, buried inner voice out of her 'deep' (530.35) past:

> I awed to have scourched his Abarm's brack for him. For the loaf of Obadiah, take your pastryart's noas out of me flouer bouckuet! Of the strainger scene you given squeezers to me skillet! As cream of the hearth thou reinethst alhome. His lapper and libbers was glue goulewed as he sizzled there watching me lautterick's pitcher by Wexford-Atelier as Katty and Lanner, the refined souprette, with my bust alla brooche and the padbun under my matelote, showing my jigotty sleeves and all my new toulong touloosies. Whisk!
> (531.10-18)

This passage is typical for its subsidence into a private memory which eventually becomes so vivid that Kate begins acting it out in dialogue, taking both her own part and that of her remembered interlocutor — here the importunate lover who told her that as queen of his heart she reigned alone. Though all the *Wake*'s females talk to themselves, she is the most dramatic, the one behind the Willingdone-lipoleum cross-talk of the museyroom. Add to this the testimony that she is a nonstop talker, plus one other piece of information, and I think we can see that, like Sackerson, she is more prominent in the *Wake* than we thought.

The additional datum is that Kate is the Mullingar's washerwoman, the one stuck with handling 'the sales of Cloth' (141.30), so inured to her routine that her face is said to resemble a tub of Monday wash (333.23-4). Which is to say that I/8, the 'Anna Livia Plurabelle' chapter, always taken as the dialogue of two washerwomen, is hers, the dream-mediated record of her talking to herself while going about her chores. (So, for instance, one of the washerwomen describes herself as, like Kate the cook, 'marthared mary allacook' (214.23).) The washerwomen derive from Kate's ongoing conversation with herself:

> Welland well! If tomorrow keeps fine who'll come tripping to sightsee? [Cf. Kate, 141.35-6] How'll? Ask me next what I haven't got! The Belvedarean exhibitioners. In their cruisery caps and oarsclub colours. What hoo, they band! [cf. Kate, 8.33-4] And what hoa, they buck! [Cf. Kate, 531.23 — the comic song 'What Ho! She Bucks' is behind both passages] And here is her nubilee letters too. Ellis on quay in scarlet thread. Linked for the world on a flush-caloured field. Annan exe after to show they're not Laura Keown's. [Cf. Kate, 141.30] O, may the diabolo twisk your seifety pin! [Cf. Kate, 531.18-20] You child of Mammon, Kinsella's Lilith! Now who has been tearing the leg of her drawars on her? Which leg is it? The one with the bells on it. Rinse them out and aston along with you! Where did I stop? Never stop! Continuarration! You're not there yet. I amstel waiting. Garonne, garonne! [Cf. Kate, 221.16] (205.03-15)
> (See also 64.15-21, 586.05-15.)

With this identification, we can confirm some earlier observations about Kate and come to understand more of her story. At 209.14, for instance, one of the washerwomen says, 'I aubette my bearb'; it is surely unlikely that the book contains *two* bearded ladies. 214.09-31 confirms that she is a seer of ghosts (although part of her is skeptical), supports indications elsewhere that she is lame, and tells us that she is going deaf, which perhaps accounts for 'Fortissa's' alarming loudness, and explains why summoning her should be the production it is.

Most of all, I think we can hear in the obsessive interest in ALP, in the alternately catty and moony tones in which ALP's story is gone over, the voice of Kate as the 'other woman', alternating between vicarious identification and sour grapes. The other woman: that in fact is just what she is called at 603.14, 'the alter girl they tuck in for sweepsake'. Her story is, I believe, essentially the same as that old warhorse of the Victorian stage, *East Lynne*, the novelistic original of which is one of the few books Molly Bloom remembers reading. It is the story of a wife and mother who, having disgraced herself and been cast out of her home, returns in disguise as a servant in the home where once she was mistress, watching pathetically as the oblivious husband and children lavish affection on her replacement.

242.25-243.36, a passage too long to quote, seems to sketch in the story behind this role by alternately blending and contrasting the careers of ALP and Kate. It occurs in II/1, the 'Mime' chapter in which the children act out the story of their parents' courtship and marriage. As usual, Shem has a disgraceful secret about the whole business, about some second helpmate ('Helpmeat two'), a 'fiery goosemother', a 'woman who did' who is 'wronged' by her lover, and who seems to wind up as, at different times, beggar, cook, pious churchwoman, and 'widders'. In any event, that *Genesis* word 'helpmate' recalls the original other woman, Lilith, the ungovernable, demonic first wife said to have been put away by Adam so that he could marry Eve. Mrs Glasheen, who detects an allusion to Lilith at the beginning of this passage, notes hints that HCE 'had an earlier wife or concubine before he married Anna Livia' and adds that 'these hints point to Kate', 'while Lilith is part of the Lily . . . theme.'[10] I think that in the sleeper's scenario Lilith *is* Kate, as is at times the temptress Lily, especially the Lily Kinsella whose last name, as Mrs Glasheen notes, weds her to the Dermot MacMurrough of Kinsella whose wife (hold on now) was Devor*gilla* (my italics), lured from her rightful husband in a manner which the *Wake* parallels to Dermot's elopement with Grania, and who shows up in the trial of III/4 as Gillia, a permutation of Kate (Kate as Fortissa is paired with Mauritius; Gillia is paired with Magravius; Magravius — 'McGrath' — is a derivative of Mauritius/Sackerson), and whom we are told HCE is secretly soliciting by proxy. Or, as ALP says about Sackerson and Kate: 'He's for thee what she's for me' (620.33). As Sackerson has come to embody ALP's old lover, so Kate embodies HCE's old flame — his first lover/fiancée/wife, his Lilith.

As the washerwomen, Kate seems to join ALP in her odium

for Lily Kinsella (the *'eau de Colo'* she smells in her clothes (204.33) is a nasty version of ALP's *eau de cologne* (624.24)), but perhaps gives herself away: the initials she finds in those clothes, 'Ellis on quay in scarlet thread' (205.07-8), display her own signatory K, and although she has distorted them in order to implicate ALP ('L' changed to 'Ellis' and 'K' changed to 'quay' are two short jumps away from 'ALP', since the 'Ellis' implies 'Alice' and 'q' is throughout the *Wake* interchangeable with 'p'), she winds up re-affirming the connection with herself, since 'quay', pronounced 'key', recalls her introduction as (8.08) keeper of the keys. 'You child of Mammon, Kinsella's Lilith!' (205.10-11): Remember that she is talking to herself.

As 'mistress Kathe', keeper of the keys, she is doubtless an incarnation of the Mrs Keyes who owned the Mullingar around the turn of the century.[11] But 'mistress' is a double-edged word, indicating not only 'proprietress' but 'other woman', husband's queen and husband's plaything. She is a slavey where once she was queen, an imprisoned 'wan warmwooed woman scrubbs' (579.33-4) whose recollection of the days of her warm wooing is wormwood. Her attendant emblems are chamberpot, washtub, sink, mop, broom, feather duster, dish-drudge's clout, with kitchen hearth and various kitchen utensils. One of these is a steam-iron-*cum*-rolling pin, which no doubt accounts for the fact that Sackerson, under her influence, can imitate a flatfish (221.07). A rolling pin, of course, was in Joyce's day an invariable symbol of wife-as-battleaxe, lying in wait to whack her erring husband as he tiptoes in the door; with Kate around (or for that matter his wife: see 495.15-16), HCE has cause to fear that he may be imitating a flatfish himself one of these days.

In sum, she is one of those astonishing old women that are so striking a feature of the landscape of Ireland; impossible to imagine an Irish epic without her. She is the latest in a line that began with the 'sisters' designated in the title of Joyce's first published work of fiction, a title which, such is Joyce's way, *Ulysses* (p. 394) explains: 'The aged sisters draw us into life; we wail, batten, sport, clip, clasp, dwindle, die: over us dead they bend'. Kate, she of the wax-works and museum, she who says to herself while running through ALP's history 'But O, gihon! I lovat a gabber' (213.08), has the same frightening power exemplified by the Misses Flynn in 'The Sisters', the power of defining the lives of the males with, simply, talk, endless talk: she is posterity. Shem may be the book's resident artist, but the excrement out of which he makes the ink to write his books began as the food he ate, and that food is eggs, as laid by Biddy the hen, one of Kate/ALP's main incarnations. The mime of II/1 is 'adopted from the Ballymooney Bloodriddon Murther' (219.19-20) — the blood-ridden mother, the post-menopausal Kate.

Kate also ensures that its telling will continue to be a female affair by training the already 'uncontrollable' night-talker (32.07-8) Issy in the ways of semi-historical narrative. That is part of what is going on in II/2, and as Shaun remarks later at 431.28-33, in a passage which blends appreciation of Issy's story-telling with recollections of Kate's bedside tales, the lesson has been learned well.

At times *sidhe*, these endlessly vocal females can also be scops. They are all singers: there is ALP's 'lilting' (627.21), Issy's 'song of a witch' (251.11), and Kate 'dirging a past of bloody altars' (276.04). This last gives a fair idea of what kind of singing they go in for. They like old songs recalling pagan days, as confirmed by Shaun's memory of his mother's 'callback' songs, which start Shaun 'dreaming back' and which 'haunt the sleeper' (294.27-295.12) — in fact work their way, through the porches of his ear, into his dreams: 'We just are upsidedown singing what ever the dimkims mummur allalilty she pulls inner out heads' (373.33-5) say the customers at one point, speaking for a dreamer who is constantly hearing the lilting voices of the females, turning them into the dreams of *Finnegans Wake*.

'Issy'

The voice that the dreamer hears most often is Issy's, that 'avoice from afire', coming through the fireplace flue his room shares with hers. If ALP is the *Wake*'s muse, the one who shows the dreamer how to dream, and Kate is the *Wake*'s quarry, its rumour repository, Issy is the *Wake*'s occasion, theme, reason for existence, prime mover — the one for whom and because of whom the dream is dreamed.

Aside from being fairy, sorceress, and druidic priestess, Issy is repeatedly envisioned as a regal female on high (Beatrice, Rapunzel, Blessed Damozel), fiery, and connected to the dreamer by a secret and shameful route, a 'Secret Hookup' (360.16) which at times suggests the hidden passageways of Gothic novels, at times — considered from her vantage — as a wishing well to some spirit or troll below. These overtones derive from that chimney flue connecting her third floor room with the dreamer's bedroom underneath. Thus for instance we first see her as 'the fields of heat and yields of wheat where corngold Ysit? shamed and shone' (75.10-11); thus she and her double are imagined coming 'Ous of their freiung pfann into myne foyer' (538.26-7). As temptress, she is placed to arouse in the dreamer the familiar madonna/whore dichotomy: her person is on high, amidst the stars, but her voice reaches the dreamer from a fire-hole on the floor, one which, when he stands before it, literally speaks to his crotch. Of the roles conjured by the dreamer out of this circumstance, Cinderella is the most prominent, and it is likely relevant that scholars of Joyce's day were revealing in the British/Welsh 'Cinderella' a story of father-daughter incest. In one of the three main versions, according to Alfred Nutt, 'Moved by his daughter's likeness to, or by her ability to wear some special part of, the dead mother's attire, a king seeks his daughter in marriage. She resists, and is cast forth or flees.' The original version is Geoffrey of Monmouth's story of Lear's banishment of Cordelia, the story invoked on the last page.[12] Add to this dimension the folk motif of conception-by-fire ('The beautiful, marriageable daughter of Daolgas came over to him, and having stooped down to kiss him, a red spark of fire flew from his mouth into hers, and she became pregnant in consequence'),[13] and we can see how the dreamer's imagined calls up the chimney are functions of his desire to rekindle the early passion of his love for the young ALP through her reincarnation in Issy.[14]

It is important to keep in mind how much of this is a product of the dreamer's projection. Mainly, Issy is a voice, intermittently audible but apparently non-stop, since in addition to the unplotted and endless tale of her daytime monologue she is a Scheherezadian uncontrollable nighttalker (32.08), 'sleepytalking' (459.05) like her alter ego Marge. So, for example, she promises Shaun that she will be repeating his name after she has got into bed and gone to sleep (461.25-6). She occasionally speaks with a lisp (61.06-11, 265.18-19, 302 fn.2), especially, it seems, when reverting to her pubescent or infantile self — a fact which, when we add that ALP apparently also lisped in her youth (139.19), possibly explains why HCE should find the sound particularly arousing (147.36-148.02, 459.28, 138.10). Another Issy-sound that excites him is of her urinating into her chamberpot; in fact, considering her fondness for the little-girl euphemisms 'siss' (e.g. 158.06) and 'whiss' (e.g. 148.26), her nickname probably has to do with this. Most of her manifold sprinklings, makings of wit, sissings, and so on seem to originate in her lispings and whisperings, combined with the high-pitched sound of the wind up the chimney and, especially, the drippings of the faucet into the basin next to the fireplace; see for instance the 'Rosepetalletted sounds' of 561.35-562.15.

As Kate is well and washtub and ALP a river, Issy is rain and dew, whose 'dewfolded song' (359.32; see also 158.19-24) is cued by the plink-plonk of drops from the leaking faucet into the room's basin. Which in turn makes her a harpist, it having been a Joycean convention since the first poem of *Chamber Music* that moving water sounds like string instruments: 'Lissom! lissom! I am doing it. Hark, the corne entreats! And the larpnotes [harpnotes plus *larmes*] prittle' (21.02-4). When the water flows she becomes ALP playing a rivery fiddle; Kate rounds out the combo by using her washtub as a kettledrum (531.09).

Aside from her voice, the two most solidly established facts about Issy's appearance are that she wears cosmetics and has blonde hair. But even these details fade under scrutiny. First, the makeup has contributed to her uncertainty about her identity: envision an adolescent girl seeing her made-up face in her mirror while still feeling one with the fair unpainted self of her childhood, and you can see how she has divided into Issy and Marge, light and rainbow. (The makeup days also correspond to her menarche, about which more later; the self-dividing accounts for the juvenile voice — a mature woman splits into two girls, each half her age.) Second, more conspicuous in the text than her shadows and tints is her jar of vanishing cream. *Vanishing* cream.

As for her blonde hair, it seems at times to have been another of the dreamer's conjurations. The evidence begins with this excerpt from ALP's farewell:

> it was between Williamstown and the Mairrion Ailesbury on the top of the longcar, as merrily we rolled along, we think of him looking at us yet as if to pass away in a cloud. When he woke up in a sweat besidus it was to pardon him, goldylocks, me having an airth, but he daydreamsed we had a lovelyt face for a pulltomine. (615.19-24)

One of the locations being specified here is, as Louis Mink says, the Rock Road tramline between Williamstown and the intersection of Merrion and Ailesbury Roads. But as Mink also notes,[15] 'Mairrion' includes Merrion Square. It happens that James Joyce and Nora Barnacle first met on Nassau Street, at some point along the line between Merrion Square and the statue of King William which used to stand before Trinity. We have here an account of that meeting: Joyce spotting Nora and being momentarily spellbound (compare the Blooms' spellbound meeting: *Ulysses* 771), then walking up to her in a sweat and speaking his first words, along the line of 'Pardon me, goldilocks, my heaven on earth', and the 1904 equivalent of 'You ought to be in pictures.' It is probably a fairly accurate account of James Joyce's first words to Nora, although other evidence suggests that instead of 'Pardon me' the phrase was 'I beg your pardon', thus, as in this version of that Nassau Street encounter, establishing the remembered suitor as a beggar: 'he hestens towards dames troth and wedding hand like the prince of Orange and Nassau while he has trinity left behind him like Bowlbeggar Bill-the-Bustonly' (135.11-32).

Why 'goldilocks', though, seeing that Nora, like ALP, was auburn-haired? ALP still remembers being struck by this bit of fast-talking flattery (619.29-30), and hopes he will repeat his act, *'wake himself out of his winter's doze'* (201.11) like (remember that rug by the fireplace?) the Papa Bear of the story; HCE has been told that if he would 'talk to her [Issy] nice of guldenselvear' her 'lips would moisten once again' (28.11-12).

Why 'Goldilocks'? I think the answer may lie in the twenty-seven year-old Joyce's admission to Nora that she had not, in fact, been 'the girl for whom I had dreamed and written the verses' of *Chamber Music*.[16] That ideal woman, we know from Poem V of *Chamber Music*, was golden-haired. Leopold Bloom considered 'hallucination' as a possible explanation for Milly's blonde hair — an hallucination, presumably, by the mother, envisioning, during conception, the blonde hair of her first lover, Lieutenant Mulvey; ALP remembers of the night Issy was conceived, 'But that night after, all you were wanton! Bidding me do this and that and the other. And blowing off to me, hugly Judsys, what wouldn't you give to have a girl! Your wish was mewill' (620.24-7). And what he wished for, it seems, was a gold-haired girl, the gold-haired girl he had at first imagined or pretended his future wife to be. Thus the pantomime courtship of II/1, as always a product of the dreamer's imagination, features a blonde female (220.07-8) that the lover met, apparently near Trinity (257.11-12).

This one definite fact about Issy has the effect of making her seem to the dreamer even more like, to paraphrase Joyce's letter, the girl of his dreams: she is 'my deepseep daughter which was bourne up pridely out of medsdreams unclouthed when I was pillowing in my brime' (366.13-15). That is why he should be described as dreaming upward — 'droming on loft till the sight of the sternes' (199.06-7) — to Issy in the star-bedecked bedroom over his, from which her voice descends trickling, dripping, sissing, plink-plunking, the distillation of the cloud formed from the ascending vapours of his dreams.

If Issy is the dreamer's dream-girl, then it seems natural for her to be identified with his dream, which is to say, with the *Wake* itself. If her presence in the *Wake*'s here-and-now is especially attenuated, especially prone to be absorbed into patterns of mythopoeic dream-making, those patterns should be correspondingly rich and central, involved in those complexes of images which emerge when *Finnegans Wake* contemplates itself. The *Wake* sees itself in images of kaleidoscope, broken mirror, phoenix, dream; Issy is rainbow-girl, handglass-breaker, 'fiery quean' (328.31), dream-girl.

There are reasons for this correspondence, which will lead us into the question of Joyce's relation with his daughter Lucia. The equation is established by a number of intricate tropes linking Issy/Lucia to the book and to its author's history. I have already described these in my previous *Notes on Issy*,[17] and will here give a brief summation of the main points.

First, in part because of her correspondence to Lewis Carroll's *A*lice *P*leasance *L*iddel (hence A.P.L.), Issy is identified with apples, especially the apple of the fall.

Second, because of those signals from above, she is the book's temptress, ever 'flispering . . . to Finnegan, to sin again' (580.20). That 'flispering', with its two 'i's, is typical of her messages, perhaps because of the fireplace's prickly 'tinct tint' sound recorded at 244.13, certainly because of the various sissings and plink-plinks which descend by way of its flue. As a result she is insistently associated with doubled sounds, especially with double i's — and thence with the two-dot Morse code signal for 'I', broadcast to a distant lover who, as *Tris*tram, invariably responds with the two dashes which in Morse code indicate two t's; thence also with a host of doubled verticals and doubled dots, including the two peas in a pod which are the subject of the prankquean's troublesome overture to the father. Her 'sissing' connects her — as 'apple' — with the book's snake and doubtless accounts in part for her name; the double i's are also a pair of eyes, and must remind us that Joyce's daughter was named Lucia, patroness of vision. Add to this the fact of Joyce's glaucoma, the identification of Issy with *Iri*s and *Isi*s — healer of the dismembered Osiris — and her refraction into the rainbow girls (especially as the perception of rainbows around lights is an early symptom of glaucoma), and Issy emerges as the guardian of the author's eyes — often, in fact (those two dots) the eyes themselves.

Guardian, but also in some way the affliction: rainbow girl equals glaucoma's rainbow; the girl who 'broke the glass' (270.21) is implicated in the light's fragmentation into a spectrum of colours. There are two Issys, Issy herself and her looking-glass double 'Marge', figured in for instance an opposition between Issy's golden butter and Marge's working-class 'marge' (cf. *Ulysses* 152), innocence and seductiveness, girl without makeup and young woman with makeup, translucent moonstone and red-flecked bloodstone or 'heliotrope', and *Finnegans Wake* is full of evidence that the division between these two corresponded to the onset of Issy's menarche and ('mensuration makes me mad' (269. fn.3)) schizophrenic madness, that behind that it corresponds to Lucia Joyce's decline into madness and coincides with the onset of the author's glaucoma, that both events are identified with the *Wake*'s 'heptachromatic' vision and its splitting of the father into a similarly paired clear-eyed Shaun and purblind Shem. The onset of this catastrophe is throughout *Finnegans Wake* associated with a flood (because glaucoma is caused by excessive fluid building up in the eyeball: as Joyce put it elsewhere: 'My left eye is awash and his neighbour full of water, man/I cannot see the lass I limned for Ireland's gamest daughter man'),[18] and a rainbow (because an early symptom is the perception of rainbow arcs around lights), Wakean analogues to Issy's first menstrual flow and the prismatic disintegration which followed from it.

The biographical facts behind these conjunctions are straightforward enough. Lucia Joyce was born in Trieste while her father was in hospital with the rheumatic fever which, according to his brother, was to initiate his lifelong history of eye afflictions. One of the worst attacks of glaucoma, beginning a series which lasted throughout the composition of *Finnegans Wake*, occurred in July of 1921, as Lucia was turning fourteen, the age at which Milly Bloom had her first menstrual period, and either exactly or approximately the mid-point of Issy's life so far.

These considerations, along with others which will follow, have led me to a cruel conclusion: The Original Sin of *Finnegans Wake* is the act of intercourse which produced Lucia Joyce. I agree with Margot Norris that the central calamity of the book is what Freudians call the 'primal scene'[19] — the intercourse of the parents, as witnessed by the child or children. (Joyce seems to have been familiar with the term. See 263.19-21.) Specifically, it is the marital copulation at which Issy was conceived, as witnessed by the boys. The story of this event has seven main constituents, not always in this exact order:

1. Preliminaries and overtures by the father, usually seen as an incursion against the mother.

2. The copulation itself, at the climax of which man and woman cry out.

3. The boys, especially Shem, witnessing the parents through the keyhole of the bedroom door.

4. The boys flee, crying out in fear, after cursing the father and being cursed. It is at this thunderous moment that for both father and sons Vico's first, 'Heroic' age begins: the father knows shame, the sons know fear, and an absolutist patriarchal society is in the making.

5. Having according to Vico's scheme retreated into a cave or similar enclosure (such as the 'Haunted Inkbottle' of 182.30-5), Shem insists on talking about and interpreting the events to Shaun, introducing the 'shame' which 'sunders' them.

6. The birth of Issy, nine months later, on or around the time of St Lucy's Day.

7. A general disintegration which culminates the divisions between brother and brother and parent and child opened up at the primal scene. The newborn Issy becomes a problematic redeemer of the Fall which her conception precipitated, light shining in darkness.

Before the sequence begins, the father has unwittingly ensured that it will carry violent overtones. Recalling Issy's conception, ALP reminds her husband,

> You were pleased as Punch, reciting war exploits and pearse orations to them jackeen gapers. But that night after, all you were wanton! Bidding me do this and that and the other. And blowing off to me, hugly Judsys, what wouldn't you give to have a girl! Your wish was mewill. and lo, out of a sky! (620.27)

Their minds thus filled with images of battle and rebellion, Shem and Shaun, hiding, as Shaun will recall at 504.09, in 'my invisibly lyingplace', perceived the event in their parents' bedroom as an act of military violence, and rebelled against it.

The first and fullest account of these events occurs in I/1. The Battle of Waterloo is — as always, among other things — a boy's eye view of the parents' intercourse. Its name forecasts the flood associated with the daughter's — and glaucoma's — 'rain'; to fix the connection with Lucia, it is called 'water-loose' (8.02-3), later 'waterlows' (202.17). 'Willingdone' is the father ('Your wish was mewill'), with his extendible and contractible phallic 'tallowscoop'; his 'big white harse' is his big white arse, first moving towards the bed and then bucking up and down. (The boys are viewing him from behind, from the door opposite the foot of the bed, so that during the copulation they see only his bottom extremities, e.g. at 8.18-21.) Waterloo's triangular Mont St Jean, fronted by its 'living detch',[20] is the mother's pubic region. Napoleon's aim at Waterloo was to dislodge Wellington's forces from Mont St Jean; here as 'lipoleums' — diminutive insurrectionary outlander/exiles; 561.06 calls them 'The Corsicos' — the boys are witnessing their father's possession of their mother and, reacting with hostility and horror, challenging his position. Like Napoleon, they never reach the goal. Instead they stop at the keyhole: after applying for the 'passkey' (8.08) at the entrance, they spend the battle 'grouching down . . . stooping' (8.22-4); later they will be remembered as 'killing fellows' (an echo of 'inimyskilling inglis' (8.23)) 'kneeling voyantly to the cope of heaven' (248.24-5) — kneeling valiantly to the pope, no doubt, but 'voyantly' contains French *'voyant'* along with 'violent', and 'cope' is an Elizabethan term for 'debauch'. (See also 115.11-17, 178.26-8, 193.10, 204.21-2, 496.19-20, and 615.34-6.) In the eyes of the twins, the scene is full of blood, of 'bluddle filth' (10.08-9), perhaps because the wife is (531.10, 583.34-6) in the habit of stimulating her husband by digging her nails into him. During the Waterloo scene the wife's limbs and extremities are personified as the 'jinnies', who as part of their 'handmade's' strategy 'irrigate' Willingdone, producing the 'thin red lines cross the shortfront', later — even more provocatively — a 'bissmark', the mark of a bite. Thereafter there is much insinuating testimony about those red lines and marks, along with confusion about whether they are to be found on the father's chest, back,

bottom, or even face (see, for example, 84.19-22; 583.29-30)
— perhaps not surprisingly, considering the 'arminus-varminus'
state of the witnesses. The Shem-Nick of II/1 concludes that
'she bit his tailibout' (229.25), a report confirmed by the
'scarlet pimparnell' later witnessed on HCE's bottom (564.2-
(564.28-30). Despite the confusion, the sight of red blood on
white skin is, from Waterloo on, a powerful symbol of alternately shameful and sacred secrets, whether as the 'red
raddled obeli cayennepeppercast over the text' (120.14-15)
of the letter, later metamorphosed to the bible's red print
for Jesus' words, 'his X ray picture turned out in wealthy red
in the sabbath sheets' (530.08-9), the 'blooding paper' on
which we hear of Buckley and the Russian General (101.19-20)
or the shameful 'scarlet' letters 'on a flushcaloured field'
commented on by the washerwomen when doing Lily's
laundry (205.07-9). When the Russian General is shot in II/3,
a red mark on his bottom seems to be the target.[21]

To the twins, of course, it all looks (and sounds) like the
most ghastly carnage. Shem remembers it as a bloody mother-
murder, an interpretation which leads him, like the character
in Rabelais, to view his mother's vagina as a mutilation
(229.23-4). Aside from the blood, noise, and frenzied to-and-
fro (10.12 sums it up as 'Hit, hit, hit!', a commentary no
doubt taking in the ugly etymology of 'fuck'), the sight of
ALP's kicking legs is what makes the greatest impression.
Many of the later recollections of those legs indicate that
ALP was wearing red stockings throughout, perhaps in defer-
ence to her husband's Bloomian tastes, and that consequently
stockings in general and red stockings in particular have
become potent synechdoches for what the witnessed event
signifies, whether to the insinuating Shaun asking Issy 'had
she read Irish legginds' (431.04) or to the terrified Shaun recalling the 'Redshanks' (500.10) of his mother's goring; see also
128.09-12, 130.01-3, 193.11-12, 337.15-22 (where 'hosen'
and German *rosen* combine to make rose-coloured hose),
354.22-3, 437.01-8, 445.15-18, 496.18-21, 531.20-25 and
557.17-21.

The climax occurs at 9.23-8, as 'Willingdone' 'orders fire',
and with it the beginning of all ruin — of the flood ('floodens'),
the smashing of everything into smithereens, mob rule, and

any number of battles.[22] There is a hint of the eventual consequence ('Arthiz too *loose*!' — my italics), and then Willingdone curses — 'Brum! Cumbrum!' — echoing a piercing orgasmic shriek from ALP which will reverberate throughout the book's memory banks: 87.29, 178.11, 198.03-4, 548.35-549.01, and 583.32-3. Also, the unexpected burst of fire or lightning is the popping of a flashbulb, recording the damning image of the father. Throughout the *Wake* there will be many reminders of this picture-taking; in particular the word 'snap' (98.19, 148.14, 171.31, 332.01, 379.08) usually seems to recall an incriminating snapshot.[23]

With that, Shem — Hebrew for 'watcher' — is like Noah's son cursed for beholding his father's nakedness, mainly with the retribution visited on Peeping Tom, blindness. (Other analogues used by the *Wake*: Harold was blinded in one eye by an arrow at the Battle of Hastings (Willingdone is William the Conqueror); Rory O'Connor blinded his son to prevent future rebellions; song-birds (see 169.12) were once blinded to make them sing better; Shem becomes a drunk because of what he has seen, drinking at one point 'wood alcohol' (70.27), famous for causing blindness.) The cue for all this trauma is the sound of the father's imprecation heard by a frightened little boy while looking through that gauzy green gown spread across the keyhole, thus seeing the whole Waterloo scene as occurring in 'some greenish distance' (8.02), who is later to discover himself afflicted with an eye disease, glaucoma, the first stage of which causes him to go 'green in the gazer' (193.10; Joyce designated the disease's three stages as green, grey, and black) and which will wind up stigmatising him as a 'peepestrella' (178.27) — once peeper, now blind as a bat. And indeed what he/they witnessed is an 'insoult' (10.14), of the sibling rivalry sort — the inadvertent creation of Iseult, of the new monarch of the nursery. Thus HCE next 'tinders his maxbotch to the cursigan Shimar Shin' (10.18) — an intimation of the 'lausafire' ('If she had only more matcher's wit', 620.29)), patroness of light and fire, whose arrival will indeed botch everything.

After this catastrophe, HCE falls asleep with the defective implement at his side and the brothers, divided into innocence and knowledge, have fled from the sight: 'Under his seven wrothschields lies one, Lumproar [Lord Northcliffe, Chapel-izod-born newspaper magnate,[24] with his photograph — the scandal will be publicised...]. The three of crows have flapped it southenly, kraaking of de baccle' (10.35-11.02). At 246.26-9, it will be recalled that 'these are not on terms, they twain, bartrossers, since their baffle of Whatalose when Adam Leftus and the devil took our hindmost, gegifting her with his painapple'. The daughter is a combination of Eve's apple and the classical apple of discord, the offspring of her mother's 'birthright pang that would split an atam' (333.24-5), an Adam into Cain and Abel.

There follows a family chronology (13.20-14.15) which, as we will see shortly, recapitulates the main events connected with Issy's conception and birth, a lyrical interlude, and then the Mutt and Jute cross-talk routine. Here, forecasting his role in II/2 and elsewhere, Shem as Mutt tries to educate his brother about what has just happened in an account of the Battle of Clontarf which is also a recollection of (a similarly watery conflict) Waterloo: 'Just how a puddinstone [Willing-done] inat the brookcells [Bruxelles] by a riverpool [Waterloo]' (17.06-7); it is a story of pollution ('Dungtarf'), father-slaughter, and the *Wake*'s usual punishment for such violations ('one eyegonblack', 16.29). As cavemen, they are in Vico's 'Heroic' age — hiding in caves, scared by thunder which they take as a patriarchal curse.

There follows an interlude featuring hints of the mother's pregnancy (e.g. 18.03, 20.07), then the prankquean tale, describing the daughter's arrival and her disruptive effect: 'fireland was ablaze' as she makes her debut (21.16-17), becoming suddenly a scene of 'skirtmisshes' (21.19) and 'falling angles' (21.25). As 'lausafire' she is the principle of foreign, forbidden knowledge, occasionally a forbidden book, spoiling the happy family that was frolicking away when she showed up: she teaches happiness to Tristopher and sorrow to Hilary, and forces the Jarl out of his castle by asking him a question he cannot answer; her door-opening expedition recalls Isis ('The Opener of the Ways'), Ishtar (the 'knocker at the door' who threatens the 'porter of the under-world' that she will 'smite' and 'shatter' his door),[25] and Janus, opening his doors for war.

Doubtless the dynamics of sibling rivalry are part of the problem, but do not explain the father's reaction to her, especially his 'indigonation' (23.02). For that, I think we must turn to her question, 'Why do I look so much like a [in lower case this time] porter?' — that is, like the pub's porter, Sackerson, whose blonde hair she suspiciously shares. Suspiciously, indeed: her conception will later be recalled as 'the flaxen flood that's to come over helpless Irryland' (583.19-20) — glaucoma-flood and flaxen-fire, forecasting a flaxen-haired girl bringing ruin. And here, keeping in mind the incendiary manner of the prankquean's debut, we may recall that fire-starting is, after all, Sackerson's job. Noting that, we may note as well that in retrospect 'Willingdone' was himself a fire-starter — with poker, firefork (8.15), and scoop (8.35), who gets the wind up, 'order[s] fire' (9.23) at the climax, and then presents his witness(es) with a matchbox (10.18) — that in coming together at the end of the Waterloo episode the sons are combining into the father, and that the blindness visited on Shem for seeing what he saw is partially the father's own. The usurpation (16.27) later complained of by Mutt is double-edged at least, meaning one thing (*Oedipus Rex*) to sons and another thing altogether (*Othello*) to the father, who through the usual Wakean displacements has, like Leopold Bloom at the keyhole in 'Circe', been envisioning his cuckolding, and who accordingly reacts to Issy's question with 'indigonation'.

To be precise, he reacts by becoming 'a rudd yellan gruebleen orangeman in his violet indigonation' (23.01-2), turning into the rainbow which here as usual is accompanied by intimations of glaucoma (23.23) and the *felix culpa* of the *Wake*'s rainbow-vision that will accompany it (23.16). It seems that the forbidden book which Issy as 'Gutenmorg' brought with her, the forbidden knowledge which split the boys, shattered the family, and broke the glass, like the suspicion of betrayal which according to Stephen Dedalus was the motive behind Shakespeare's art, is also redeemed by the fact that it makes possible the book we are reading.

So the daughter of *Finnegans Wake* deserves gratitude for the 'ruinboon' (612.20) of madness and semi-blindness which has coincided with her birth and menarche. What the father has done he 'would [do] again . . . and may again when the fiery bird disembers' (24.10-11). May in December, the fiery phoenix resurrected in winter: this passage explicitly connects the daughter's creation to the figure of Christ-as-phoenix, sun returning after the winter solstice. The connection seems inevitable: St Lucy's Day, in the old calendar the darkest of the year, has traditionally been a feast of light, an obvious analogue to Christmas[26] and in some cultures inseparable from it. The child conceived during the *Wake* mating, 'along about the first equinarx in the cholonder', as Butt remembers the primal scene (347.02-3), would be born on the winter solstice — the old St Lucy's Day, just preceding Christmas, arriving like the Issy-type 'Hetty Jane' who according to 27.11-14 will be coming 'with a tourch of ivy to rekindle the flame on Felix Day'.

This story is repeated in many places throughout the book, often in fragments jutting out of the text here and there like remnants of some primordial catastrophe. Sometimes the whole sequence is repeated by tale-tellers unaware of how the story being told — of Clontarf or the Russian General, for instance — is really a creation myth, a displaced account of how their world came into being. Like the children's songs that Joyce, following the scholars of his day, took as echoes of historic and prehistoric concerns and events, a nursery rhyme can tell part of the tale (134.36-135.04; 511.32-4). So can a geometry problem in a schoolboys' lesson: as Diane and Paul Thompson have observed, the Euclidian exercise of II/2 describes 'a sexual union — between HCE and ALP',[27] and its caption, 'The family umbroglia', suggests umbrage felt by someone towards someone else — and most of the *Wake* umbrage is either between father and sons or between father and manservant. As in I/1, the sons are watchers (284.08-9), and Shaun is the one who can't understand it. Its sequel is the 'regeneration of the u*rut*teration of the word in pregross' (284.21-2 — my italics), and when that word arrives it is a 'rainborne pantomomiom' (285.15-16) leading inevitably (286.02) to chaos, later a brother-battle at the climax of which Shaun smites Shem, probably in the eye, causing him to see the 'rayinbogeys rings' (304.09) of Issy-Isis and glaucoma.

Two such recapitulations occur in I/1. First there is the

chronicle which occurs midway between the Waterloo episode
and the Mutt and Jute routine. It is presented in four ages:
1. 'Men like to ants or Emmets [the twins as 'Emmets' or
rebels] wondern [wondering] upon a groot hwide Whallfisk
which lay in a Runnel' [HCE's organ in ALP's] '. 2. '. . . after
deluge [the climax] a crone that hadde a wickered Kish [a
wicked — whiskered — wicker basket: her vagina] . . . as she
ran for to sothisfeige her cowrieosity [both 'fig' and 'cowry'
are traditional vaginal symbols] . . . found hersell sackvulle
[found she had been impregnated — by Sackerson?] of swart
goody quickenshoon and small illigant brogues ['illegitimate'
consorts with 'elegant' in 'illigant' — the two i's, as always,
give Issy away — and 'brogues' cues Sackerson, the 'Boots';
ALP's womb — cf. 444.20, 'babybag' — is full of Issy]' 3. '. . . a
brazenlockt damsel grieved (*sobralasolas!*) because that
Puppette her minion ['Puppette' echoes Swift's nickname of
'Ppt' for Stella, hence Issy] was ravisht of her by the ogre
Puropeus Pious [Latin *puerperus*, bearing young: the damsel
is ALP crying out during childbirth as Issy is wrenched from
her body]. Bloody wars . . . [ALP's womb opening was also
the door to Janus' temple, which had been 'brazenlockt',
opening as in the prankquean story to initiate the bloody
wars of Issy's 'rain'].' 4. Shaun (Primas) and Shem (Caddy)
split into two polar opposites and head off for Windsor
('Winehouse')[28] and Santry. They are now two warring fac-
tions, in this case English and Irish, as elsewhere they divide
into north and south.

Finally, we can return to the first page, to those introductory seven clauses:

1. (3.04-6) Tristram, lover-violator, arrives on the scene
to wield his penis.

2. (3.06-9) Copulation commences: 'rocks' by a stream at
the centre of which is the French *con* swell and gorge; their
'topsawyer' is doubling his number and humping a mother.

3. (3.09-10) Bellowing voices, male and female: the usual
love-making fanfare.

4. (3.10-11) Three butt-endings from the life of the eye-
sick Isaac: the cad-kid (Shem) sees his father's butt-end
through the keyhole; a kid supplants Isaac in Abraham's
sacrifice to the Lord; Jacob in his goatskin tricks his father

into giving him the blessing due his brother, butt-ending not only blind old Isaac but bland old Esau. Usurpation, and murderous father-son and brother-brother rivalry.

5. (3.11-12) A sister is 'wroth' — wrought, bringing wrath (against 'nathandjoe', HCE — Jonathan Swift, turned upside down — Sackerson, who is introduced (141.27) as a 'Joe', and, of course, the twins) and the colour red, Issy-as-blood-stone's colour, first colour of the rainbow.

6. (3.12-13) *Felix culpa* in the form of liquor, which we are reminded is rotten malt: elixir from decay. Noah's sons brew it by the 'arclight' which symbolises Joyce's glaucoma in three ways: it conveys the ark and its flood, the rainbow's arc, and the arclights whose iridescent refraction, we know from Herbert Gorman, first signalled the disease.

7. (3.13-14) The end of 'rory', the father as Rory O'Connor, last king of Ireland, whose reign is ending; the end of vision: nothing can be seen, not even one's face in the mirror; the end of the flood, signalled by a rainbow; the end of the rainbow, where there lies, of course, gold[29] — the daughter whose gold hair, like her begetting, is source of both consolation and consternation. It is this daughter, as 'lause'/Lucia,[30] whose gift of this rainbow book is relinquished at the end: 'Since the lausafire has lost and the book of the depth is. Closed.' (621.02-3)

FIVE

'Dreamer(s)'

FINNEGANS WAKE is a portrait of the artist, another consideration of what he might have been had he stayed in the land of his birth — the work of a man in Europe imagining a version of himself at home, growing and accumulating his own history. That alternative self is to a great extent John Joyce, the father who in the year that James sailed away from Ireland was one year younger than the father figure of *Finnegans Wake*, three years older the last time father and son saw one another.

This point has been urged before, by Hugh Kenner, who in *Dublin's Joyce* argued that John Joyce was the *Wake*'s main source.[1] And thereby hangs a tale. Kenner's argument has not fared well because it relies heavily on what is generally called the John Joyce interview, a transcript of an interview described as 'given to an unidentified journalist who called on Mr. Joyce *pere* at the request of his son in Paris',[2] which has come to be widely regarded as a hoax perpetrated by the inimitable Brian O' Nolan.[3]

I am convinced that the John Joyce interview is genuine, for four reasons. First, Dr John Garvin, formerly a colleague and acquaintance of O'Nolan's, reports that the story of the hoax was itself a hoax.[4] Second, Padraic Colum confirmed that Joyce had sent a newspaperman to Dublin to interview his father.[5] Third, the interview contains at least one (correct) datum which was not likely to have been known to O'Nolan: that the proprietor of the Mullingar Hotel during John Joyce's stay in Chapelizod was a man named Broadbent,[6] a man whose connection with the inn, incidentally, ceased before O'Nolan was born. Fourth, no one has ever made clear how O'Nolan, in Dublin, is supposed to have introduced his spurious document into the carefully guarded Joycean collection of Mme Jolas, in Paris.[7]

If the interview is authentic, the argument based on it is entitled to be taken seriously: the sleeping giant of *Finnegans Wake*, his body crawling with latter-day Lilliputians, is John Joyce, to a certain extent. To a certain extent: there remains the fact that the ages of the principals work out to those of James Joyce and his family in 1938, nine years after John Joyce's death. If the dreamer is in one way the John Joyce (renamed Porter, by all accounts an appropriate choice) whom his son last saw in his fifties, he is undoubtedly in another way James Joyce, approaching and reaching that remembered paternal age.[8] *Finnegans Wake* unfolds as James Joyce in Paris dreaming of being John Joyce in Ireland dreaming of, among other things, being the type of wild fellow who would not have stayed put, who would have run off to, for instance, Paris. When at the beginning of the *Wake* we observe the 'roundhead staple of other days' as an 'eyeful hoyth entowerly' (4.34-6), both Howth Head and Eiffel Tower, each dreamer is fondly imagining himself as being where the other in fact is.

The son-dreamer dreams, consubstantially, of both dreaming and being his dreaming father's dream, and thus generating the book in which the two are, after much pother, problematically reconciled: 'I go back to you, my cold father'. Following through to the first page, we find that the journey, recirculating, has taken us back to Howth Castle and Environs, and shortly thereafter upstream to the Chapelizod where John Joyce once roistered, collecting stories about Russian generals and Norwegian captains. It makes sense, after all, that the man who in his previous book had cast himself as an Odysseus, a home-comer, should now be ready to consider himself as a Nestor — or, as the *Wake* has it, 'nester'.

Which is to say that in aspiring to dream his father's dream the Joyce of *Finnegans Wake* is seeking the atonement — at-one-ment — initially repudiated by the son. The re-arrival of the first page is the prodigal son's as well as Sir Tristram's — the re-arrival of James, coming home to John.

Or, as the names occur most often in the *Wake*, Shem is coming home to Shaun, to 'reamalgamerge' in one fatherly figure. Reconciliation between brother and brother mirrors atonement between son and father, between exile and homeland. Shaun feels about his wayward brother's return just as the prodigal son's siblings felt about his. (See e.g. 190.24-32, 424.11.) Behind both of Shaun's fables lies an aggravated concern that things not turn out unfairly in the end, that the Gripes not get the grapes, the Gracehoper not get the girls. Returning prodigal is also usurper, a Jacob/Cain who in expropriating the birthright intended by father for brother becomes the enemy of both, and who in several versions of his homecoming is greeted (e.g. 316.22-3) with ambush.

This is an old story with Joyce, about whom we can say what Stephen says of Shakespeare, that the theme of the usurping brother is 'always with him'. Why? I suggest the answer lies with the child, mentioned on the first page of the Gorman biography, who was born on 23 November 1880 to John and Mary Joyce and who died eight days later. According to its certificate in the Dublin Central Registry Office it was a male, and its name was, as we might have guessed, John[9] — which no doubt explains why the next son was named something else, James. That James Joyce knew about this ghostly predecessor is certain. That he turned over in his mind the subject of its death and his own assumption of its privileged place seems to me evident from his writings. So Stephen on the first page of *Portrait* is what in fact the infant Joyce's father used to call him, 'baby tuckoo', named for a bird that takes over the nest rightfully belonging to another. So, especially in *Finnegans Wake*, where Shaun's name is repeatedly traced to some variant of 'John', and Shem is of course (e.g. 169.01) James and Jacob, archetypal usurper. The forked father is 'Jarl von Hoother Boanerges' (22.31-2), that is, both James and John, given to drinking Guinness from James's Gate and Power's from John's Lane,[10] and the two brothers continually 'joustle for that sonneplace' (568.08-9) that James had long ago wrested from John, just by being born.

James Joyce came into life as a Jacob, seizing the privileged position supposed to pass to his brother, from one John Joyce to another. That sainted infant, saved by his early death from the 'lessions of experience' (436.20-1) which so mark his brother (when asked what his autobiography would be like, Shaun replies proudly that it is a 'Heavenly blank' (413.30-3)), returns in *Finnegans Wake* in his 'puerity', baby fat still intact, to ascend to heaven (191.15-6) and judge the living. He can be heard alternately addressing and being addressed by, alternately attacking and joining, his brother, in, for instance, the conclusion of I/7 (see 193.32-194.13), where John-voice complains that James is a 'cannibal Cain', flourishing on the grave of his brother, James that he has spent his life haunted by an image of the kind of total innocence possible only to the dead. 'I guess to have seen somekid like him in the story book', gushes the narrator of III/4 about John/Shaun/Kevin (562.33-4), contrasting him with the 'posthumious' James/Shem/Jerry (563.04-5), and pitilessly sums them up as 'the one loved, the other left' (563.10).

As the good firstborn named for the 'father foresaken' by James, John represents the domestic life chosen over the lures of adventurous destiny-forging abroad; the bourgeois heaven towards which he ascends in Book III is the reward the father can look forward to. Like those other Joycean stay-at-homes Robert Hand, Gabriel Conroy, and Leopold Bloom, he is portly. Young John is the proper and plethoric life the Chapelizod dreamer more or less chose, James the life that his lower self entertained following into the subterranean realm of dreams but which was eventually repressed. Shem's exile is also an expulsion, a kicking-out as much as a leave-taking, a bottling-up as much as a kicking-out, and the animus against him derives as much from the fear that he wants to return as from the fact that he once left. Both homebound Johns stand guard against the overtures of the 'inwader and uitlander' (581.03) for a latter-day atonement, paternal and fraternal.

That is one of the *Wake*'s dreamers: the mustachioed John Joyce, origin of the Simon Dedalus who in *Portrait* had announced 'with fierce energy' that 'We're not dead yet, sonny', lies like Finn McCool in the landscape, a sleeping giant if Ireland ever had one, and as the book's 'John a'Dream's' (61.04), 'johnajeams' (399.34), 'all-a-dreams' (597.20) and 'John-a-Donk' (614.29-30) dreams over all he did, might have done, or wishes to do, hoping to rise up like the Finnegan of the song. The Mullingar's landlord-publican is the first of his dream-emanations, and from him, pinched, earwig-like, in two, with young man asleep upstairs and the ominous Sackerson down below, comes Earwicker and his filial upper and lower half-selves, each recognisably derived from one of the sleeper's two first-borns: the Paris-Shem 'an allblind alley leading to an Irish plot in the Champ de Mors' (119.31-2), the domestic Shaun a 'mothersmothered' darling (191.25). 'If one had to name a character, it would be just an old man',[11] Joyce told a friend, and John Joyce was his archetypal old man.

The other dreamer, in Paris, is James, the son whose image glimmers through and blends with that of the father, in one pattern or other, for example by playing skeleton (422.09) to John's fat. We have already noted some of that double-focus portrait's features. John-dreamer is fat; James-dreamer is the wiry rover he renounced, and buried in bulk, by staying put. In his John incarnation the dreamer has a moustache, in his James incarnation a black eyepatch. Both drink too much; both are accomplished tenors who tend to moon about a singing career as what-might-have-been, personified in the John who died. Both have children, and at times the two sets are indistinguishable: Giorgio can melt into any combination of Joyce *père*'s first three sons, Lucia/Isabel into the 'Margaret Alice' who was born between James and Stanislaus. Both made marriages in the grand romantic manner, spurning all family objections and sweeping their beloveds off their feet, Tristram-style, and both at least occasionally have second thoughts now, as do their wives: is there a more ironic moment in Joyce's work than HCE's boast that the descendant of the young Ibsenian iconoclast who eloped with a free spirit named Nora has now settled down with her in a 'cagehaused ducky-heim' (533.18), Scandinavian for 'doll's house'? As for John Joyce, 'murrayed' to his 'queen . . . Of the may' (208.33-5), May Murray, the resulting children and debts are partly why he envisions himself as a sleeping giant, held down. Both are consequently prone to romanticise their pre-nuptial states, which each associates with the life chosen by the other: see for instance 131.16 for an example of how carefree a Dublin publican's life can sometimes look from the perspective of a soul-forging Parisian wordsmith.

At other times, the son's visage shows through distinctly, his story fusing with the father's own. Its events fall into a few categories which, like all Wakean categories, tend to mingle with one another: childhood, usurpation, fall, elopement, exile, eyes, father, family, art, envisioned return.

All but one of these categories have been noted earlier. Probably because of that earlier John Joyce, James represents his *childhood* as that of a precocious *usurper*, battling brother and father in an enmity which his eventual *exile* confirms. He both repeats his crime and reaffirms the *father*'s mutual guilt in it by witnessing the primal scene, from which event comes both his *eye* affliction and the girl, on one level his sister and on one level his daughter (in turn a reincarnation of his wife) who as Iris/Alice embodies the *Wake*'s 'heptachromatic' glaucoma-vision, as Isis/Lucia its transcendence. Rainbow book — *art* — and rainbow girl are alike agents of atonement, new covenant, and *return*.

The one item in the catalogue not yet covered is the *elopement* from Ireland to Europe. For the *Wake*'s dreaming James, it was the decisive event of his life, the act through which he became exile and lover, Shem and Tristram, ocean-going adventurer: all the recollections of it involve an ocean voyage during which, speculates a washerwoman, they may have been 'captain spliced' (197.13). Just as Joyce's image shows through, so does that of the woman with whom he made that move, Nora Barnacle. She shares his divided feelings about that move. The *Wake*'s two clearest instances of her conversation — 'O, I can see the cost, chare!' (148.09-10) and "tis thime took o'er home, gin' (114.01) — among of course other things (the first, Iseult speaking to Tristram, on deck, spotting the coast, the second, any long-suffering wife to any tippling husband named Jim) convey on the one hand her excitement at leaving Ireland and on the other her desire to return home. The choice, after all, was made by two people. In II/1, for instance, both young lovers repeatedly feel the lure of the companions they have abandoned, 'To part from' whom, we are told at the outset, is to go 'into overlusting fear' (222.29-30), and both feel spasms of homesickness.

Joyce acknowledges his debt to this woman, who ran off with him and stayed with him, by setting the book on her birthday, working her birthstone — heliotrope — into the book's symbology, turning the Liffey the colour of her hair, remembering her Finn's Hotel address in the title, re-enacting the first meeting with her on Nassau Street, and giving her, like Molly, the last word. The continental exile she shared with her husband registers in the affectations of her daughter, who wants to marry 'an engindear from the French college ... *nomme d'engien*' (146.19-20), styles herself *la princesse de la Petite Bretagne* (157.32-3), and uses Parisian cosmetics (143.36). As Tristram's lover both mother and daughter divide into Iseult of Brittany and Iseult of Ireland, French self and Irish self; the 'North Armorica' from which Tristram arrives on the first page is the home of the former (Brittany is part of the ancient Armorica), the Chapelizod to which he is heading the home of the latter. Like the male homecomer whose image of his arrival wavers between welcome and ambush, his partner can envision herself on her return as either exalted or rejected, either Queen of the May or Kate, especially in her *East Lynne* role, ignored and debased where once she reigned.

Both husband and wife are returning at the beginning of *Finnegans Wake*, problematically completing the circuit of the exile they began together in their youth. It is a time for summing-up and putting-in-perspective, for measuring what was gained by the life chosen against the imagined life left behind. The seven clauses of the first complete sentence, which we have already looked at twice, do just that, thereby establishing the framework of the book. As if to affirm the centrality of this pattern, the *Wake* repeats those seven autobiographical clauses at three other pivotal places — at the start of I/5, the 'Letter' chapter (104.10-14), at the start of I/6, the quiz chapter (126.16-24), and at the end of Book III, just before the Ricorso (589.20-590-03). Here is the story they tell:[12]

> I. a. 'Sir Tristram, violer d'amores, fr'over the short sea, had passencore rearrived from North Armorica on this side the scraggy isthmus of Europe Minor to wielderfight his penisolate war'
> b. '*Amoury Treestam and Icy Siseule*'

    c. 'thought he weighed a new ton when there felled his first lapapple'

    d. 'First for a change of seven days license he wandered out of his farmer's health and so lost his early parishlife.'

Stage 1. Ocean voyages: the Shaun/Tristram who was sailing to North America in Book III is coming back again, *encore*, as wandering passenger; the prodigal son/Shem/Tristram ('*fr'over* [my italics] is a cue) returns to Ireland from Armorica (doubling as Patrick, who also reached Ireland from Armorica)[13] and the Paris in 'parish', mirroring his earlier departure from his father's hearth. Elopement: as young lovers the couple are the amorous Tristam and Iseult, but there are signs that their return voyage, contrasted with the memory of their elopement, lacks romance or beauty. We hear of loss of former health, of a fat man and an 'icy' woman, of the isolation of both man and wife, of violated love. The departure was a fall, all right, taken ('lapapple') with a young woman who as we have seen often *is* the *Wake*'s apple, but despite present remorse a happy one, since we are reminded of Newton's lucky bop on the head from another apple. Because of the following stage of the sequence, it should be noted that one of the first things Joyce did on reaching Europe was to deflower Nora and beget Giorgio. The year is 1904.

II. a. 'nor had topsawyer's rocks by the stream Oconee exaggerated themselse to Laurens County's gorgios while they went doublin their mumper all the time'

    b. '*saith a Sawyer till a Strame*'

    c. 'gave the heinousness of choice to everyknight betwixt yesterdicks and twomaries'

    d. 'Then ('twas in fenland) occidentally of a sudden, six junelooking flamefaces straggled wild out of their turns through his parsonfired wicket, showing all shapes of striplings in sleepless tights.'

Stage 2. The birth of Giorgio — 'gorgios' — envisioned as occurring in Dublin, which doubles here with its American namesake on the Oconee (both are, therefore, in 'fenland'; Trieste, Giorgio's actual birthplace, is also built on a fen) in Laurence County, Georgia. Perhaps from the author's ignorance, this young Georgian boy is identified with the faraway Tom Sawyer. (Peter Sawyer, founder of Dublin, Georgia, is in there too.) In any event, we are in the proverbially provincial west — 'occident' — so far from Paris as makes no difference, one fen being pretty much the same as another. That the baby should be 'junelooking' probably recalls Joyce's fears, as expressed in one of his letters to Nora,[14] that Giorgio was really the child of one of his false Irish friends, a paternity that would require him to have been born in June at the latest (he was in fact born in late July), since the couple had sailed from Ireland on 8 October, and first made love shortly afterwards. The 'six junelooking flamefaces' struggling through their wicket may also be the six female offspring of John Joyce, who when it came to doubling his number far outdid his son James; the 'striplings' are doubtless the sons. All of them, every Tom (Sawyer), Dick and Mary of them, is given the heinous name of Joyce. Having established himself, John/James is multiplying his establishment. The year is 1905.

III. a. 'nor avoice from afire bellowsed mishe mishe to tauftauf thuartpeatrick'

    b. *'Ik dik dopedope et tu mihimihi'*

    c. 'had sevenal successivecoloured serebanmaids on the same big white drawringroam horthrug'

    d. 'Promptly whomafter in undated times, very properly a dozen generations anterior to themselves, a main chanced to burst and misflooded his fortunes, wrothing foulplay over his fives' court and his fine poultryyard wherein were spared a just two of a feather in wading room only.'

Stage 3. As 'gorgios' signaled Giorgio, so 'bellowsed' — along with three sets of double i's — gives us the Lucia (along with the mother, *'nor a*voice'), whose birth is here remembered. Appropriately enough for the girl who will grow up to lure her brother with 'the song of a witch', her arrival is accompanied by portents: first the voice from the druidical fire, then an incantation (also, of course, a baptism), then the appearance of a multi-coloured seven-girl in the middle of a chalked circle, a white draw-ring, then ruin from the womb, a miss/fortune-teller forecasting foul things. Again, James's continental family blends with John's, stuck in the peaty

Irish bog: the one seven-coloured girl is also several maids; the domestic drawingroom, as 'drawring*roam*', also recalls the son who left his father's hearth. For reasons explained earlier the daughter's birth forecasts flood, rainbow, and redemption, *felix culpa* and glaucoma. Coming from 'afire', it also forecasts a phoenix-rebirth. It is 1907, beginning of Joyce's eye problems.

IV. a. 'not yet, though venissoon after, had a kidscad butt-ended a bland old isaac'

  b. *'Buy Birthplate for a Bite'*

  c. 'is a Willbeforce to this hour at house as he was in heather'

  d. 'Next, upon due reflotation, up started four hurrigan gales to smithereen his plateglass housewalls and the slate for accounts his keeper was cooking.'

Stage 4. Half-blinded after the glaucoma attack of Stage 3, our hero, with two children and diminished prospects, has become a vulnerable father, subject to the storms of the world and the oedipal antagonisms of his offspring: he is Isaac Butt supplanted by Parnell, Noah after the flood of Stage 3 having his butt-end spied on by his son (and, at the same time, the son being insulted by the display of his father's butt-end), Wilberforce beset in the 'house' of Commons, and both the eye-sick James Joyce and the John Joyce whose rapid decline in life coincided with the arrival of his children. The children — gals and Gaels — beating on the windows of his establishment are also bill-collectors, calling in accounts, and the four old men who are forever passing judgment on HCE. 'Venissoon', as Joyce explained,[15] signals the 'venison purveyor Jacob' tricking Isaac into granting him the birthright due to Esau, and so introduces the theme of usurpation. That theme is complicated by 'kidscad', which should remind us that Isaac was himself supplanted once, benignly enough, by a kid, on his father Abraham's altar.[16] Consider these two stories together, and you get something like this: the sacrificed other, the one who died in Isaac's place, is returning, metempsychotically, outfitted in the animal skins in which he was once butchered, to seek retribution simultaneously against the old usurper (Isaac) and his chosen heir (Esau). The brother-battle of James and John, one as challenged supplanter, one as returning ghost, is under-way in earnest, as is the parallel father-son struggle of James and the other John: as the reminders of the primal scene (Willingdone as Wilberforce, son spying on father) indicate, one cause of both battles is the witnessed outrage. Overlaid on all that is the story of a resentful local populace — epitom-ised as the 'cad' in much of Book I — taking revenge on the returned exile who once, like Esau, sold his birthright and, like James Joyce, spurned his birthplace. The time is around 1915-16: war on the continent, uprising in Ireland, fractious-ness in the family, which is sitting out the hostilities — in Switzerland, surrounded by combatants; in Ireland, with the fighting just outside the door.

V. a. 'not yet, though all's fair in vanessy, were sosie sesthers wroth with twone nathandjoe'

b. *'Which of your Hesterdays Mean Ye to Morra?'*

c. 'pumped the catholick wartrey and shocked the prodestung boyne'

d. 'Then came three boy buglehorners who counter-bezzled and crossbugled him.'

Stage 5. The daughter is now two persons, the son three — the numbers they assume in accounts of the father's disgrace. The daughter is w*roth* — red — because she has had the men-arche which makes her mad, divides her in two; that she was 'wrought' in the first place was the beginning of all the trouble, especially when we consider that her creator, 'nathandjoe', implicates 'Pore Ole Joe' (141.27), the manservant; the 'nathandjoe' with whom she is wrathful is not only the father as topsy-turvy Jonathan (Swift) but the brothers — the Nathan who in *Ulysses* is by way of Mosenthal's *Deborah* established as a type of the apostate son, a Shem (at 181.36 Shem is 'nate Hamis') paired with 'joe', foreshortened Jones/John/Jonathan. The resulting fracas is also an Irish civil war: Catholic against Protestant, brother against brother, sibling against sire, rebel against patriarchal authority. In the ongoing account of the returning exile's reception, this is the nadir. *Everyone* is indignant at him: the plural 'sesthers' of V.a, the voice of society which in V.b demands that he do the decent thing

and choose one woman, the Protestants whom, according to
V.c, he has 'shocked', the soldiers razzing him in V.d.
As of now, his homecoming has been a disaster. The time is
1921-2: Lucia has her menarche; the Irish Civil War rages;
Joyce antagonises the bourgeoisie with *Ulysses*.

> VI. a. 'Rot a peck of pa's malt had Jhem or Shen brewed
> by arclight'
>   b. *'Hoebegunne the Hebrewer Hit Waterman the Bray-*
> *ned'*
>   c. 'killed his own hungery self in anger as a young man'
>   d. 'Later on in the same evening two hussites absconded
> through a breach in his bylaws and left him, the infidels,
> to pay himself off in kind remembrances.'

Stage 6. Considering the vengeful violence of the last three
entries here — Hebrew hits Waterman, young man kills
'hungery self', abandoned father 'pay[s] himself off' — we
may take the brewing of VI.a as yet another form of retribution, especially considering 'Rot': the sons are brewing the
liquor which is a cause of the father's 'arclight' glaucoma.
The popular indignation of Stage 5 has reached the level of
outright attack, although the righteousness — and distinctness
— of the returner's antagonists is undermined in the telling:
the young male fermenting the blindness-inducing liquor
suffers from 'arclight' himself; pious Hebrew smiting the
'Waterman' returning by water is also brewer striking tee-
totaler; the 'young man' of VI.c is referentially ambiguous,
so that the character in question is either killer or killed,
either the angry one or the 'hungery' one, and in either case
is killing himself; the 'hussites' of VI.d are both righteous
Hussites and fallen hussies, and the phrase 'the infidels' seems,
again, to be doubly referential — the civil war is both a family
conflict and a struggle of self against self, of suicidal self-
immolation. John Joyce is here as always, drinking not only
his family but himself into ruin: rotting himself, addling his
brain, killing himself, paying himself off, all with 'pa's malt'.
Son James, under attack from himself and others, is suffering the same fate. John Joyce in decline is reduced to reliving
his past, sometimes bitterly (killing his own young self), sometimes nostalgically ('kind remembrances'); James Joyce is doing

the same thing, sinking into the intermittent blindness of the post-*Ulysses* days, reviewing his past 'by arclight', the result being this book: '. . . whenever I am obliged to lie with my eyes closed I see a cinematograph going on and on and it brings back to my memory things I had almost forgotten.'[17] Both John and James are dreaming *Finnegans Wake*. The time is the 1920s. Joyce's eye condition, beginning with the severe attack of 1922, is worsening.

VII.a. 'and rory end to the regginbrow was to be seen ringsome on the aquaface'

b. '*Arcs in his Ceiling Flee Chinx on the Flur*'

c. 'found fodder for five when allmarken rose goflooded'

d. 'Till, ultimatehim, fell the crowning barleystraw, when an explosium of his distilleries deafadumped all his dry goods to his most favoured sinflute and dropped him, what remains of a heptark, leareyed and letterish, weeping worrybound on his bankrump.'

Stage 7. Joyce's exposition of 'Arcs in his Ceiling Flee Chinx on the Flur' divides this seventh stage into symbols of ruin and redemption, terminus and re-beginning: on the one hand the flood has come, 'The ceiling of his (E) house is in ruins', 'He is a bit gone in the upper story, poor jink', and the 'larks' he saved have abandoned 'the zooless patriark'; on the other hand there is rainbow, a recession of waters, free drinks downstairs, switched-on arclights, and larks: 'God's in his heaven All's Right with the World'.[18] Clearly, this is the *Ricorso* stage of the sequence, represented in all four passages as a hope for the redemption from the flood which is Joyce's main symbol for glaucoma: VII.c and VII.d compound the ruin of the deluge with an allusion to Ibsen's sonnet about torpedoing Noah's ark; in VII.d the torpedo explodes. But even a torpedo can be an agent of rebeginning, as we will find in I/4, where HCE's 'thorpeto' (77.07) becomes a kind of submarine ark in which he makes his escape, and in fact *Finnegans Wake* insistently equates immersion in water with rebeginning. So the end of this bankrupt king -- Rory O'Connor, Lear, Leary, 'heptark' crowned on his 'regginbrow' -- marks the beginning of a new 'rain', and new vision; Leary was, after all, followed by Patrick, messenger of the resurrection and Irish originator of the alphabet and whiskey, water of life. And so of course there should be 'free drinks downstairs': this, remember, is Finnegan's wake. And since, as the Ricorso, Stage 7 should lead us back to Stage 1, let us recall the place from which Patrick departed on his first trip to Ireland: Armorica, as in 'North Armorica'. The time is the 1930s, some time after the Wall Street crash, with both father and son awash in booze (the 'rory end . . . on the aquaface' may be an allusion to James's red nose)[19] and James, Noah-like, trying to gather his family together into some shelter against the assaults of that terrible decade.

This is the master plan of the book, overlaying and complicating the four-stage Viconian sequence which Joyce advertised. The sequence of extended autobiographical mythmaking structures not only the first page but the first chapter as well — and also, we will see, the first half of Book I (I/1-I/4), Book I itself, and finally, *Finnegans Wake*, from start to finish. The overlaps are made possible by the carefully arranged co-extensiveness of odd-numbered stages with one another and even-numbered stages with one another: numbers 1, 3, 5, and 7 all pertain to mother and daughter, begetting, gestation, and birth; numbers 2, 4, and 6 pertain to the sons and their relation to the father; the members of each set are highly congruent with one another, so that for example I/8, the 'Anna Livia Plurabelle' chapter, corresponds to both the Stage 3 of *Finnegans Wake* as a whole (arrival of Issy, the 'raining' rainbow girl) and Stage 7 of Book I (flood and rainbow). Indeed we may envision the book as having the shape of a stretched-out bull's-eye, like the pattern of concentric ellipses with which Joyce sketched the stages of gestation and the design of 'Oxen of the Sun':

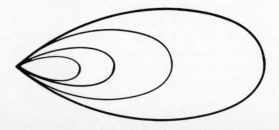

We have now taken three looks at those first seven clauses, the first time as a point-by-point circuit of the sleeper's room and its fixtures, the second time as an event-by-event account of the primal scene and its aftermath, the third time as double biography. Consider them all together, and two conclusions suggest themselves. The first is that, like the halls of those classical orators who used furnishings as cues for the main heads of their speech, the sleeper's room has by dint of being lived in for years become a repository of memories which, when evoked, recall the story of a life which is also a universal history. For our sleeper, to go around the room point by point is to re-live the past, stage by stage, age by age. The second conclusion is that, just as history is contained in one small place, so it is contained in one moment: the primal scene refracts from its instant of conception into the seven stages plotting all of human time. When Joyce lent Eugene Jolas the first hundred and twenty pages of *Finnegans Wake*, he told him that it 'contained the outline of the whole book'.[20] He might as easily have said the same thing about the first page, in one dimension, or the first chapter: they are all the same multi-layered story, writ large or small.

SIX

Book I, Chapter 1

'RIVERRUN': We begin the book in French: *Riverain*, river-dweller; *Reverons*, let's dream,[1] *Reverrons*, we will see, again. French is the right language, after all, for a dreamer in Paris envisioning himself as returning from Armorica, to see again his native land, the old home on the river. Mrs Glasheen observes of the first page that its manifold voyagers 'are exiles who cross the sea to Ireland';[2] we may add that the dream-voyaging James Joyce is chief among them.

What it is that we are going to see again? For answer, we may recall that the book ends with two voyages, of which this is the continuation. One is of the river, which on 628 was heading out into the bay and has now circled around and begun flowing back, to Chapelizod. The other is the picnic outing taken, or imagined, by the publican and his wife, to the top of Howth, from where like Molly and Leopold Bloom they can survey Dublin and environs: 'We can sit us down on the heathery benn . . . To scand the arising . . . At the sight of salvocean. And watch would the letter you're wanting be coming may be. And cast ashore.' (623.24-30) That letter is ALP's famous letter, in its bottle, the descendant of the Shaunian barrel of III/1 and III/2, floating downstream with its 'missive' (111.31), and the place it is cast ashore and found will be Chapelizod, upstream; having been sealed and sent with a kiss at 628.14-16 it floats back now to fight its 'penisolate' war ('penicillate': marked as with a pencil or brush — the letter is 'Of eyebrow pencilled, by lipstipple penned' (93.25)) against the complacent natives; at 63.32-5 a bottle will be hammering against the gate, and forty-one pages later it will have been opened.

So we begin panoramically, noting the main points of

interest, in a professorial idiom at times resembling a tour guide's patter: observe this; look down here; watch your heads; let's be going, shall we? Our returning voyager, after all, has some reorienting to do. But we are also watching the river with the bottle with the letter, heading towards one small point in the landscape beneath us, and are going to be especially interested in scrutinising that point: by page 8, the grass/glass through which we passed (628.12) to get here ('l' and 'r' are often interchangeable in *Finnegans Wake*), with one version of the viewer on each side, has become a different kind of glass, a telescope ('tallowscoop'), with a magnified image of the viewer ('big Sraughter Willingdone') at one end and a diminished image ('petty lipoleum boy') at the other,[3] peering down into the backyard of a Chapelizod pub, scene of that avatar who stayed behind in Ireland.

A telescope is not a bad symbol for the double dream on which we have embarked.[4] The word means, literally, 'far-seeing', an epithet twice applied to HCE, as 'farseeker' (548.14) and the 'Farseeingetherich' whose 'rerembrandtsers' seek 'those yours of Yesterdays' (54.02-4); re-arriving at John's Chapelizod, we are simultaneously remembering/tele-scoping two main points of departure — the last pages of the book, and Paris. The book ended with a rivering voyage into the ocean which was also a flood, and in I/1 'the length of the land lies under liquidation (floote!)': the flood waters are just beginning to recede; the 'brider' day promised in last night's forecast and glimpsed in IV is now succumbing to the 'lucal drizzles' (324.32-3). Two other events (at least) from the last chapter have their continuation here. First, as reported indirectly at 604-7, HCE has dipped his head in the bedside basin of water, the 'lethemuse' (272. fn.3) which will permit him to 'Begin to forget it' (614.20), like a Platonic soul being purged of its past life before reincarnation. (The act is recalled at 4.21-5.) Second, he has swallowed a morning laxative (613.22-5), as a result of which his first act of I/1 will be to visit the privy in the backyard.

In Paris, our principal is a usually late riser getting up now only because of biological need and the shock of the early-morning traffic noise outside — the 'rollsrights, carhacks . . . tramtrees . . . tournintaxes' (those famous Parisian taxis), even 'aeropagods' (Joyce, in a letter, about a bird which flew into his Paris apartment: 'Perhaps he . . . sought refuge from the air squadrons then over the city'[5] (5.30-33)). Brékkek Kékkek Kékkek Kékkek! Koax Koax Koax! Ualu Ualu!' (4.02-3) is a fair imitation of those old automobile horns that one sometimes hears in movie comedies of the thirties; compare 294 fn.1, where Issy comes forth with a similar sound ('Makeacakeache') in imitation of the traffic on 'Carpenger Strate'.

He is hung over. He hiccups (4.11), stumbles and falls (6.09-10) more than once, suffers from migraine headache (4.04), a 'big head' (6.08) and — like Simon Dedalus after a night of excess (*Portrait* 93) — a shaking, 'Stuttering' hand (4.18). Worst of all, he is prone to the kind of morning-after self-recriminations (5.10-11) which in the course of the book will magnify into a battery of accusers. When he begins to wake up, the first thing he sees is a room whirling around, from *swerve* of shore to *bend* of bay, in 'recirculation'; the first thunder of the 'fall' is among other things the first awful instant of consciousness.

Already, clearly, we are dealing with two main — to use the limited but sturdy metaphor — levels of action: crapulous dreamer in Paris, old dreamer in Chapelizod. Each is an extension of the other, one of them, at the end, heading out towards France, the other, at the beginning, heading back to Ireland. The duality is complicated by the fact that each dreamer is capable of sending out ghostly emanations from himself in a process which resembles a popular special effect of the movies of Joyce's day (the 1937 hit *Topper* is a good example), in which a double-focus image of a sleeper or corpse is seen rising from its horizontal form and setting off on a series of adventures, after which it frequently returns and melts back into its original. That, I think, is the best way to envision, for instance, the picnicking man of the last few pages in relation to the figure dreaming him. The *Wake* actors take many trips, but the shadowy figure of their dreaming horizontal begetter is their origin and terminus, the boxy room in which he sleeps is their stage, and the many stimuli which manage to filter through to him are their cues.

Our dreamer, then, startled by the noise outside while

dreaming of return to Ireland, goes through the following motions:

3.15-25: He checks to see if he's all in one piece, head to toes (3.20-4). The memory of the vista he was surveying before the rude shock is enough to transform his body, seen from the vantage of his upraised head, into the landscape below Howth Castle and Environs, stretching as far as the border of Phoenix Park: many names for parts of the anatomy are discernible in the text.[6] He is now a giant asleep under Dublin. Phoenix Park is especially prominent because things look green, from glaucoma and/or the green quilt across his body.

4.01-18: The racket of the traffic combines with his homecoming fantasy to beget visions of battle, of the sort that an unwelcome French invader might expect in Ireland: partisans of Baudelaire[7] (like Stephen Dedalus, back from bohemian Paris at the beginning of *Ulysses*) clash with local 'Malachus Micgranes' (cf. Stephen's antagonist, all-too-Irish Malachi Mulligan); Verdun veterans attack Whiteboys; Irish and French imprecations mingle.[8] As always, peace is signalled by the rainbow girl, arching over the battlefield as 'the skysign of soft advertisement'. As 'Iseut', with one French, one Irish incarnation, she is the perfect peace-maker for this battle. The conflict has adumbrated the Battle of Waterloo (8.09-10.23), which was also a fight between an Irishman and a Frenchman.[9]

4.18-5.04: Issy has got into a dream largely because of the sound of the water trickling into the basin between bed and fireplace — always one of her cues. Conscious of this forbidden prize the dreamer — this is where the double-focus begins — steels himself and leaves his sleeping form behind. The language of this paragraph is the language of stern resolve, culminating with the now upright and partially dressed male gazing out the window at, simultaneously, Howth Head and the Eiffel Tower onto which, according to Arthur Power, the Joyce apartment on the Avenue Charles Floquet looked.[10] If the reader protests that apart from being vertical objects topped by lights[11] these two look not the least bit alike, Joyce lies in wait: the object is 'in undress maisonry upstanded', and indeed the skeletal Eiffel Tower does look undressed, rather, compared to the Howth which in *Ulysses* Joyce clothes with a 'fell of ferns'. Being temporarily in his upstanding — and standing-up — posture, the dreamer chooses to cast the trickling Issy-stream as his beloved 'liddle phifie Annie', though 'liddle', with its clear allusion to Alice Liddell, gives the game away.

5.05-12: The risen post-wassail boozer continues dressing, putting on his 'arms', with a sense of beleaguered self-importance which results in this mock-heroic picture of 'Wassaily Booslaeugh of Riesengeborg'. The 'hoe', first instance of HCE's stick-like sign, is probably really a cane.

5.13-6.12: No sooner does he stand erect and give us a look at him than a 'shebby choruysh' of ridiculers begins taunting him. He now sees himself mainly as a different sort of majestic outsider, Mohammed, set upon by infidels. One of his favourite roles, Mohammed suits him because in legend it combines the best of both worlds, piety and promiscuity: it allows him to be holier-than-them and still get the girls, like the polygamous Mormon-elder incarnation which will later cry out 'Bringem young, bringem young, bringem young!' (542.27). In this new scenario Issy returns as a prophetess/houri and — appropriately, for this 'bedoueen' setting — a 'dreamydeary'.

Having prayed in vain to his cane to 'Stay us . . . O Sustainer', he wilts under the din of his attackers, the source of which din is, again, the traffic horns from outside, echoing in his 'cubehouse'. Thus begins a frequent pairing of the book: the braying attackers, often the sons, are horns; the plink-plunking girl a soothing (usually string) instrument of some sort.

Our hero falls again, back into bed. Or rather one of him does: that double-focus division between bedridden self and ambulatory self is now cast as fallen-vs.-risen, so that for the next two pages the horizontal figure, stretched out like a sacrificial victim, will be juxtaposed with the figure who, outfitted with stick and hat, plodges down the stairs — 'latter' (= 'ladder' = ship-talk for 'stairs') — from which he will stumble out to the backdoor and yard.

6.13-28: Probably because the privy-bound figure is passing through the downstairs, where the bar is, his 'corass' of noisy tormentors now consists of 'hoolivans'. That their 'ululation' should be notably wet and windy suggests — as confirmed at 10.29-31 — that it is blustery out there in the yard we are about to enter; horn-noise is fading into wind-noise. The weather is wet: at 6.27 the walker at the doorway has water 'fore his feet'. Meanwhile, back with the sleeper, the howling has become the keening of a wake, with some disturbingly cannibalistic overtones.

6.30-8.08: With comparative neatness, these two paragraphs consider, one at a time, the figure in bed and his double entering the backyard. In the first paragraph we catch a glimpse of the latter — in the rotund shape of Joyce's stay-at-home Irishman — as the 'owl globe [who] wheels in view', but mostly we see the former, as a fat little baby being served on a platter. In the second paragraph we are in the backyard, sloshing through the rain, 'Anna Rayiny' and her 'piddle med puddle' (prompted by the sound of that trickling Issy-stream, by the sleeper's ear). Dublin and in particular Phoenix Park landmarks come into view; the purblind traveller, seeking his destination, 'peer[s] yuthner in yondmist'; his white feet in the green grass (and, back upstairs, in the green quilt, and, always, in glaucoma's green fog) are 'swarded in verdigrass', later 'two quitewhite villagettes . . . minxt the follyages'.

8.09-10.24: The vision of the fat baby was also a vision of the father, stretched out like 'a mummified pharaoh, an overgrown babeling' 'peep'ed at' by mourners.[12] They are also voyeurs, kneeling at a keyhole. Remembering that green gown spread across the bedroom door's keyhole, we are now ready to re-enact the primal scene which I have already described: the blurry image of the father through the keyhole is 'a fadograph of a yestern scene', and that remembered yester-scene is the primal scene.

Remembering the direction of our downstairs traveller, we can account for the undeniably excremental cast of the 'Waterloo' episode. As Stephen puts it in *Ulysses* 571, 'Waterloo is a watercloset' — also a 'loo', a spelling which may remind us of the O O symbol once common on public toilets, which symbol will hereafter be connected with enactments of sex, creation, and sexual creation.[13] Thus do events establish a reason for what J. S. Atherton has discerned to be the great heresy on which *Finnegans Wake* is based, the belief that creation and fall are one,[14] the act of generation an act of pollution.

'Mind your hats goan in!', we hear on entering, recalling Leopold Bloom 'bowing his head under the low lintel' of his jakes (*Ulysses* 68). Using Kate's key to get in, our 'invalids of old guard' — we are partly in Paris, at the Napoleon museum by *Les Invalides* — having entered 'to sate the sort of their [his] butt', is by 8.21 squatting down on a 'big white harse', mirrored by the lipoleums 'grouching down in the living detch'. After preliminary exertions, evidently with the aid of the cathartic 'Wonderworker' of *Ulysses*, there is a climactic, flatulent evacuation (9.23-28) followed, like Bloom's, by a stream of urine (9.27-30). The 'Fire!' and accompanying 'solphereens' trace both to the sulphurous stench and to the match struck to light a cigar. This juxtaposition will be remembered elsewhere, perhaps most strikingly in Butt's description of the Russian General 'smooking his scandleloose at botthends of him' (343.24-5). The meaning of the 'silvoor plate for citchin the crapes in the cool of his canister' is obvious in itself, but we may add these two overtones: 1. The silver canister alluded to was a chamberpot called 'The Emperor'.[15] Wellington's insult to Napoleon is of the most degrading kind. 2. The sentence is followed immediately by 'Poor the pay!', and Kate will later show up, complaining bitterly, with a plateful of shit (142.07). She has received her 'tip'. After this, the outhouse's visitor wipes himself with a sod of turf (a 'threefoiled hat' = trefoil = shamrock; Napoleon's tricorne hat is there too, completing the earlier insult), hikes up and wriggles into his pants, and exits.

For the watcher, the sequence in the privy blends with the primal scene because both are shameful acts of his father which he has witnessed through a keyhole while — because of those war stories — imagining himself to be a soldier: 'We must spy a half a hind on honeysuckler [father as 'Goldilocks' bear as honeymoon bridegroom] now his old face's hardalone wiv his defences down [pants are down] during his wappin stillstand, says my Fred [one of the *Wake*'s watching soldiers]' (588.03-6). Those watching soldiers are the same as the 'courtin troopsers' that 'Pukkelsen' later says have been put 'behind the oasthouse' (319.22-3), their usual haunt. For the

watched, defecation and (among other sexual acts) copulation
are alike triggered in his mind by a trip to the privy because
this is the place where he goes, or used to go, to masturbate,
stimulated by the pictures in *Lysistrata*. We can, I think,
catch glimpses of that text in the 'handmade's book of
stralegy' being read by the 'jinnies', who from it are, like
Lysistrata's minions, learning to 'irrigate' and 'fontannoy'
their men for purposes of political strategy.

That Waterloo should be the central battle evoked is owing
partly to that battle-scene picture (or memory of same) hanging up in the privy, partly to its wonderfully apposite name,
Water-loo, partly, since the ground here is wet, to the fact
that the rain-soaked condition of its field was decisive to the
outcome, partly, since the Mullingar's backyard was at one
time a bowling green,[16] to Wellington's apocryphal remark
that it was won on the playing fields of Eton, partly to its
opposition of Iron Duke and pudgy 'frog', reactionary and
revolutionary, and partly — the returning-voyager level — to
its being a battle between a Frenchman (problematically:
Napoleon was born in a recently Neapolitan Corsica rebelling
against the French) and Irishman (problematically: Wellington
once remarked that he was an Irishman only if a man born
in a stable was a horse, a nasty crack for which Joyce pays
him back by making him a 'harse'), meeting in a land,
Belgium, which by a convoluted onomastics evidently known
to Joyce could be either part of Ireland or part of France.[17]

The Irish-French conflict precipitated by the exile's re-
arrival is here at its peak, with the usual complications:
Wellington, whose rear-view squatting pose should doubtless
remind us of 'those throne open doubleyous' of his cursive
initial ω, 'seated with such floprightdown determination'
(120.28-33), is also Joyce's contemporary the Marquis of
Willingdon, Viceroy of India in the waning years of the Raj.[18]
(W's attackers are sometimes sepoys.)[19] Napoleon, fighting
the Irishman, is an admirer of Ossian; Wellington, invading
the continent, doubles with the William who invaded from it
in 1066. Wellington's conquest is undermined in the telling:
we hear at the climax (9.26) that 'Arthur [Wellesley] is to
lose',[20] and it might be added that the echoes of World War I,
in which the main antagonists of Waterloo were, a hundred

years later, to join forces against Blücher's descendants, remind us that in reversing history the *Wake* is doing what history itself does all the time.

As in all Joycean victories and usurpations, Waterloo is a contest of two versions of one self, here as one figure seen from two ends of one telescope. It is as if the father were attacking himself — which of course in Oedipal terms is exactly what a man does when he has sons. One alternative self he is attacking is definitely his manservant, suspected cuckolder and sire of Issy, who in Joyce's diagram of the battle shares the disputed Mont St Jean with the father,[21] and whose presence is signalled by Willingdone's horse 'Cokenhape' — an allusion not only to the Scandinavian Copenhagen but to the Cape of Good Hope, off which sails the Flying Dutchman who is one of the father's obsessive personifications of sexual usurpation.

10.25-12.17: Pants pulled up, Waterloo over, the first of the confrontations between one dreamer's home and another dreamer's home, invader and native, father and son, brother and brother, brought to its unresolved close, our ambulatory figure comes out into the yard and remarks, naturally enough, on the clean — 'keling' — air. 'Phew!' indeed. He gazes sentimentally up at his daughter's window overlooking the backyard (10.27-9) and, like Bloom with the 'Chookchooks', talks a brand of silly chicken-talk to the family hen (11.03-8) — who, thus anthropomorphised, becomes a type of the wife, the change being mediated by her identification with the old 'biddy' Kate. The 'peacefugle' woman, letting 'byes will be byes', takes over, declaring 'armitides' and pecking up out of the leavings of war the makings of ALP's letter. Her feed is also the remnants of the picnic (see 110.29-31) and the father's seed (chickens eat seeds). 'I wrote me hopes and buried the page', recalls ALP about that letter (624.04), remembered on that picnic, and here they are, unearthed: 'ills and ells with loffs of toffs and pleures of bells and the last sigh that come fro the hart . . .' Her blessing embraces both the battle of son with father ('a gorgeups truce') and the daughter to be born, from that seed, on 'muddy kissmans'. The second paragraph extends the wife-as-hen conceit and brings it full circle: as hen she will lay an egg which will be brought by the wife for the dreamer's 'forebidden' breakfast, fulfilling the prophecy of *Ulysses*, where Molly thinks she has been bidden to bring her husband breakfast.

12.18-13.05: 'Review' is the word that establishes the action of this passage. The walker strolls around to the front of his building, surveying the grounds with satisfaction. In the process he reactivates some parallel re-views: the picnicker looking down on the Dublin landscape, feeling lord of all he surveys, the upstairs dreamer surveying the 'flagpatch quilt' over his globular body, the returning exile re-viewing (*reverrons*) his native land. This last comes in at the end — 'So This is Dyoublong?' — because he has arrived at the front door and is about to seek admittance. (Did he lock himself out? Bloom did.) The re-arriving invader of the first page has now got as far as the door of his old home.

13.06-13.19: Seeing the white horse in the fanlight above his front door, our observer is reminded of two things — of the recent scene in the privy with its 'outwashed engravure'; and the calendar picture in the bar within, in the *'inn*kempt' house, with its own white horse. Recalling such landmarks, he is here very much the traveller returning after long absence, nostalgically revisiting the spots where he 'Used' to do all kinds of things. The elegiac mood eventually transforms that recurrent trickling sound — 'Hear?' 'List!' — into the strumming of an Irish harp/lyre. It is also the sound of the doorbell: our traveller wants his manservant to let him in.

13.20-14.15: The vignettes recalled, of primal/privy scene and calendar picture, combine with the antiquarian mood encouraged by the harp sound, now an ollav's 'harpsdischord', to generate an ancient four-stage chronicle — horse-riding man with pot-on-pole, woman, serving maid, sons juxtaposed with pot-on-pole — which as we have seen also distills the family history. In this retrospective mood, we meet the four old historians.

14.16-15.28: The antiquarianism gradually reaches a lyric pitch. 14.16-27 is a somewhat indignant commentary on the events just reviewed, behind which we can detect these questions: Where's that Sackerson? Did he die? Run away? In the next paragraph (14.27-15.11) the cogitator admonishes himself to snap out of it and notice what's around him, and we are treated once again to the returned exile's appreciation of his recovered home. How nice that so many beautiful things have remained unchanged through the wreckage of time! Chief among these are flowers, whose scent has been brought out by the rain. Cued by associations with that flower-decorated 'elopement fan', the story that dominates from 14.35 to 15.26 is of plighted love withstanding (male) assaults, including the Sackerson-like 'Danes' and 'Firebugs'.

15.27-18.16: Speak of the devil, here at last is Sackerson — 'Comestipple Sacksoun' — to let us in. And thus commences the *Wake*'s prototypical encounter — as Waterloo is its prototypical trauma — one that will be recalled many times, perhaps most plainly in this passage from Joyce's early drafts:

> At the time of his last disappearance in public petty constable Sigurdsen, who had been detailed to save him from lynch law & *mob mauling* ran after greeted him just as he was butting in through the door with a hideful saying as usual: 'Wherefore have they that a ~~dog here~~ herring?[22]

(Compare 16.04-5 and later greetings; for the final version, see 186.19-32.) The usual signs are there: he is an imbecile (15.18), a stupid drunk,[23] a regressive 'dragon' man who speaks virtually no English. He is also, it seems, deformed — one reason for thinking that he, not HCE, is the book's hunchback. Most of all, he is 'evident the michindaddy' — the 'miching', skulking, father of Issy, the *'mich-in-daddy'*, in other words 'myself in primitive form',[24] an identification confirmed at 72.13, where 'Miching Daddy' is one of the epithets hurled at the father. So the first person our returning exile meets is a variant of his scapegrace self, a fact which will come into play when this event is recast as a meeting with a 'cad' — 'cad' being short for Swift's Cadenus,[25] one of HCE's identities. He is also, at this point, Patrick, Ireland's most famous invader, having arrived from France with the 'crook-head staff' (HCE's cane) of the druidical prophesy.[26] He crosses the threshold (16.02-3) — imagined as the 'fire defences' of a caveman's cave because Sackerson is a fire-tending brute, because HCE has a cigar (remembered as the 'cheroot' of 53.21-6, elsewhere as a pipe), and because Patrick's famous fire is an assault against druidical custom — and,

confirming the interchangeability of these two males by exchanging hats, initiates the book's first dialogue, between me
(Mutt) and you (Jute), 'abast the blooty creeks', about bloody,
wet battles like Waterloo and Clontarf.

Not surprisingly, the main difficulty in the ensuing cross-
talk is in keeping the two separate. Though Sackerson is introduced as 'Jute', 'Mutt's' 'Aput the buttle, surd' is a sure-fire
sign that Sackerson is the one speaking through him, 'sir!'
and references to bottles being part of his limited repertoire.
Mutt is the one who says he 'became a stun a stummer' at
the primal scene — a phrase which in Scandinavian just means
that he became mute, 'Mutt', for a while — but Jute is the
one who thereupon proceeds to begin stuttering, revealing
his paternal guilt as a begetter, a copulator.[27] Though the
pubkeeper is the one who is chronically anxious about being
usurped, Mutt/Sackerson, the displaced former lover, is the
one who starts wailing about usurpers (16.27). Typically, the
publican tries to buy him off with (wooden) coins ('coyne'
— a Gaelic cognate of 'Barnacle') and typically, the illiterate
Sackerson reads the pictures of the currency: 17.09-10 indicates that he is seeing the bull etched on a one-shilling
piece (cf. 321.22-9) although he seems at first (16.35) to mistake it for a bear.

Talk of Clontarf — where Sackerson's ancestors were driven
out — is also talk of Waterloo. (For 'One eyegoneblack' see
Joyce's *Scribbledehobble* note, 'Mark blind when he sees T & I
do it'.)[28] Let in the door, HCE becomes imperious towards
his welcomer, a Shaun rejecting a Shem, while Sackerson,
the vanquished Viking, advocates an ideal of racial live-and-
let-live ('Mearmerge two races, swete and brack'), pointing
out placatingly that things rise and fall and intermingle, that
time levels all. The publican is having none of it: 'See you
doomed' . . . 'Stench!'

18.17-21.04: Sackerson's conciliatory message is given the
last word, and carries over into this next section. As we would
expect from this illiterate 'Mousterian' *naïf*, it is full of child-
like wonder, particularly about writing (on the coin, for instance). We are still 'stoop'ing, looking at that coin and considering the symbols which give it meaning; at the same time,
incidentally, the semi-blind walker is going up the steps of his

stairway, 'stoop' being etymologically close to 'step' — 'Stoop) . . . (please stoop)' — guided by the manservant. The definition of knowledge given at 18.24-8, beginning in 'ignorance' and ending in experience, is Lockean because Sackerson is a mental blank.

Through his eyes we consider written language and its 'all-forabit' from outside. At 19.20-30 his helpful directions to his master — one foot after another, that's the way — stimulate a reverie of childhood ignorance as a kind of pre-literate pastoral: we were all ignorant 'sons of the sod', with no paper or anything else, but my weren't we happy! and so on. 19.31-20.18 considers the complications introduced by print, of which *Finnegans Wake* is the supreme example: that's what you're in for when you start letting people write. At 20.17-18 'Daleth' (= 'door' in Hebrew = 'porter' = Sackerson) opens and closes the door to his master's bedroom, and in the next paragraph — calling him as usual 'sir', asking him to 'lay it easy, gentle mien' — escorts him to his bed through the green glaucomal fog with enticing words about the woman whose bed he is rejoining.

21.05-23.15: The female promised at the end of the dark journey has also been the daughter-as-houri/Scheherazade — all set to tell the father a story when he settles down. That story, the prankquean fable, begins with the usual Issy-sounds of plink-plunking water, here as 'larpnotes', and windy whispering. That Issy's voice is coming or imagined coming from the room above via the chimney near the bed explains why in the opening sentence the Jarl should have 'his burnt head high up in his lamphouse'. As ambulatory dreamer here fades back into stationary dreamer, the first sound he heard — 'riverrun' — returns to the foreground, reconfiguring the initial tableau of dormant mountain listening to trickling water (see, for instance, 175.21-4), 'madameen spinning watersilts, when mulk mountynotty man was everybully'.

As 'duppy'/'dummy' Sackerson as usual gets kicked around here, not only by twins and father (in addition to being the twins the 'jiminies' are, like the 'jinnies' of Waterloo, feet) but by the prankquean, who as a mischievous piratess is identified with the figure most frequently called the 'Welsher'

(322.08, 480.12, 590.13), from his habit of asking the bar-keeper to tote up his drinks on the slate — the 'p' and 'q' of 'prankquean' traces to the tally of pints and quarts on that slate — and never paying for them. (See 390.15-30 for one example of how the story of welsher and prankquean can merge.) The prankquean, as outlaw the natural enemy of Sackerson in his constabulary bouncer/till-watcher/account-keeper role, shows up three times asking for a pint of porter, in each case running away without paying and, adding insult to injury, 'converting' each ill-gotten pint into urine. (In earlier drafts this part of the story is clearer: the prankquean says, 'I want a cup/2 cupsa/3 cups of porterpease'.)[29]

Over this simple memory of trust-breaking are overlaid a dizzying number of other tales, all involving analogous viola-tions, all traceable to that story of the returning exile (Shaun at one point types Shem as a welsher, who 'escapa sansa pagar' (464.11)), seeking entry to the country he once spurned, that was established with the opening sight of Tristram, coming from Armorica. (The prankquean is a 'queen of Prancess' (312.22); the 'westerness' from which she comes is simultaneously Galway, Wales, and Brittany.) I have earlier noted that the story incorporates an account of the daughter's birth, suspected by the father of being illegitimate: so the publican, like Leopold Bloom undergoing *couvade* (*Ulysses* 494), is laying hands on himself, and the two spells of forty years during which the prankquean is off in Tir Na Mban, Land of Women, translates into forty-two weeks,[30] almost exactly nine months. The innuendo of illegitimacy is con-veyed by the echoes of 'Rumpelstiltzkin' (discussed earlier), of the many child-stealing games which Joyce read about in Alice Gomme's *The Traditional Games of England, Scotland, and Ireland*,[31] and of any number of folk-tales involving fairy child-stealers and changelings. All these analogues involve the disruption of a settled society by a trouble-making out-sider: *La lutte continue*.

23.16-24.15: Following orders, Sackerson closes the room's shutters. The resulting noise signals the first of the *Wake*'s new covenants, along with the calamities attendant on the daughter's arrival. The traveller has finally come all the way home from exile, the door slammed behind him, the window boards closed on him (corpses before burial are said to be 'under board') which is to say that like that other returned exile, Father Flynn of 'The Sisters', he faces the terms of such reconciliation: death-in-life, the company of importunate yokels, in sum the state of being 'Landloughed by his neaghboormistress and perpetrified in his offsprung'. It is all worth it, if he can hear her voice — and hear it he does, lying in bed, with his woollen nightcap on (23.21),[32] in his darkened room, buffeted by 'soundwaves', fading into a corpse at a wake: 'With lipth she lithpeth to him'.

24.15-28.35: The traveller's return voyage comes to its logical conclusion: he is home again, stretched out in the detested Tim Healy's 'Healiopolis'. The sound of his daughter's voice has aroused visions of marriage, of re-beginning, but Dublin voices prevail, and the wedding subsides to a wake. He is in a way a returning hero — his cane is now a 'supershillelagh', the sweat of his palm venerated like a saint's excrescences — so long as he will consent to be 'duddandgunne'. The voice here, appropriately, is of the twelve customers, speaking in chorus rather like Flann O'Brien's 'The Plain People of Ireland'.

There is news aplenty, all of it dull or dismal stuff. That news (plus the usual improper interest in the daughter-as-temptress) spurs our hero to try once more to rise, only to be forced down again by one of the drinkers who assumes — such is the ubiquity of projection in the *Wake* — that he has been aroused by the smell of liquor on someone's breath. There follows more news, the assumption of which is that the person being addressed is dead, culminating in an account of the daughter upstairs, reading a romance based, ironically, on the father's youthful elopement.

28.35-29.36: As a final insult, the dreamer learns that even his role as prodigal son, patronisingly returning to 'our paroqial fermament', has been assumed by another, the 'Humme the Cheapner, Esc' whose story is indeed a cheapened copy of his own. Outlander-dreamer having subsided back into inlander-dreamer, thus bringing the saga around one full cycle, we are ready to re-begin with yet another emanation, a bloated earwig-shaped publican whose person and life resemble the dreamer's own more closely than he would care to admit. Poor Earwicker, here introduced, enters the scene with two strikes behind him, a predicament which he shares with Joyce's picture of humanity: not only out of place in his adopted home, barely tolerated by the natives, he is ever on the verge of being repudiated by his resentful and exasperated creator: 'his own fitther couldn't nose him' (322.12-13).

SEVEN

Book I, Chapter 2

THE FIRST eight episodes, Joyce told Professor Ernst Robert Curtius, 'are a kind of immense shadow'.[1] We have seen how much of I/1 is memory, the shadows of earlier events. The next seven chapters, especially I/2 to I/5, extend this 'shadowy' quality, trailing behind it like a tail on a kite, recasting the story brought forward by that brief spell outdoors.

Not that these chapters are without event. Three occurrences are particularly exigent: the breaking of the window and blowing-open of his windowboards at the end of I/2, the arrival of a (late) breakfast in I/5, and the arrival of Kate, to clean up the mess, in I/8. In each case, the room-dweller's semi-conscious mind exhibits that extraordinary capacity for retrospective accommodation which Joyce, like many another dreamer, observed[2] — the way, for instance, someone who falls out of bed is likely to remember that in the dream-narrative before the crash he was going over the edge of a cliff. So I/2 ends with the sound of a 'Glass crash' (44.19-20) — the breaking window — which is immediately made over, retrospectively, into the smashing of glasses by his persecutors.

Those persecutors are there in the first place because of the dreamer's abiding, recently aroused guilt, fixated as previously on the sound of Issy's whispering. Here (compare *Ulysses* 563-7) that initiates a chain of *sotto voce* chatter about the events of I/1 which reminds me of the children's party game called 'Consequences' or 'Rumour', in which 'Uncle Joe is a pip, pass it on' becomes 'Ugly John is a pimp, pass it on', and so forth.

Identities, in such a game, are largely a matter of factitious synechdoche. A man holding an earwigger[3] is known thereafter as Earwigger/Earwicker. An assailant is, simply, a 'cad with a pipe'; a crowd consists of loafers (cigars in mouths, hands in pockets), pawnbrokers (three gold balls), hunters (rifles), ladies (in sedan chairs), schoolboys (blue coats) and so on (42.17-43.21). That is just how the mind functions in this chapter: when Treacle Tom takes a room in 'Block W.W.', the initials become for him immediately emblematic of Winny Widger, rider of the horse he failed to back (40.03-4).

Out of the concatenation of such mis-takings is literature — for instance 'The Ballad of Persse O'Reilly' — evolved. It is fetishistic, deteriorated, distributed in pieces which are then cobbled randomly together. It is, in other words, a process of dissipation, and the characters who produce it or figure in it here are accordingly 'dissipated'. HCE is, as specified at the end of I/1, a 'Cheapner' of his legendary original; the 'Napoleon the Nth' who officiously patronises a drama about his illustrious namesake is a sad commentary on what has become of his stock; equestrian victor Wellington is reduced to (apart from his memorial) the jockey 'Winny Widger', who with his 'neverrip mud and purpural cap' is also good at winning muddy contests: the cast of characters declines from royalty to mob.

The weather is deteriorating too.[4] The weather forecast/focus has predicted/reported wind from the northeast with fog and varying precipitation, and its influence is detectable throughout the chapter, both in the wretched state of the principal (the cold front, we were told, encounters a 'sotten retch' (324.32)) and in the frequent sounds of splattering (rain), rattling (hail) and whistling-moaning-screeching without (wind), climaxing in the assault on the window and windowboards; we can also sometimes hear the 'sybelline' branches of the elm at the window, wind-whipped against the boards. 'Assault' is the proper word: it is here that we have the experiential source of Stage 4's 'hurrigan gales', 'smithereen[ing] his plateglass housewalls', and the many depictions of HCE's attacker as a stone-thrower; as we shall see it is also pertinent that Joyce thought that many of his eye-attacks were brought on by bad weather.

30.01-33.13: We begin with our male principal, hereafter called HCE, lying in bed, attending to the sound of weather outside his room and the daughter's whisper within, con-

tinuing the retrospective meditations begun in the previous
chapter's last few pages. In the interests of equanimity he
will try, unsuccessfully, to 'forebare' thinking of the two girls
whose mention so aroused him at 27.22. Wishing to return to
sleep, like Leopold Bloom at the end of 'Ithaca' he tries to
compose himself by recalling a bedtime story, a little Kipling-
esque fable about how Mr Hump Earwigger got his name.
The story reveals three main determinants: the remembrance
of how some wag compared his pinched-in-two figure to that
of an earwig; the calendar picture — regal equestrian dram-
drinker with retinue, suppliant innkeeper — which the traveller
most likely glimpsed when downstairs; the impulse to palliate
the disturbing associations of the last chapter. The 'king' (he
will later return as the disreputable 'Festy King'), 'long-
sighted from green youth', with his 'retinue of gallowglasses',
is a sanitised derivative of the one/two/three watchers at
Waterloo, struck green-eyed from what they witness, as his
'none too genial humour' is some dream-censored hostility
which will eventually become a direct assault. The name-
giving process he begins will be completed by the hostile
Hosty: 'I parse him Persse O'Reilly else he's called no name
at all.' (44.13-14)

Everything in this paragraph, and the chapter as a whole, is
similarly displaced: the 'catholic assemblage' at the theatre
is a happily subservient version of the Catholic mob feared
by the Protestant dreamer; the menacing sound of hail
beating against the windowboards becomes first the king's
laughter ('One still hears that pebble crusted laughta'); and
then, most probably, the sound of 'Pinck poncks that
bail for seeks alicence' (the pub's licence is right above the
window), then the applause of the theatre-goers ('the *inspiration* of his lifetime and the *hits* of their careers'; my italics).
The paragraph ends with HCE-as-returning exile in his zenith:
a latter-day Napoleon, back in France for good, the pacified
mob safely at his feet, watching an amusement about Waterloo,
his rival, and his marital problems, all safely reduced to literature.

33.14-34.29: The attacks begin in earnest. The applause
and laughter of the previous paragraph takes on a nasty edge:
we hear of 'wisecrackers' (like firecrackers, perhaps — the hail

cracking against the outside) with some heavy-handed sarcasm: 'Hay, hay, hay! Hoq, hoq, hoq!' Ominously, the scene shifts to 'the people's park'. As he did in I/1 when faced with similar rumblings, HCE gets on his Mohammedan high horse, anathematising infidels, particularly the one stumbling (because blinded) 'in leaky sneakers' — the latest derivative of the lord of Leix who just a few pages ago was attending his sovereign. (In a few lines he and his mates will re-emerge as 'shomers', Hebrew for 'watchers' and our first glimpse of Shem.)

Also as in I/1, the Mohammedan pose recalls the girl(s), prompted by the green (34.27) silk (34.23) gowns (34.20) opposite (34.19) the bed. As before, the subject of the daughter has insinuated itself, and seems to be winning through: the narrator admits to a 'partial exposure' before her, and a partial exposure of his guilt is what we are getting.

34.30-36.34: The dream-censor forces rush back, led by 'Wives' doubtless alarmed by the male's predilection for younger flesh, ordering the blackmailers — 'malers' — to keep back. There follows a long denial in which the voice, like an American politician caught in a cover-up, tries to minimise the damage by conceding certain obvious facts the better to gain credibility for the suppression of others. The displacement continues: the phrase 'ides of March', for instance, with its parricidal overtones, is adjusted one month over to the harmless 'Ides-Of-April'.

The story that emerges owes most to the earlier encounter between ambulatory dreamer and Sackerson, with the wet 'ambijacent floodplain' recalling both Waterloo and the rain-soaked grounds. HCE, sloshing with his cane through the wet, meets a 'cad with a pipe'. Like all Wakean encounters this is partly a meeting of HCE with himself, cap-a-pie (also, of course, Hamlet meeting the ghost, son meeting father), but the translation of pipe-carrier into 'luciferant', i.e. light-bearer, is a clear signal of Sackerson, 'torchbearing supperaape', and his first question (35.15-16) is a bastard Gaelic version of the first question asked, in bastard French, at the earlier meeting with Sackerson (16.04-5).[5]

This and a second question, about the time, arouse the usual fears of not belonging, of being displaced. HCE asserts

his right to be where he is, in Ireland, as the legitimate double
to the nearest landmark, the Wellington monument, named
for another dubious son of the sod. The change from French
to Gaelic shows that the tables have turned. On one level he
is the returning Patrick, coming from France into a hostile,
unenlightened island, and the cane he carries is the 'crook-
head staff' prophesied by the druid priests he will supplant.[6]
Like Patrick he is haunted by the memory of a past sin. His
peculiar expression 'Me only, them five ones, he is equal
combat' expresses anxiety that he first, is outnumbered and
second, has been overseen masturbating.[7] And there is one
other anxiety, revealed in his stuttering reference to 'our
mewmew mutual daughters': is the feared and despised
Sackerson his cuckolder, the father of Issy?

36.35-42.16: Another reason that HCE finds Sackerson
disturbing is that he owes him his wages. The encounter in
the park was also taken as a demand for payment, for
'Guinness', as in 'guineas', hence a holdup. 'Bradys' signals
Joe Brady, the Invincible; the cad will often be remembered
as a holdup man, for example a 'betholder with his black
masket . . . [on] the bawling green' (517.09). The 'five ones'
of HCE's answer are apparently shillings as well as fingers,
totalling a crown (at 38.01 the cad will recall his 'happy escape' as a 'crowning'), and over the next few pages the passing-
on of HCE's story from party to party also tracks the progress
of the money from hand to hand, 'hands between hahands'
(38.32-3), from man to wife to priest to racetrack tout to
thief to bar and flophouse to various 'wasters' and wanglers
and 'stonebroke' low-lifes, like everything else in this chapter
becoming more dissipated at each stage.

Sackerson's reaction to the payment is typical: he sits
down at his customary hearthside to have his customary meal
and become, as usual, drunk, but his newfound wealth leads
him to get above himself and see castles in the air (37.22-3);
his bottle from the Phoenix Porter Brewery, for instance,
becomes 'a bottle of Phenice-Bruerie '98'. (Again: the Parisian
exile longs for home; the Irish exile dreams of France.) The
pious Kate overhears his maunderings about their master,
and the rumour is off — from Kate to her priest to his friend
and so on. The gossipers are for the most part recognisable

variants of HCE's sons, especially Shem;[8] here as elsewhere Sackerson has been the source of the twins.

Tracing this sequence adequately would take too long, but three influences should be briefly noted: the increasing chilliness (hence visions of poverty, especially outdoors — for instance 'O'Mara' sleeping outside on 'the bunk of iceland'), the sleeper's biliousness (hence puking, drinking to excess, sea voyages), and the rising wind outside, which near the end of this section we hear as a 'cremoaning' fiddle.

42.17-47.29: In the final section the storm outside grows fiercer: the wind's fiddle is now a higher-pitched flute; the hail beats against the window (the windowboards have blown open) with a 'felibrine trancoped' metre; the mob's murmur rises to a roar; the elm, whipping against the window, becomes a looming 'woodmann'. At the climax that tree breaks through with the sound of a thunderword crash; the hostile outside has come in. All this culminates in the ballad: as ALP later tells her husband, 'Once you are balladproof you are unperceable to haily, icy, and missilethroes' (616.31-3). Like the aged Wellington,[9] HCE has his windows attacked by a mob.

The disaster revives memories of an attack of glaucoma's blinding flood, caused by 'an overflow meeting of all the nations in *Lens*ter [my italics] fullyfilling the visional area', as a result of which we soon meet the blind Joyce as 'Caoch O'Leary'.[10] The incriminating photograph of HCE is also here, hewn from the tree and blown around, like a leaf, by the wind: 'an excessively rough and red woodcut, privately printed at the rimepress of Delville, soon fluttered its secret on white highway and brown byway to the rose of the winds to the blew of the gaels'. The source of this image is those bloody 'thin red' wounds, from 'excessively rough and red' love-making, on HCE's skin. Mutt, we recall, suffered an 'eyegonblack' at that encounter, a blacked-out eye in the *augenblick* of a camera's shutter opening and closing, and the 'shutter' of HCE's room has now just blown open, exposing the 'Lens' of his window.

Hosty's ballad challenges, again, the re-arriver's claim to acceptance. Like Patrick he is attacked by his past. The ballad runs through the charges against him, especially his role as *arriviste*, a meretricious 'Cheapner' recently 'washed to our island'. As a crowning insult, it equates him with ('the deaf and dumb Danes') Sackerson, whose inferiority is, in an in-. stance of Freud's 'narcissism of small differences', a mainstay of HCE's sense of his own integrity. The disintegrative assault against the re-arrived exile is well under way.

EIGHT

Book I, Chapter 3

THE WEATHER news at 324.26-34 says that the front which 'incursioned' our 'sotten retch' is/was 'haralded by faugh sicknells', and sure enough I/2's window-breaking is now followed by a 'cloud barrage' (48.05), wafting through the open window and fogging things up. (Compare 270.20-2, where Alice's breaking of the 'glass' brings 'mistery'.) The influence of this fog registers with the narrator in three main ways. First, things are wet and clammy (e.g. 51.21). Second, it evokes conventional associations with 'misty London' (602.28). At least partly as a result, I/3 is the *Wake*'s 'English' chapter, in several ways. The scenes and characters tend to be English. HCE's *'regifugium persecutorum'* is now England, and he is uncommonly, and unguardedly, proud of his British connections (e.g. 54.23-6), so much so that at the chapter's end the one hundred and eleven epithets directed against him are, as Frances Boldereff has suggested[1] and Hugh B. Staples shown,[2] equated with the one hundred and eleven anti-English votes of the Irish Parliament against the Act of Union. Most of all, the chapter is stereotypically 'English' in its voice. The normative idiom is wistful-plummy Edwardian, with the affected fogginess that Joyce despised in, for instance, Whistler's 'nocturnes'.[3] The author even parodies his own Edwardian production, *A Portrait of the Artist as a Young Man* (53.01-6), seconding Wyndham Lewis's charge of preciosity.

Third, things are, simply, foggy. Appearances blur and mix, people change sex and 'reamalgamerge'. (Appropriately, Nicholas of Cusa makes his debut here.) I/2's dissipation continues.

48.01-50.32: Fog obscures, but it also refracts, as we are reminded at the beginning of III/1, when the 'fogbow' produces a 'remembrandts' of red nose, green eyes, and blue teeth against a violet background (403.05-22), or at 176.18, where '*his Steam was like a Raimbrandt round Mac Garvey*'. I/3's identities are fractured and 'spectrally' recombined, as in a kaleidoscope. (As always, rainbow follows flood.) The earlier story — recalled in I/1, 'dissipated' in I/2 — is acted out by a repertory company in a series of productions trying to evoke some ancient story dimly sensed to be the primal drama. It is as if D'Oyly Carte were attempting to stage the Eleusian mysteries. The gossipers return in this opening section, although the parts they 'mime' mutate at a dizzying rate. One example: the 'O'Mara' of 40.16-20 was 'an exprivate secretary of no fixed abode' seen sleeping on a step of the Bank of Ireland, former seat of the Irish Parliament and thus a re-minder of stolen nationhood, dreaming that the icy step was the stone on which of old the Irish kings had once been crowned. At 49.03-15 he returns as 'A'Hara', now one of Ireland's wild geese, still with 'no fixed abode' but taking revenge on those who robbed him of his home, seeking refuge in 'the home of the old seakings'; his final gesture, handing on a letter, is the act of a private secretary. We may, I think, take his second incarnation as the dream of his first.

The recapitulation is complicated by the recorder's reten-tion of the events accompanying the rumour — the whistling wind (49.01-2), the 'leaves' of the tree coming through the window (here dramatised as the message in the hand of a dying hero (49.13-15)) — and the 'slopperish' atmosphere. Beginning as 'Sordid Sam' (the two S's are a signature), Sackerson is also prominent. He is introduced as hearing in his sleep the knocking (in I/1, the walker 'banged pan the bliddy duran' to be let in) at first interpreted as a call from 'Israfel the Summoner', which will later come to dominate the narrative. (The source may be the windowboards, swing-ing loose in the breeze.) It is the thunder of divine displeasure (cf. 64.14-15), then kicks, then a bottle falling into a crate, finally the butcher or baker knocking at the door.[4] Then comes fellow-servant Kate, as 'her wife Langley, the prophet', identified first with 'Levey' — that is, a variant of the Liffey — then one of 'Padre Don Bruno's' 'yarnspinners' (cf. 620.35-6). As at 38.09-39.13, the combination of old woman and priest is enough to get the scandal circulating.

50.33-54.06: HCE, roused to do something about the window, gets up from the bed and looks at himself in the mirror,
probably the one over the mantel. What with fog, eye troubles
('he's never again to sea') and the ravages of age, it is difficult
to 'idendifine the individuone'. The tête-à-tête between himself and his mirror-image recalls the park meeting of I/2, this
time with 'free boardschool shirkers in drenched coats' who
in a typical instance of Wakean projection ask to hear about
the meeting of a haberdasher with some lads in coats. This
request brings forth an account re-enacting HCE's rising —
'His Revenances . . . rose to his feet' — in order to repeat the
meeting, the request, the story in answer to the request . . .
then the circle goes round again. Standing erect, the arisen
HCE becomes an ancient monument whose 'fall and rise'
from his bed is passed in legend and retailed from cicerone to
spectator as they ride by, peering at him through the touristy
Irish twilight. At the end of this sequence he puts on his hat
(54.01).

54.06-57.29: Dressed, hatted, and risen, HCE assumes the
pose of a public person, a 'Mass Taverner' (as Jack Dalton
showed, 'Travener's' is a misprint) and hotelier. He puts on
his public smile, which along with others of his features will
be much discussed in the next four pages.

There is a good deal of false heartiness in that smile,
prompting a Jamesian comparison of his image in the mirror
to 'a beam of sunshine upon a coffin plate'. Standing before
the round mantel mirror, as always when in that position
'cordially inwiting the adulescence [Issy, up the chimney]
who he was wising up to do in like manner', his feet at the
ashes in the grate, 'averging on blight', he waxes philosophical
about cyclical ups and downs, phoenix falls and resurgences:
'Life, he himself said once . . . is a wake', in both main senses.
55.10 begins a reversal of perspective: we pass through the
looking-glass and the image in the round mirror becomes the
spectator, looking out 'Cycloptically', 'with eddying awes' at
HCE; it is also the 'windowdisks' and 'round eyes' of an English
party (we are back with the tourists) circling him, this time
as a tree, noting the 'asches' at his feet, making patronising
comments, blandly wishing they could bridge the 'abyss'
separating viewer from viewed. At 56.20 they merge in a

tourist-customer, a 'Traveller' peering through the mirror at HCE's outfit of cap, stock and collar, hat and brogues, and reading into it various inn signs.[5]

Hoping to be taken in, the melancholy down-and-out smiles wanly, appealingly, from the mirror. The prospect of himself as a Shem-type as always brings out the censorious Shaun-self. What, he asks in effect, is that fellow smiling about? Who does he think he is and where does he think he's from? This last question is taken literally: we look around, consulting the points of the compass, and, perhaps to steady ourselves, sit back down (57.05; cf. 57.25), obliterating the mirror-image. HCE becomes a judgmental, disillusioned, compass-consulting sitter — and mutates into the four old men, from the four points of the compass, sitting in judgment, explaining away the exaggerated myth-making of the last few pages. Now very shrewd about the 'unfacts' in 'our notional gullery', we look with the old eyes of the professionally disabused at a 'flashback' of the 'lifeliked' wax-works figure.

57.30-62.25: The voices of the crowd below are given a prosecutorial cast by the courtroom scenario just conjured. In a sense, HCE is sitting in judgment on himself — 'sittang sambre on his sett . . . holding doomsdag over hunselv' (198.34-199.05; cf. 134.33) — and the charge is the by now familiar one transferred 'mid pillow talk and chithouse chat'.

The word 'tapatagain' introduces the Coldstream Guards,[6] chief among HCE's accusers ('cockaleak' signals their affinity with the king's retinue of 31.17-18, 'cappappee' with the cad of 35.11 ff.), who add homosexuality to the charges — an easily understood accusation considering that during the primal scene HCE must have been repeatedly thrusting his naked behind back towards the watchers on the other side of the keyhole opposite his bed; as the ballad remembers it, '. . . some bugger let down the backtrap of the omnibus/And he caught his death of fusiliers' (47.09-10).

The man-on-the-street testimonies that follow are typical Wakean projections: a pious martyr testifies about a saintly 'Sankya Moondy', a 'revivalist' reveals a repressed obsession with liquor, a matador addresses the subject as 'matadear', and so on. All these windy 'outrages' have been enough to make HCE flee 'beyond the outraved gales of A*tree*atic' (my italics): if the broken window was a breach for invaders, it can also serve for escape, out of the house and beyond the gale-blown tree, away from 'manslaughter' — slaughter by men, laughter of 'man', the accusation of manslaughter. HCE's exile, which Roland McHugh calls the 'unifying theme' of the next chapter,[7] properly begins here. It is two exiles, fused: first, a recollection of Joyce's elopement from Dublin, with a 'papishee', to Trieste on the Adriatic (and even 'beyond'), the easternmost point of his odyssey; second, yet another re-telling of his rearrival to Dublin, 'the seventh city' (cf. *Portrait* 167) where he assumes the identity of a master-brewer (62.03), only to experience, as before and always, rebellion, condemnation, and entombment. It is the old double story: John escaping to James, James returning to John.

62.26-69.29: These next seven (quite disorienting) pages are united by at least two things, the framework of inquiry, especially judicial inquiry, established at 56.31-57.29 and recalled by the story of HCE's return to/escape from those who 'condemn' him, and a banging noise which most probably originates in the whacking of the windowboards but which in any case is generally identified as the knocking first recalled by Sackerson at 49.21-50.05. (The sound also fits the courtroom scene, as gavel.) As the returning exile evoked in the last paragraph HCE, hearing that banging sound, relives the return-and-ambush retailed in I/2 as the encounter with the waylaying cad, which encounter was in turn a transmogrified re-run of his I/1 return from the privy (here 'the second house') to bang on the door for Sackerson to let him in. 'It was after the show at Wednesbury' — scene of an ancient battle between Saxons and Britons,[8] like Waterloo, Hastings and Clontarf a type of the struggle between Sackerson type and HCE type. The background banging makes the encounter more violent than before, with threats of exploding pistol or bashing fist, and the memory of that burglar-like 'shrievalty entrance' recently forced into HCE's chamber by tree and weather. The source of the imagined burglar's crowbar, introduced as a 'fender' — as in 'fend off' — is almost certainly the cane which the dreamer of I/1 took with him to the privy (at 63.20 it becomes a parasol). As door-knocker HCE becomes a drunken process-server, hammering on his own door, though in self-defence he claims to be a type of Sackerson, merely banging a bottle, expecting the milkman predicted at 604.12-17 — hence the garbled talk of a 'cattlepillars Mullingcan', and other variations on the milk/milkman/cow theme. He has been dreaming 'that he'd wealthes in mormon halls', a standard old-man-and-young-girl's fantasy (cf. 542.26-7) which, combined with the thoughts of milk and Issy's connection with fruit (from the 'apple' association) leads to the story of Daddy Browning and his 'strawberry frolic' with a girl named 'Peaches' in 'the real cream', with 'Creampuffs' 'by the jugful' amongst the Milky Way; the background banging contributes to the 'popguns' and, finally, the 'Ack, ack, ack' of the newsreel's flapping film.

We then go from milkman to postman, possibly carrying ALP's letter. About that letter ALP will tell her husband, 'I wrote me hopes and buried the page', and this introduction of the subject indicates that he (cf. 621.31-2) is what she buried it in: when she gives directions for the removal of his 'remains' she specifies that 'earnestly conceived hopes' are to go with them (617.28). He is the 'Fierceendgiddyex' postman at the door, then the 'huge chain envelope', then a herm/pillarbox, containing the letter; the transition at 66.27 from letter to coffin is not as disjunctive as it appears.

The coffin is apparently, as in I/4, made of glass, reminiscent of the glass coffin in which Snow White sleeps until awakened with a kiss — and here again it is continuous with the letter theme of 66.10-27, since ALP has said of that letter that she 'left it to lie till a kissmiss coming' (624.06), and we have just learned that the letter buried in HCE will 'lurk dormant' until pecked out by 'Mrs Hahn'.

All this is getting away from the subject of the knocking at the gate, to which our guide returns us at 67.07. This time the knocker, encountered by Sackerson as policeman — 'Long Lally Tobkids', 'peeler' — goes from milkman (with his 'bottled heliose') to tradesman, a butcher wishing to deliver muttonchops, doubling with the coffin-maker trying to remove/deliver 'carcasses'. The macabre prospect of being delivered as meat to his own establishment by a firm of butchers/morticians — 'mattonchepps' probably takes in his whiskers — is just the latest stage in a story starting with the premise that the ballad at the end of I/2 was the death of HCE, that the encounter with the cad was mortal.

Which leads to the question of what brought this tragedy about. The girls, of course: as 62.32-4 established, 'womanhood' has been responsible, through 'an agent male' — HCE's waylayer. 67.28-69.04 re-evokes the mirror-girl Issy as *femme fatale* sending 'many a poor pucker packing to perdition', whispering provocative messages down to her defunct old victim — dog, king, 'ravenous' raven-eyed blind relic of a 'dead era'. The 'whole of the wall' to which HCE now 'turn[s]' has a triple meaning at least: he is a dying man turning his face to the wall, the enamoured father/lover turning his attention to the fireplace hole in the wall from which Issy's voice comes, and that fellow who some time ago roused himself to see to the hole punched in his wall by hail, tree, and wind, anthropomorphised as rock-throwing balladeers. When the narrator reports that the applegate/'iron gape' has been 'triple-patlockt' on HCE, we can infer that the windowboards have been closed on the weather. Thus is he locked in his 'shack', protected from 'being freely clodded', although the protection is double-edged: the windowboards double as grave-boards.

69.30-74.19: With that, HCE is ready to return to bed. There is one last blast from the chilly north wind: the 'northroomer' who after blowing 'through the houseking's keyhole to attract attention' 'bleated through the gale outside', 'opened the wrathfloods of his atillarery', concludes his attack with 'a few glatt stones . . . at the wicket', and, leaving behind a trail of hailstones already turning to water, thence to evaporate into 'nubilettes', deliquesces into the hypnotic pitter-patter of 'Rain'. He is a journalist, working for a 'payrodicule', according to the equation (journalism = wind) that governs the 'Aeolus' episode of *Ulysses*, combining previous antagonists — Hosty, the cad, and especially the 'crude man' Sackerson, blowing Quaker's oats through the keyhole as at 586.36-587.01 he will bring him 'waker oats'. He is also the twins, mainly Shem (earlier they were the cold stream of wind, as 'Coldstream Guards') looking through the keyhole, drinking himself blind with wood alcohol, publishing scandal. He thus becomes HCE himself, confronting his '*brocken*dootsch' (my italics)[9] in battles that amount to such mirror-image conflicts as 'Potts Fracture . . . with Keddle Flatnose' — compared to a kettle, a pot, after all, is noseless — achieving peace as an act of 'Patself on the Bach'. As Campbell and Robinson observe, 'A striking feature of this chapter is its tendency to let the figure of the hero and his antagonists become merged'.[10] That *Brocken* fog reflects as well as refracts, doubling as well as dispersing HCE's image. The peace at the end is the peace we all make nightly with ourselves in order to go to sleep.

NINE

Book I, Chapter 4

75.01-79.13: Shuttered in, hatches battened down, rain weeping outside, HCE envisions himself, first, as a lion in a 'teargarden' (zoo), then in the glass coffin of I/3, buried underwater in Lough Neagh, legendary preserver and home of what Moore in 'Let Erin Remember the Days of Old' calls the 'long-faded glories' under 'the waves of time';[1] the submerged coffin then changes into a submarine, complete with 'conning tower' (chimney heading up to Issy), 'ground battery fuseboxes' (and heading down to the kitchen below) and an 'aerial thorpeto' in the 'sternebooard', which 'thorpeto', with its overtone of French *peter*, recalls his favourite revenge against his antagonists: 'sends boys in socks acoughawhooping when he lets farth his carbonoxside' (128.9-11).

A submarine is a kind of mobile coffin, appropriate for both static moribund self and wandering, invading-exile self, a fit container for both John and James, the 'Two dreamyums in one dromium' (89.03) of this chapter. It is as if the glass coffin launched in the previous chapter had, like the letter-in-bottle of which it is a version (at 75.04 we can see it being 'sigilposted' in a 'brievingbust', Dutch for letterbox), come bobbing back into the bay. As prepared for at 66.10-67.06 (and particularly 66.27-8: '. . . a pillarbox. [new paragraph] The letter . . .') letter and coffin go together, the former first imprisoned in and then escaped from the latter; I/4 begins with one and ends with the other, released. In all his manifestations here, HCE is a submerged or buried form threatening/hoping for escape while biding his time, remembering 'the baregams of the Marmarazalles' (Issy's legs again) and brooding on 'the wrath of Bog', the hostility of the native bogtrotters. All the earlier expressions of resistance to our returning exile converge in this chapter, combined with the earlier hostility to the established publican, reaching new heights of intensity even as it becomes more difficult to tell who is fighting whom, who is inlander and who outsider.

By forcing him underground or underwater, HCE's enemies have in a sense blinded him, 'obcaecated' him like the architect of his 'underground haven'. The room has been darkened with the closing of the shutters (more on that later), leaving him 'involved in darkness' (79.01) to exercise 'his deepseeing insight' — retrace, relive, and consider events. One event he finds himself reliving is the one which started it all, the trip to the privy. His chamber is among other things that outhouse,[2] opened up again by Kate ('insteppen, alls als hats beliefd!' (77.20-1)), in which he sits once again, 'a kingbilly whitehorsed . . . on anxious seat', perusing the pictures 'of those lililiths undeveiled'. Looking within, he becomes a hibernating bear, feeding off fat accumulated by having eaten a 'rainbow trout' — that is, the letter, 'written in seven divers stages of ink' (66.14), buried inside a figure who need only sink within himself to see the rainbow light.

79.14-81.11: A mystery of the previous chapter was, How do those shutters get closed? The answer comes at 102.01-2, when we learn that ALP 'shuttered him after his fall'. Is she still there? I think so, introduced here as 'Kate Strong, a widow'. ALP becomes Kate here because with his back to her HCE does not see her, because she is on the Kate-like chore of cleaning things up and makes a Kate-like remark about the wet mess on the floor made by the 'beggars' bullets' — [hail] stones — and 'smithereen planes', and because HCE's submergence has an atavistic dimension which, beginning at 79.14, takes us back to 'those pagan ironed times' (before the invention of toilet paper, 'when a frond was a friend inneed'), of which Kate is the pub's symbol. ALP-as-Kate emerges as the guide to the area around the privy, thus to the primal scene and its repercussions, especially the repercussion by now remembered as the encounter in the park. The scene is also a Viconian turning point: HCE cursing the boys and scaring them away becomes the 'Allhighest' terrorising the free-living pagans.

81.12-85.19: With his 'deepseeing insight', the somnolent

HCE retraces the past, back to the HCE-Sackerson 'Mutt and Jute' meeting of I/1 and to other memories evoked there, notably Sackerson's troubles with the caddish character I have called 'the Welsher'. The 'oblong bar' with which 'he rose the stick at him' signals that, like the last such encounter, this is a 'stickup', but then 'stickup' is elsewhere identified (315.17, 512.04) with the beerpull which Sackerson mans at the bar — which helps explain how when his antagonist becomes a beggar holding out his bowl, the stick becomes the 'worm' of a distillery, from which he pours him 'refleshmeant'. In return, the intruder tricks Sackerson by inveigling change for a 'woden affair' (recall the wooden 'coyne' of Mutt and Jute (16.31)) which, since the ruse is in effect a robbery, is also a 'webley', a gun, after which he levants, leaving the manservant to go to his colleagues the police.

Other stories are going on too. Brother fights brother, tall father short son. Somewhere along the line, as the narrative tells us they should (81.33-82.02), intruder and defender switch identities: the outsider who opens 'his billy bowl to beg' becomes 'Billi with the Boule' (Gaelic for 'sacred tree', French for 'globe': symbols of beggary have become symbols of sovereignty, sceptre and orb, belonging to King Billy of the Boyne) whose defensive stammer identifies him with HCE; the intruder becomes a type of Sackerson, with his linguistic ineptitude: his expression 'that the thorntree of sheol might ramify up [my] Sheofon to the lux apointplex but' is a mangling of the idiomatic 'Bugger me, but . . .' In sum it is a 'boarder incident' over 'mutual tenitorial rights', at the conclusion of which the defender emerges with the bloody 'thin red lines' of Waterloo (84.19-20), and his adversary, with his 'danegeld', has, like the sons, paid for his intrusion with his teeth (84.03; cf. Shaun, 410.25), some of his hair (84.23, cf. Shem, 169.13), and perhaps — 'dane*geld*' — his manhood as well.

After this, HCE continues tracing back in his memory, to the subject of 'our forebeer', who is depicted first as thwarted invader/exile with ship stuck in harbour or lost at sea (also, again as letter, stuck in 'the bottol' in the river), being ambushed by natives, then as back in that privy, 'upon a public seat', where it all began.

85.20-93.20: The confusion is getting out of hand: time for a trial, to sort things out. As the case of one 'Festy King' set in England's Old Bailey, it is a case of 'Crown vs. King', self vs. self; examining his memory, HCE is, again, 'holding doomsdag over hunselv'. The charges against 'King', 'flying cushats out of his ouveralls and making fesses immodst his forces on the field', recall the Waterloo sin, but when elaborated by the prosecution a greater grievance emerges — that the accused, now in 'dry dock', has recently sailed back to Ireland and tried to pass himself off as a native. (In this light, 'flying cushats' recalls Noah, letting loose the doves before striking land.)

Accordingly, 86.07-31 shows what you have to do in order to be taken for native: first you cover yourself with peaty dirt, then you get yourself a pig, then after assuming an absurd name you show up at the quintessential Irish gathering, a pig-judging contest in a mudstorm. So much for the romance of the ould sod. Festy King, *'elois* Crowbar, once known as Meleky', a derivative of the housebreaking crowbar-armed assailant of earlier encounters, soon bifurcates into 'Tyking-fest and Rabworc', who are in turn recognisably the sons. (At 86.07-18 they are 'their two and trifling selves', and the two-three combination is an unmistakable signature of the twins. Joyce was twenty-three at the birth of Giorgio, who was thirty-two at the time the book is set.) The conflict is becoming more and more one between alternative selves, Shem-half versus Shaun-half. The testimony, beginning at 86.32, can perhaps best be understood as that of a returned ex-exile trying to pass as a life-long local, as someone who belongs at the Irish pig-show — that is, a Shem/James type trying to pass for the native Shaun/John — hence the white and green hat (cf. *Ulysses* 483) and the fulsome praise for the local weather. His account of the usual sin amounts mainly to an excessively enthusiastic account, full of Irishisms, of a local faction-fight, 'on the fair green'.

Despite the affected chauvinism, 'it oozed out in Deadman's Dark Scenery Court' — that dark, shuttered room — that he is lying and/or, perhaps, blind, a 'greeneyed mister'. Suspicion of his bona fides increases when he uses expressions like 'As cad could be' and 'Holy Saint Eiffel'. Questioning of witness becomes inquisition over suspect, the purpose of which, increasingly, is to trip him up with local idioms and 'mathers of prenanciation', until, as Mrs Glasheen discovered, by the bottom of page 89 he is being asked about terms gleaned from a book called *The Secret Languages of Ireland*.[3] Seldom can the 'shibboleth' test have been applied so rigorously. Before long the imposter, his 'stucckomuck' disguise removed, stands exposed as 'Pegger Festy', a derivative of the original 'Festy King' but also (cf. 26.36, 537.01) the outlaw-assailant who 'pegged' stones at the father's window and threatened him with a stick — charges he confirms, typically, by denying (91.11-12, 30-2).

At the end the testimony comes down to the real issue — 'why he left Dublin'. He tries unsuccessfully to ingratiate himself by making 'the sign of the Roman Godhelic faix' (as in 'fakes'), but ends up 'perseguired and pursuited'. The crowd becomes the leap-year girls, a bouquet of misses who flutter around the Shaun-type while berating the Shem-type who just disgraced himself, and nominate as messenger of their wrath one of their number, 'a lovelooking leapgirl', who instead joins with Shem in unmistakably sexual union. It is the first of the *Wake*'s elopement scenes, with the usual symbols of flowers (that elopement fan), sea, and sex. Blind Shem is driven from Ireland with the one woman who would not join in the general odium.

92.33-96.25: With the reminiscing HCE, we have traced back to the event 'which had just caused that the effect of that which it had caused to occur' — the exile which made the rearrival of the *Wake*'s opening necessary. Shem's 'Brythonic' 'loudburst' turns out to have been a fart, 'gash from a burner' like Joyce's own scurrilous 'Gas from a Burner', sent from exile to his native land. The disgusted 'advocatesses' chase him into 'Drinkbattle's Dingy Dwellings' — author's inkbottle, author's exile, dreamer's dark room, sinner's privy (at 93.21 we ask Kate for the key again), purblind author's benighted world, and, most of all, the bottle containing the letter.

The paean to the letter, which follows, confirms what ALP tells us about it at the end, that it is the repository of hopes — a sigh, a beaming eye, a song, and so on. Which is to say it is a type of Pandora's box of all the yearnings which undo us, it being one of the *Wake*'s saddest axioms that 'First we feel. Then we fall' (627.11). Whatever else the scribbling Shem now enclosed in that inkbottle/letter-bottle may represent, he is the remembered hopes and errors of the dreamer's audacious youth. Old men trying to recapture their youth are objects of fun, and so the four judges now return to give us a scornful portrait, inspired by Shem's recent mephitic contribution, of 'that old gasometer with his hooping coppin' and 'his sayman's effluvium', returning to Dublin and trying to reclaim the girl he remembers. Yet at the same time they find themselves moonily re-enacting that young romance, until called by duty to 'forego the pasht' and return to the business of passing judgment.

96.26-103.11: Skipping uneasily over the fact that all the *Wake*'s creation is the result of some man's guilty fascination with some young girl — Issy's outline discerned among the stars in 'the fields of blue' of her bedroom upstairs, Issy's 'funner's stotter' (Finn's daughter, Finn's stutter), coming down the fire-place flue, at the 'root' of all speech — the judges resolve to become 'special mentalists', in other words denatured, 'spatial' Shaun-types, judging and condemning the Shemian exile/immigrant. Perhaps inspired by the calendar picture, he is a hunted fox, harried by 'bugles', 'louping the loup' and 'doubling' back, chased back home where he hides in 'covert', as such a version of the subterranean, submarine, boarded-up figure of the chapter's beginning. He flees again and returns again to 'this country of exile', where he is reincarnated as both John type and James type, prosperous public man and backdoor beggar. Once again he is thought to be safely finished off, 'lion . . . in a pureede paumee bloody proper', like the caged lion at the chapter's beginning, listening to (the sound returns here) 'the ruining of the rain' submerging him, and once again his supposed extinction brings forth a call for that sea-born letter — 'The Latter! The latter!' echoes *'Thalatta! Thalatta!'* — the opening and reading of which will resurrect him.

As usual at the end of the war — declared finally 'o'er' at 101.07 — the woman is summoned to make peace. At 100.05-8 HCE 'Besights' daughter, companions and wife, and soon thereafter he is established with his woman, the burning homefires signalling, like the smoke announcing a papal successor, that order has been re-established and the line continued. He is not barren, dead for good; he is a 'tesseract', extending through time as well as space. That is, he is a married man, whose relationship with his wife brings forth those two Shakespearean antidotes to mortality, literature (the letter) and children (the litter). With which rousing assertion we meet ALP, in the vicinity for some time, who now 'stood forth' to dismiss HCE's antagonists with her 'babalong' talk.

With her arrival, another cycle of the book's seven-stage sequence is coming to completion, having gone as follows:

I. (3-10) Waking up, recall of fall, trip outdoors to privy ('wandered out of his farmer's health'): voyage outward fused with return voyage, elopement, primal scene, fall.

II. (10-18) Return to house, encounter of male with male: birth of son, brother-battle, father-son battle.

III. (18-29) Re-established in bed hearing Issy's voice: birth of daughter, first occurrence of blindness and flood.

IV. (30-47) Noise from without and breaking of windows: vengeful mob, often identified with children, attacks the re-arriving intruder.

V. (48-74) Cowering in room, hearing banging sound and wind outdoors alternating with daughter's seductive voice from upstairs: imagined male-fight over woman, intensified attack, cries of indignation from without; the fog is the worsening glaucoma which progressively 'overclouded'[4] Joyce's sight.

VI. (75-101) Shuttered in, turns inward: Defeated, ruined, starting to brew up *Finnegans Wake*.

VII. (101-) Sinking deep into self, at the end of the tether, turns to woman, remembers youth with her, starts cycle over again: final blindness, flood, rainbow, the letter, the book, *Ricorso*.

I/4 ends where I/1 began, with the female sound of running water: 'riverrun' — 'babalong'. Perhaps that faucet near the bed has been turned on again.

TEN

Book I, Chapter 5

THE *Wake*'s famous letter is the ever-reinterpreted memory of HCE and ALP's life together, as called forth during one exchange in this chapter. Even the much discussed letter-paper on which it is written is, as I/1 defines 'papyr', 'hides and hints and misses in prints' (20.10-11), a tissue of signs and gestures, interpreted and misinterpreted. It is, first, the 'hopes' of young love — 'the mains of me draims' (623.31) — 'buried' in HCE by his bride, till 'kissmiss coming' (624.06). Originating in the woman, deposited by her words and fermented in the man, called forth by the woman's act, it is indeed, as I/5 says many times, a 'duplex' (123.30-1), a 'pen-product of a man or woman' (108.31), a synthesis of 'un-brookable' female script and forceful male punctuation (123.32-124.03; see also 123.08-10): writing, like reading, is collusive. As at the end of the book, where ALP's last kiss (628.15) gives us the 'keys' to the beginning, so in I/5 ALP's kiss of her moribund husband, like Biddy's analogous peck at the dungheap, will revive old memories, 'in the baccbuccus of his mind' (118.16 — '*bacbuc*' = bottle in Hebrew: the letter is also the letter in the bottle) and start the ball rolling again.

Thus unearthed, the letter is brought forward as an exhibit for examination, subject of the 'rude rule of fumb' (283.20) of a no-nonsense Shaun (113.25-6). The events enacted and recalled in I/1 have been dispersed (I/2), refracted (I/3), reviewed and amplified (I/4); now we begin to sort them out and purge the disorderly elements. I/5 introduces the apparatus of scholarship; I/6 will be a numbered list, with the subject of the unruly Shem relegated to those numbers, eleven and twelve, beyond the pale of Shaun's ten-digit 'rule of fumb'. I/7, which as E. L. Epstein suggests is an extension of

the twelfth question of I/6,[1] continues to anatomise and
anathematise that rotter; I/8 washes the last traces away.

All this begins, prosaically, with breakfast. Hence 'Butt'
will report indignantly that he originally mistook HCE's
noxious 'gospeds', God-sped gospel, received and sent, for
the innocent reception of breakfast (343.31-3); hence Shaun
will accuse his girlish congregation of 'turning breakfarts into
lost soupirs' (453.12), breakfast into the 'sigh' which I/1
(11.25-6) identifies with the letter. As recalled in I/8, ALP
arrives with that letter, 'forebidden' in *Ulysses* (11.29-30):

> . . . he durmed adranse in durance vaal . . . And there she
> was, Anna Livia . . . for to ishim bonzour to her dear
> dubber Dan. With neuphraties and sault from his maggias.
> And an odd time she'd cook him up blooms of fisk and
> lay to his heartsfoot her meddery eygs, yayis, and staynish
> beacons on toasc and a cupenhave so weeshywashy of
> Greenland's tay . . . and a shinkobread (hamjambo, bana.)
> for to plaise that man . . . (199.09-20)

Accounts of this breakfast vary, but a few definite facts
emerge. It wakes HCE up (cf. 102.02). It includes an egg or
eggs, a roll or toast, fruit and, most emphatically, a cup of
tea. It comes accompanied with chatter about news from
back home, and, as the wife leaves, a farewell kiss.

104.01-109.36: Besides the seven-stage sequence noted
earlier (104.10-14), the 'plurabilities' of which ALP is the
'bringer' include pictures of her housebound '*hosenband*',
memories of her youthful hopes and their consequences
and the contents of the arriving breakfast (see e.g. 106.18,
106.19, 106.21). The document is, after all, a 'mamafesta' —
a mother's feast.

After the list comes this account:

> There was a time when naif alphabetters would have
> written it down the tracing of a purely deliquescent recidi-
> vist, possibly ambidextrous, snubnosed probably and pre-
> senting a strangely profound rainbowl in his (or her)
> occiput. (107.09-12).

As snubnosed bowl-shaped teapot being brought with breakfast, the letter mingles vegetation and water to produce its

solution. The bowl is also a head, the 'occiput' of the 'aysore' (107.23) glaucoma-smitten HCE and the rainbow in his cranial bowl (the besieged HCE of I/4 was said to 'get outside his own length of rainbow trout' (79.07-8)), peering through the 'kitchernott darkness', groping through the obscurity with his eyes like an old owl, reading the tea leaves ('now lief . . . then frond') for signs, as if the leaves were the letters of some mysterious alphabet, or the shifting tiles of some symbol-laden mosaic, or stars being anthropomorphised in the eyes of a myth-making astrologer, or (cf. 96.26-9) the daughter's starry ceiling on the floor above anthropomorphised and coveted as the lusting father's displaced object of desire, or microscopic pheromones leading an insect from flower to flower (107.12-18).

The world seen from the eyes of our eye-sick dreamer is refracted, rainbow-coloured, ever-shifting, 'moving and changing every part of the time' (118.22-3; cf. 19.12-13). The simplest way for the viewer to cease being so 'bewilder-blissed' by his vision's 'night effluvia' is just to shut his eyes — as he does, at 107.28, thus allowing the impressions to sort themselves out in his mind, to 'coalesce, their con-trarieties eliminated, in one stable somebody'. (He is also waiting for the tea to draw — hence the admonition to be patient.)

The emerging letter is now a 'radiooscillating epiepistle', coming in through the ears only — but, as we are reminded on 109, the coalescing impression which results represents what would today be called naïve essentialism, achieved by HCE's 'preferring to close his blinkhard's eyes' to the 'enveloping facts', abstracting a 'vision' of his wife as 'plump and plain in her natural altogether'.

110.01-111.24: Accordingly, we begin, tentatively, an en-gagement with the incongruous facts of this 'inharmonious' creation, allowing 'a few artifacts' to swim into our ken. Since, after all, we're about to have an egg, let us go back to the 'original' hen — more reductivism, arbitrarily declaring that chicken comes before egg — the one we saw (10.25-13.03) pecking away after Waterloo back 'in his mistridden past' (110.31) — back at the primal scene (Waterloo), back with the leavings of an 'outdoor meal' (the picnic in prospect

during the *Wake*'s closing pages), back to the memory of
what the father was at the time the letter was sent off, the
time he sailed off with his woman. It becomes clear, I think,
why the bottle-letter should be compared to the Ardagh
chalice: this is an invocation, a calling-up of spirits, from a
place — Boston, Mass — which is never spelled out, is always
'Mass'.[2]

   The letter itself (111.05-24) hardly seems to justify such
claims. The events are prosy enough: the tea having drawn,
the wife presents her husband with a cup ('largelooking tache
[*'tasse'* as well as 'stain'] of tch'), poured, we are assured,
from the spout of a genuine piece of Irish pottery, while
filling him in on the latest news and, I think, thanking him
('Dear, thank you' is one of the letter's motifs) for her birthday gift, the *'lovely'* gown. All this is complicated with what
at 66.18-21 is called 'inbursts of Maggyer . . . semposed . . .
in . . . siamixed twoatalk' — interjections from Issy's dark
double, Maggy. As much as ALP, Issy is the one whose voice
is heard here (closing his eyes to his wife, HCE has envisioned
her as her younger Issy-self); in fact all the regular elements
of the letter occur again in her monologue of 143.31-148.32,
from opening 'dear' to Arrah-na-Pogue 'lucksmith' kiss, and
the letter includes Issyan subjects, for example the piece of
wedding cake, letting the recipient know that she's taken
(cf. 147.22-4, 232.11-15, 279.32-5). In resurrecting the
dreams buried years ago in the figure of her then dashing
young husband, ALP is resurrecting her young self as well,
from the days of a romantic match consummated far enough
from home that family and friends were informed of it by
mail, the event more or less coinciding with the death of
the 'Father Michael' whom Mrs Glasheen, correctly I think,
associates with the Michael Bodkin behind 'The Dead'.[3]
Above all, the letter is a return to the time recorded at
202.23-204.20 and elsewhere, when the young ALP chose
between priestly lover and sailor lover, Shaun type and Shem
type, John and James, life at home and life abroad, departed
Father Michael and the rover whose memory her kiss now
tries to bring back.

   111.25-119.09: With the arrival of the 'letter' begins the
commentary on it. First, we get a dismal account of the fate

of any photographic 'negative', for instance of a white horse, that *Wake* symbol of male promise and prowess (see, e.g., 621.30-2) recorded in the snapshot of Waterloo, now a 'distorted macromass of all sorts of horsehappy values'. Trying to get it 'unfilthed', the egg-bearing ALP becomes, once again, a hen, pecking up the past, whom we are urged to follow to an age of rejuvenation.

Also to an age of re-integration: as the purblind viewer notices the 'cop of her fist right against our nosibos', her hand reaching the teacup to his mouth, he sees the Claddagh ring on her finger whose insignia of two joined hands holding a crowned heart — 'And she has a heart of Arin!'[4] — is the *Wake*'s invariable symbol of fraternal reconciliation (brothers shaking hands) and young love, the ring having been ALP's engagement band. The wife is evidently feeling rejuvenated herself, in her new gown: her hair shows the 'rudess of a robur', and she enjoys showing herself, dazzlingly, in her 'graith uncouthrement of postmantuam glasseries' — she is looking at herself in the glass — while reviewing the 'old story' of the elopement and its consequences.

Next, her husband, as he was urged, follows her ('after you, policepolice') — gets himself up and peers in the mirror into which she was just looking, 'Drawing nearer to take our slant at it'. Upright, feeling like a Shaun-type, 'a worker, a tombstone mason', he confronts in the glass the image of a dissipated Shem, 'a poorjoist', with a Shemian night-person's version of the room scene behind him (114.23-31). He initiates a prosecutorial line of inquiry of the letter's story as seen under a 'pudendascope': the 'Maggies' become magdalenes; 'Father' and 'Michael' are darkly suggestive of incestuous fathers and lecherous priests; the sender of the wedding cake is a lubricious 'nympholept' who cannot get over the 'drauma present in her past', that traumatic separation from the homeland of the Father Michael who, in the next, Marxist, interpretation, represents 'the old regime', contrasted with the 'social revolution' of the 'Margaret' who ran off with the Spartacus-like upstart.

Various other interpretations of the old story just resurrected by ALP and her tea, the story of lover chosen and lover left, flight, marriage, resentment, rivalry, and regret, follow in various forms, for instance 'this oldworld epistola of their weatherings and their marryings and their buryings and their natural selections . . . like an ould cup on tay.'

The letter becomes a kind of 'charter', validating that momentous choice, its deteriorated state therefore a source of worry: looking in the mirror, HCE now sees that feared rival, the 'olmond bottler' Sackerson, and commands him to accept the *fait accompli* of which the letter is the symbol: 'the affair is a thing once for all done'. The anxiety is all the greater because the ultimate source of the deterioration is 'all in his eye': its signs are changing and moving around so bewilderingly because of the glaucoma-flood (tracing to the daughter's birth, conceived because of that elopement) which leaves scarcely a 'dried ink scrap of paper' to which we now cling 'as with drowning hands', hoping for the deluge to 'clear up'.

119.10-125.23: Having been broken down to its narrative components, the letter is further reduced to the alphabet. Purblind HCE staring in mirror sees first his eyelashes ('whip-looplashes'), then his smitten eyes ('bolted or blocked rounds'), leading to 'the touching reminiscence' of the 'airy plume-flights' — the elopement — which preceded his 'glorioles'; thence we get the sigla for first HCE, then ALP 'following a certain change of state of grace', then the other members of the family and establishment which followed from that flight, and which lead to all the other elements of the story as touched on in the parody of pedantry extending into page 124: the exile's defiance of his pious upbringing (120.01-5), his defiantly Byronic sexuality (120.33-121.08), the winning of his auburn-haired beauty (122.06-19), the scene in the outhouse (120.28-33) which 'return[s]' us to 'one particularly sore point in the past' — the primal scene recorded in blood-red marks on a white field (120.14-15) — the cursing of the snaky Shem who at that scene witnessed 'the innocent exhibitionism', 'a rightheaded ladywhite don a corkhorse' (121.19-23), the ensuing battles (122.09-14), blindness (121.16-19), decline (122.34-5), death (123.02-3), *'funferal'* (120.10) and reviving kiss (122.32).

The man looking at himself in the mirror has commenced a kind of self-psychoanalysis, retrieving that buried Shem-self whom ALP hoped to revive. The two hyphenated scholarly schizophrenics who next show up to explore his schizophrenia and his semi-unconscious personify this activity; they soon merge into a professor murdering to dissect, who in turn becomes a facsimile of HCE at his breakfast, poking food with fork, amidst (124.07-8) the window's broken glass. The letter has set in motion the self-excavation which has brought us to where we are at the end of the chapter, scrutinising and confronting that 'Diremood' who as the romantic figure of the Dermot and Grania story defied tribe, lord, and duty to run off with his woman. We are back to, down to, Shem.

ELEVEN

Book I, Chapter 6

BEFORE scrutinising Shem close-up, we pass through I/6, which Joyce called a 'picture gallery'. HCE continues to stare at himself in the mirror. Question 9 describes him in a trance,[1] 'the states of suspensive exanimation', looking at 'seemself' through (143.24-7) the rainbow of his glaucoma, picking out 'the reverberration of knotcracking awes, the reconjungation of nodebinding ayes, the redissolusingness of mindmouldered ease and the thereby hang of the Hoel of it' — nutcracker jaw, eyes, mind-moulding ears, mouth plus 'whole' face, reflected in a *riverbero*, a kind of mirror.[2] Staring at 'seemself', he is Shaun and Shem staring at one another, through the looking-glass: Hart observes about this passage that the subject is 'seeing in the mirror of the kaleidoscope an inversion of his ego and/or id', and that he is gazing at himself as in a well, like Narcissus[3] — and sure enough the chapter begins with Shaun introduced as an 'echo . . . in the back of the wodes', 'wodes' being Slavic for 'water'.

Order-imposing Shaun-self, called forth to sort out the chaos of I/4's testimony and keep down the resurgence of I/5's letter, attempts to do just that with his numbered question-and-answer, his 'exanimation'. The attempt is only partially successful. The introduction to the exam tells us that Shaun 'left his free natural ripostes to four of them in their own fine artful disorder'. If, as E. L. Epstein suggests,[4] we take I/7 as the extended answer to question 12, then eight question-and-answers are orderly, fitting some easily recognisable formal scheme, and four are disorderly — long, sprawling, out of control. These four, about HCE (number 1), Issy (number 10), and Shem-Shaun (numbers 11 and 12) are, not coincidentally, all related to the story of brother-battle and father-son battle over a young female which was called forth by the release of the letter from the bottle, and which it has been Shaun's business to contain.

I/6 also re-commences yet another run of the ubiquitous autobiographical seven-stage sequence, just concluded in the previous chapter. Questions 1 and 2 (126.10-139.28) correspond to Stage 1, the mating of Tristram and Iseult, HCE and ALP. Questions 3, 4, 5, 6, 7 (139.29-142.29) correspond to Stage 2, the 'doubling' of the couple to produce an establishment, an inn with servants and customers (numbers 3, 5, 6, and 7) which includes, in microcosm, Dublin (numbers 3 and 4) and Ireland (number 4). Questions 8, 9, and 10 (142.30-148.32) correspond to Stage 3, the disruptively alluring arrival of the magdalene-like 'elope year girl' (number 8) coming from 'afire' (number 10) to the spellbound noodle (number 9). Question 11 (148.33-168.12) corresponds to Stages 4 and 5: brother and brother (and father and son) engage in a battle (Stage 4) from which a divided Issy/Nuvoletta/Marge gradually emerges as the apple of discord (Stage 5). Question 12, extending through most of I/7 (168.13 to approximately 193.29) corresponds to Stage 6, Shem as 'Hebrewer' and 'young man' being attacked and 'paid off' by Shaun, recalled with mixed longing and loathing by HCE. The end of I/7 and all of I/8 (approximately 193.30 to 216.05) correspond to Stage 7 — flood, rainbow, forgiveness, re-beginning and, through the chattering of the washerwomen, the redemptive power of litter-ature.

126.10-139.14: As on the book's first page, this sequence seems cued by an imaginative circuit of the room. We begin where we left off in I/5, with an excavation into the figure before us, HCE, now standing in front of the mantelpiece mirror along the southeast wall. The questioner, as Epstein argues,[5] is Shem, summoned in the preceding pages. Reflecting backward into his mind and its store of memories, HCE encounters what in II/2, under similar circumstances, will be described as 'his house of thoughtsam . . . a jetsam litterage of convolvuli of times lost or strayed' (292.14-16). Question 1 is the mind's flotsam, the drifting raw material of a free-associating figure entering the trance state, turning his past into legend, himself into a buried giant.

139.15-28: We next 'turn our optics' from HCE to the woman standing 'by his side' — to the left, in the direction of the faucet, whose 'pranklings' we can hear in the background. Shem's next question, 'Does your mutter know your mike?', is evidently a childish taunt involving — like many such remarks — a reference to Shaun's mother. Considering that 'mike' is within echoing distance of 'McCool', the name just given the father, it can probably be taken as a variant of 'Does your mother know who your father is?', with 'mike' also implicating[6] the dead Father Michael who is a major candidate for ALP's first lover, and whose spiritual son Shaun definitely is; both represent the pious, domestic virtues celebrated in Father Prout's famous 'The Shandon Bells', the model for Shaun's answer.

139.29-140.07: Shifting our vision back to the reflected male, we see simultaneously the licence over the window behind him, with its Dublin seal — the certification of HCE's domestic respectability. The picture given here is of the rotund prosperous ('Coalprince') one-eyed ('painted witt wheth one darkness') 'civilian' who settled down in the last entry, plus seal (with its three castles — 'rookeries', '*Dreyschluss*'), plus public house. Shaun's version of Dublin's authoritarian motto says that as far as he can see with his 'orb', HCE is fat and happy.

140.08-141.07: Although the X siglum assigned to this question connects it with the four old men, the main concern of those 'shehusbands' (390.20) is here, as elsewhere, the woman's marriage and its consequences. Beginning with an invocation to a goddess ('a dea o dea!'), this entry, as Ruth Von Phul observes[7] about the 'Dorhqk' passage, 'concerns marriage, and it indicates that what the suitor promises and his bride dreams of is not what she gets'. 'Delfas' is the decisive, frankly phallic wooer, overpowering the woman and giving her a gold band (in, I think, the Claddagh design — 'heart' is usually a Claddagh cue); 'Dorhqk' is a smooth talker; 'Nublid' a lazy boozer living off his wife's labour and his own dreams, hoping she will inherit something; by 'Dalway' the woman (who was riveted by the first, manacled by the second, and set to work in the kitchen by the third) is a 'trotty' 'hooked' by her no-account husband — a bitted and bridled horse being ridden, a fish being caught and netted. Much of the imagery derives from the 'wishtas' imaginable from the window, below the permit of the previous entry. The Shandon bells, so alluring in number 2, return here as wedding bells; in number 6 they will confirm the dreary wife's progress just given by becoming the servant's bell which 'Summon[s] in the Housesweep Dinah', ALP's next incarnation.

141.08-142.07: The dissolution into which the couple of number 4 were slipping is embodied in the next male-female pair, Sackerson and Kate. Sackerson is a hanger-on of the inn whose establishment was described in number 3 and of the country surveyed in number 4. (Geographically his is the most difficult of the entries to situate: he may be cued by thoughts of the yard outside the window, which he patrols and from which he is sometimes imagined spying, and the windowboards — 'fullest boarded' — which it is his job to tend; we are also told he is supposed to 'swab' the 'Baywin-daws'.) As for Kate, it seems to me that the cue for her voice is, in fact, her voice — the sound of the servant recently 'Summoned' to clean up the broken glass (141.34) on the floor. Witchy, bitter, and, like Sackerson, exploited, sarcastic-ally recalling with her floor-polishing 'beeswax' the fine words of the bearish lover who once called her his 'honey-sugger' (the 'Goldilocks' story is of course behind this), she represents the female nadir of that Irish life established by the imposing figure introduced at the outset. After this brief appearance she leaves, maybe to get her mop; she will return in I/8.

142.07-28: Having gone counterclockwise around the room from HCE to ALP to basin and faucet to permit to window-scene to door, we return, with the seventh question, to the mirror itself, through which we are soon to pass, and from which we spy, first, HCE and ALP in their degraded incarnations as Sackerson ('the doorboy') and Kate ('the cleaner'), then a diaspora. As, collectively, the 'component' impressions in a Wakean mirror they are both reflective ('re-troratiocination') and predictive ('vaticination'), both forgiving ('condone every evil') and, as 'doyles' and 'sullivans', judgmen-tal. Reflecting the male gazer's face, they are 'porters'. Like many a bedroom mirror, they have witnessed a great deal (142.24-5); like every *Wake* mirror they are alternately shattered and whole, symbol of fragmentation and reintegration.

142.30-143.28: Back at the mirror, we are back at that flower-patterned elopement fan spread out before it, here as at 220.03-6 and elsewhere personified as the twenty-eight girls who, in language whose repetitiveness may owe something to the 'he loves me, he loves me not' of daisy-picking, recall the 'elope year' which the fan symbolises. This is Stage 3, the arrival of the young girl who re-creates the young ALP of earlier days.

143.29-148.32: That is, we are at Issy's 'avoice from afire' (3.09), the 'earsighted view of old hopeinhaven' (143.09-10) promised in the previous entry, here experienced as 'a bref burning till shee that drawes dothe smoake retourne'. Standing at the fireplace, the entranced HCE hears the voice of Issy coming down the flue, talking to her cat and luring birds to it. She begins by addressing it as 'pette', and although in the usual Wakean way this name is soon distorted by the listener's fevered projections, we can still discern that original cat:

> Of course I know, pettest, you're so learningful and considerate in yourself, so friend of vegetables, you long cold cat you! Please by acquiester to meek my acquointance! Codling, snakelet, iciclist! My diaper has more life to it! (145.08-11)

(Compare 361.08-17, where Iseult, shortly before addressing 'Kitty Kelly', says 'And move your tellabout. Not nice is that, limpet lady!' Issy is playing with her cat's tail, in language that HCE takes personally. See also 146.33-36, 147.29-148.05.) The voice HCE hears becomes Issy-as-young-ALP-as temptress, thanking him for the present he has just given his wife (144.20-2, 148.07-10), scorning the recently tea-serving ALP as a lowly Kate-type Maggie-type (144.36-145.07), responding teasingly to 'The flame' of his burning appeal up the flue (145.23), luring him to 'Come big to Iran' (144.18) by apparently spurning his rival, the priestly lover (see, especially, 146.08-12).

148.33-159.23: In particular, this speech, imagined by a figure who has just had memories of his youthful elopement revived by the fan before him, precipitates the rivalry that follows:

> . . . he's so loopy on me and I'm so leapy like since the day he carried me from the boat, my saviored of eroes . . . I beg your pardon, I was listening to every treasuried word I said fell from my dear mot's tongue otherwise how could I see what you were thinking of our granny? (146.23-9)

As I have argued earlier, his first words, recalled here, were 'I beg your pardon, goldilocks'. Returning him to the brave wooer who spoke those words, Issy, as promised in question 9, lures HCE through the looking-glass (you can hear her disappearing and daring him to follow at 146.30-147.02, 148.26-32) to 'the course of his tory' (143.12), the curse of his history: at question 11 he is a wretched exile like the subject of Thomas Campbell's 'The Exile of Erin', now literally a 'beggar' — figures of speech have a disquieting way of being taken literally in the *Wake* — and intercepted by the domestic John/'Jones' who is not about to forgive him for having prevailed against his own suit, for having taken the girl they both coveted away from him. The mantelpiece picture exerts its influence over this encounter of 'exiles or ambusheers, beggar and neighbour' (163.12-13): the Mookse of the fable carries a *'lancia spezzata'*, and the Gripes is recognisably a type of the serpentine Shem/cad. A 'blind blighter', Shem will be the 'bland old isaac' of Stage 4, 'buttended' by his revanchist rival. Shaun keeps abusively naming him as Levy-Bruhl/'Loewy-Brueller'/'Levi-Brullo'/'Llewellys ap Bryllars' — that is, the Liffey-burner whose flashing eyes, we recall, set the young ALP's hair afire and lured her away from Shaun's Ireland. The main source of this animus, caused, as 517.13-14 recalls, by 'smutt and chaff' just sent down 'between' the mirror-image brothers by the trouble-making Issy, is fraternal (and of course, Oedipal) rivalry over a central woman. As such it is a 'Mr Skekels and Dr Hydes' (150.17-18) struggle between two halves of one figure. Physically it is between 'Shouldrups' and 'Kneesknobs' (157.10-12), crowned head and 'anathomy infairioriboos' (154.11), kisser ('blissim'

(156.27) — and thus we get an ad for lady-killer accessories (156.28-30)) — and farter ('Puffut!' (156.34) — and thus we get an ad for a gas-inhibitor (156.35-6)). Psychically it is between the fat, flat, petrified effigy of head-and-shoulders framed in the mirror like some monumental bust and the remembered passion just now aroused from a voice originating in a region below the waist — between, that is, a static image and memory, between space and time.

The bifurcation of HCE and hypostatisation of his two abstracted psychic constituents, which as McHugh notes[8] began with the trial of I/4, is by now in full swing. Ruth Von Phul has suggested that the much-discussed '*Semus sumus*' (168.14) occurring at the very end of the chapter's brother-battle may be translated as *se mussumus*, 'we brood over ourselves or mutter to ourselves',[9] and there are indeed times (see especially 160.25-8) when Shaun seems partly aware that he is engaged in a muttering dialogue of one. It is the latest version of those self-and-other encounters that dominate I/3 and I/4, this time defined more dramatically than ever before in terms of HCE's sense of his life as a morality play of good angel vs. bad angel. The master-servant encounter of I/1 has by now been brooded over and recast, though we can see traces of the original, most tellingly in the charge of cuckoldry exchanged between the two antagonists[10] just before the appearance of the girl whose parentage is in dispute.

As at 165.21-4, Issy sits above the combatants, in the 'bannistars', because her voice does in fact come from on high, as usual trickling and drip-dropping down. Near the end of this sequence the characteristic 'siss' of her sigh, along with the growing dusk outside, evokes a lyrical scene of gentle evening breezes blowing through waterside reeds, which reeds in turn evolve from a picture of green grass surrounding everything: 'ver grose O arundo'. Greenness, darkness, dripping water: emerging from this latest struggle is glaucoma-smitten Joyce of Stage 4, a blind old Isaac.

159.24-168.14: Dropping the fable, Shaun attacks more directly the allegations, typical of the 'Cusanus philosophism' (163.17), that he and his opposite are really doubles. Let the insinuating outsider go back where he came from, or better yet as far away as possible, to Tristan da Cunha, say, one of those remote little South Atlantic islands — St Helena is another — made to order for troublesome exiles who refuse to stay put. But even there he might be like one of those disgracefully procreative tropical trees which sends its 'self-sownseedlings' on the winds over thousands of miles, to descend like 'mannah ash' (the tree is also a volcano, like Krakatoa spreading ashes over the world) on the innocent female inhabitants of the island which spurned him (compare 235.19-21) . . . Taking another tack, then, let us consider this 'arrivaliste case' in terms of food. Shaun is butter, 'obsoletely unadulterous' (161.17); Shem is cheese, an 'eastasian import' (166.32) with (163.09) 'a hole or two' (which I suppose would make him Swiss cheese, recalling Joyce's Zurich exile). But of course both are milk products and therefore identical in 'the dairy days of buy and buy' — a point made by the arrival of 'Margareen', who is, number one, 'the cowrymaid M.', milking her cow and, number two, margarine, a synthetic product. Shaun doesn't help his case by going on to compare the brothers to Brutus and Cassius (different types, true enough, but after all allies) or to the (identical) B and C angles of an isosceles triangle. Unable to stave off the obvious, Shaun is reduced to repudiating the whole line of inquiry.

With that repudiation we have arrived at the assertion with which the next chapter begins, that Shem's 'back life will not stand being written about in black and white' (169.06-8) — precisely Shaun's medium. HCE, plumbing his past, recoils from what he finds, especially the 'shamebred music' (164.15-16) of Joyce's passionate youth. Protesting too much, Shaun dismisses 'this tickler hussy for occupying my uttentions' (166.29): 'The word is my Wife, to exponse and expound, to vend and to velnerate, and may the curlews crown our nuptias!' (167.29-30) A stirring affirmation of marriage, no doubt, but those 'curlews' cannot help but recall (see, for instance, 383.15-17) the seabirds which serenaded the elopement, and as for devotion to 'the word' . . . well. Look around the page. Clearly, 'the word' has at least as much of 'the hoyden and the impudent' about her as she does of 'the Wife'. To engage language for any purpose, however virtuous, is to be dragged down into the Shemian universe, with its 'root language'. Shaun does his best to bring things to a resounding finale, but in vain: he will continue to splutter on for the next chapter.

TWELVE

Book I, Chapter 7

AS CONFIRMED near the end of this chapter (193.12-16, 194.06-10), HCE continues to stare into the mantelpiece mirror, communing with himself. I/7 represents a movement downward — to the Shem-self — and backward: we are at Stage 6, in which the principal brews his rotten malt (3.12-13), is a 'Hebrewer' with water on the brain/hitting the brainy 'Waterman' (104.12-13), kills his young self (126.22-3), and pays himself off with memories (589.33-5), and the memories dredged up are simultaneously of the author's youth and of the events of the opening chapters.

169.01-175.28: The Shem described by his brother is a character out of the distant, unlamented past ('would we go back there now . . .?'), his introductory portrait (169.11-20) an impossible catalogue of Daliesque attributes which none-theless do — literally — add up to (count them: 'eight', 'one', 'fortytwo', 'eighteen', 'trio', 'two', 'fifths', 'two', 'one') eighty-two, year of James Joyce's birth. The scandalous 'debouch at the very dawn of protohistory', back there in the 'garden nursery', was, simply, his birth; the Satanic riddle he poses has to do mainly, I think, with death, specifically of the brother he has supplanted. Of its fourteen answers, three ('when the angel of death kicks the bucket of life', 'when wee deader walkner', 'when yea, he hath no mananas') clearly refer to someone's death, and several of the others are arguably on the same theme. As Leo Knuth points out, in the last version of the riddle (607.11-12), 'when is a nam nought a nam wheneas it is a', 'nam' conveys 'I am not' and (as Irish *anam*) soul or life;[1] the riddle, that is, may be roughly trans-lated as, when is a man/soul not alive?' As for the answer, 'when he is a . . . Sham', *asham* is a Hebrew word referring to a sacrificial victim, someone who dies that another may live.[2]

In keeping with the autobiographical story we hear a lot about the young Joyce's flight from Ireland and his fights with the kind of local piety the older brother is made to represent. Underlying this familiar account is an emerging memory of that cursed 'lipoleum' of I/1 who witnessed the father at stool, remembered the primal scene, ran away in fright, insisted on telling his innocent brother all about it, was cursed and blinded. In memory, HCE becomes the Shem spying on himself. As Clive Hart shows,[3] Joyce has fun with the Einsteinian formulae which make such a feat technically possible, but at least in I/7 the main rationale is that the ruminating father has sunk to, become one with, the peeping antagonist of the earlier pages.

Thus Shaun's charge that like the father of I/1 Shem was a reprehensible defecator (171.29-32) 'shotted' with the familiar gun/camera which, for the father, captured his incriminating image and, for the peeker, 'closed his vicious circle, snap' (98.19), put out his eye. (At 174.19 Shem is described as having a 'piteous onewinker'.) And thus it is that the father whose tale is being told by Shem is himself half-Shem, on one hand the 'farfamed fine Poppamore' but on the other hand 'his rotten little ghost of a Peppybeg, Mr Himmyshimmy . . . always bottom sawyer'. Shem's gaze is a 'focuss', both son's peeping and father's retaliating 'cuss'; the 'Haunted Inkbottle' in which he will be shut (182.31) is both that bottle containing the letter's young Shemian impulses and the boarded-up bedroom (doubling as the privy — 'SHUT' is inscribed on its door) in which HCE hides from his assailants; the rainy 'hailcannon' night of his 'departure' is both I/2's hail cannonading against his window, always associated with the son's assault, and, as McHugh notes, the 'halcyon days' of his (Shemian) youth. Hence, I think, the temporal anomaly of Shem's poem (175.07-28) surveying the familiar seven-stage sequence: from the father's perspective, it is a summary of things that have happened to him; from the son's, it is a summary of things that will happen in due course but have 'Not yet'. If father can view son as buried memory, son can view father as future fate.

175.29-178.07: The self-accusatory father-son mirroring

is evident throughout this next section. Shemian 'Darkies' from Belial/Balliol attack Shem himself while singing some of his songs, one on the theme of the father's sin. Shem, as usual, reacts to the sight of 'his pawdry's purgatory', his father's evacuation, by (177.06-7) soiling himself in turn. In fact his pasquinade, manufactured, as we will learn, from excrement, will itself duplicate the act it reviles. There are sound psychological motives for his strenuous denial (at 177.31-5) of identity with his twin/father, in language which undermines the argument.

178.07-179.16: Shem next returns to the 'thorough fright' which produced the 'dreadful' stuff in the first place. Identification between terrified, cursed son and spied-on, beset father seems complete here. The 'erstborn gore' on 'every doorpost' recalls both the sacrifice of the firstborn John Joyce and Waterloo's 'thin red lines'; the telescope through which the spier is peeping when blinded like a 'tompip peepestrella' recalls the frightening paternal 'tallowscoop' of Waterloo, turned back on him, then becomes the gun barrel of the father's I/3 assailant, pointing through the keyhole which both father and son have cause to remember with anxiety; the indictment against Shem is made on behalf of the 'incensed privy' – as in 'Privy Council', a sign of fatherly authority, as in the other kind of privy, a reminder of the father's Shemian humanity.

179.17-181.33: The returning Shem is remembered arriving by canal barge because he is a *'canaille'* (173.02). He is a 'drug and drunkery addict', taking absinthe (464.18) and wood alcohol (70.27) because of the traumatic shock he is trying to forget and expunge from his sight. Shem-Joyce reading his 'usylessly unreadable Blue book of Eccles', *'edition de tenebres'* is also HCE in the 'glaucous den' of his privy using the 'expurgative plates' (356.30-1) of his pornographic book as fodder for masturbatory fantasies ('Eccles', with its capital E, is an HCE name – see, e.g. 514.15), and also HCE still gaping into the mirror and imagining alternative lives ('Eccles' suggests 'Ecce', as in 'Ecce Homo', and as an 'espellor' HCE is a face in an *'esphello'*, Portuguese for mirror.) As in Book III, one of these fantasised lives is that of a lady-killing singer – after which, in a familiar Joycean pattern, dreary reality returns in the shape of that Shem source, the kitchen-dwelling Sackerson who was earlier (160.25-34) reading a book by the fire, and who is here seen with his slate trying to learn English, imitating his master, being fired, being repelled by Kate, being reviled by all, smelling, and, as the pub's 'boots' (63.34-5), getting 'the boot'.

181.34-186.18: Shem's 'stipple[d]' self-portrait of 'a heartbreakingly handsome young paolo with love lyrics for the goyls' continues the earlier famous-singer fantasy. ('Stippled', made of dots, Shaun's portrait cuts 'a great dash', and sports a 'long pair of inky Italian moostarshes', like so:

```
              ..............
         .     _      _     .
         .        .   .     .
         .         . .      .
         .         ^        .
         .        _ _       .  )
              ..............
```

Contrasting reality is once again a downstairs kitchen, doubling as the laboratory in which he combines perception, memory, and obsession to produce his 'chambermade music'. Written in obscene Latin to deceive HCE, the 'Anglican ordinal' whose brand of scarlet on the brow of 'her of Babylon' is remembered from the 'Derg rudd face' (582.28-31) of III/4's strenuously copulating father, Shem's formula produces a concoction which as 'gallic acid on iron ore' is both French and Irish, which 'brought to blood heat' is both excrement and blood for writing on skin, thus re-creating those 'thin red lines' on the father's skin remembered from Waterloo and *merde*, the '*mot de Cambronne*' (9.27) hurled at that encounter. The creation is brilliant at inception, but soon 'waned chagreenold and doriangrayer in its dudhud', vision decaying to glaucoma, inspiration fading to ink on paper and becoming the property of captious dullards such as Sackerson, the 'parochial watch' who now appears in his own person, to pass judgment.

186.19-191.33: We re-enact the dreamer's I/1 return to the house from the privy, his knock on the door, encounter with man-servant, and entrance ('in he skittled'). Simultaneously, prodigal son James returns to the Irish homestead 'on his way from a protoprostitute' — as Ruth Von Phul suggests,[4] Nora, as 'seen by the censorious'. Ambushing Sackerson is now associated with the forces of landed propriety, condemning the returning exile's scandalous life and works. In that capacity, like many a Joyce-reader since, he calls for 'mercy or justice', thus, in the way of the *Wake*, initiating a dramatised exchange between 'JUSTIUS' and 'MERCIUS' in which, naturally, he takes the part of the former.

His attack is a species of — to combine the critical vocabulary of Joyce's time with our own — philistine logocentrism, based firmly on a belief in some 'natural knot' of meaning which writers in particular are always trying to obscure with 'scribblative' embroidery. Stand up, he says, and drop the pretences of this literary third-person voice, and talk to me man to man in the forthright first person. Shem's literary perversion of the spoken word has a sexual counterpart: he fell away from the native sexual cycle of exchanging one pair of 'twin feeders' (mother's milk, being sucked in through a 'syringe') for another (testicles, 'feeding' the penis), of filling the cradle almost as soon as he left it.

After an interlude to glance at the calendar picture, the indictment continues with one of the *Wake*'s most overt allusions to the dead John Joyce Jr — killed by Shem/James, the charge is, because among other things he broke the spell into which Shem had fallen (compare 304.05-9, where Shaun does just that) and/or like Narcissus' reflection looked too pretty in the mirror and/or wounded Shem in the eye.

191.34-195.06: With that last round of accusations we again detect HCE staring at himself in the mirror, facing his fat and accusatory reflection. His admonitory sermon is probably derived from the 'chattiry sermon' (324.26-7) delivered last month by 'our revelant Colunnfiller' on the text of I Corinthians xiii, Paul's (see 192.13) testimony that though one may, like Shem, have power of prophecy (see 189.28-190.01) one still sees 'as in a glass darkly' (which is exactly what HCE is doing), that without charity earthly vision is worthless, 'That the host may choke me if I beneighbour you without my charity!' (193.26-7; cf. 192.09).

Beneath these high sentiments lies the envy of the dead for the living and a desire for revenge; in fact the final prescription offered is death. Shem's reply of '*Domine vopiscus*' asserts that no, it is the other brother who is dead, that he himself is still among the living: as Breandán Ó hEithir says, '*vopiscus*' indicates 'the survivor of a pair of twins' when one has died before birth.[5] Although the two voices sometimes blend in the following *apologia*, almost to the end there remains discernible a dialogue between the celestial image in the mirror (with mercury backing), 'clothed upon with the metuor and shimmering like the horescens, astroglodynamonologos', and the earthbound 'blusher in an obscene coalhole'. At 194.20-1 we can hear the voice of the bereaved father, mourning his 'lonly son' whose image is before him in the mirror — both firstborn 'only' son John and his successor, the lonely James — then a grieving female voice, soon to modulate into the chatter of the two washerwomen who first showed up (158.25) at the end of the last mirror-image brother-battle. We are beginning to hear Kate, as she arrives to mop up the mess on the floor and thus usher in Anna Livia.

THIRTEEN

Book I, Chapter 8

KATE'S arrival works the first of this chapter's transformations. Under the influence of her chatter, the two young men on either side of the mirror become two old women on either side of the river — in each case 'rivals'. As Grace Eckley has demonstrated, the washerwomen carry on the Shem-Shaun polarities established in the last two chapters.[1] As in II/2, one is the educator and tale-teller, the other an alternately fascinated and indignant listener. As in the 'Mookse and the Gripes' fable, with which this chapter is continuous, dialogue becomes dialectic near the end, when the watery female in question emerges to have the last word.

Kate, 'Moppa Necessity' (207.29), shows up with mop and bucket filled with water from the 'bassein' (207.19; the noisy pipes are heard at 198.01) and begins slopping it around while carrying on her one-woman conversation. With that, we are out by the river, which is heading out to sea and close to dead low tide — one reason that Anna Liffey is so diminutive through most of this chapter; at 196.09 'the river is narrow enough for the washerwomen's heads to collide as they bend'.[2] (This may also give us a glimpse of those two HCE's facing one another in the mirror.)

196.01-201.20: 'Mercius' was the last voice of the previous chapter, and this chapter, cued by a woman's voice, on the whole continues the merciful impulse; HCE is in a self-forgiving mood after his spasm of guilt. For the old women, time is rapidly washing away all the remaining recriminations, the fading stains on the family linen. Reduced to ancient history, HCE's story recedes into other, roughly cognate stories. We catch a trace of the Waterloo episode in 'Minxing marrage and making loof' (196.36), but this soon becomes the old story of the young man imprudently getting marriage mixed up with love and eloping with a penniless woman (197.27-8). The primal scene is now recalled as a familiar account of salmon/sailor invading upstream, the orgasmic noise reduced to the roar of breakers (198.03-5).

Most strikingly, HCE's guiltiest secret, his desire for his daughter, is excused away: ALP, who brought Issy into the world, is blamed with 'calling bakvandets sals from all around . . . to go in till him, her erring cheef'. It is a roundabout way of blaming the victim. At 199.11-200.16 ALP is, in the narrator's memory, daughter, wife, and, combining both, wife trying to revive the impervious husband's interest in her by acting out the part of a young girl in her new green gown: after serving HCE the breakfast remembered from I/5 (notably eroticised), she dances, Salome-like, for him, simultaneously re-enacting Issy, the dancer, and forecasting Kate, whose crippling 'goyt' begins to afflict her. Her gestures re-enact and extenuate the scandals of the early chapters: 'puffing her old dudheen' (cf. the cad with the pipe) and luring 'every shirvant siligirl or wensum farmerette' (cf. the girls in the park), 'making a sort of a cackling noise like two and a penny or half a crown and holding up a silliver shiner' (cf. the dispute over money, especially the 'tenpound crickler' (82.26), during the meeting with the cad), 'Throwing all the neiss little whores in the world at him' (doubtless incorporating 'gneiss'; cf. the rock-throwing accusers of I/2), she brings forth a 'wyerye rima' (cf. 'The Ballad of Persse O'Reilly') that chides rather than accuses, trying to rouse her husband.

202.21-204.20: The gossip about ALP combines two journeys, the elopement abroad and a voyage backward in time to her youth. The story of ALP's two early lovers, the 'wolf of the sea' and, 'behind that', the 'local heremite', recounts the choice she made, of Shem-type over Shaun-type, prior to her elopement; the same choice seems to have been adumbrated earlier in the form of 'Barefoot Burn and Wallowme Wade', fiery type and watery type, and certainly 'first of all, worst of all', with hound and dove. The language describing this backwards search for the source of the 'Nihil' (202.20) mirrors her ambivalence, since alongside the obvious water-passage is a backwards account of a fire-making: peat and oak are added at 202.30, flames fanned at 203.02-4, 'kindling' piled on red coals (by a 'hot' monk) at 203.22-34, a French 'souff'' given at 204.02 (which breath began as a chirrup (204.12)); at 204.15-17 Issy is ignited, lucifer to spill, while her nurse sleeps in the soot. As remembered on other occasions, the Liffey is being set afire; the girl whose voice comes 'from afire' has been given the genealogy such a distinction demands.

204.21-209.17: '. . . somebogger was wisness', responds the listener (the scene with the monk on the previous page was attended by those 'sycomores' which in II/4 (397.23-4) will turn into the four old voyeurs), returning us to the primal scene anxieties also signalled by the laundry, especially the red letters 'on a flushcaloured field' – those 'thin red lines' from the *Wake*'s definitive witnessed outrage. Protecting her husband, ALP again makes herself into a distraction. (It is the lapwing's strategy: ALP is at times transposed to LAP.) She consults one of her daughter's fashion magazines (206.11-14; cf. 28.20-1), applies the sort of makeup her daughter has just discovered (becoming a rainbow in the process: 207.10-11), and, in a passage which I think also lets us see the strands of Kate's mop dropping onto the floor after being sloshed into the bucket full of soapy water, lets her hair down: 'First she let her hair fal and down it flussed to her feet its teviots winding coils. Then, mothernaked, she sampood herself with galawater and fraguant pistania mud'. Her masquerade works: the loafing crowd by the riverside sits up and takes notice, and everyone more or less forgets HCE.

209.17-216.05: For one thing, they are curious about the contents of her sack (Kate's scavenger's sack can be glimpsed here), which are the raw material of all story-telling. Each of ALP's gifts is an individual destiny, a novel in miniature, some of them familiar to *Wake* readers, some not, each potentially as absorbing as the life which has been remembered and scrutinised for the last two hundred pages. ALP has drowned out her husband's story with scores of others in a post-Babel narrative so overwhelming that one of the washerwomen sticks wadding in her ears (214.09), so rich with circumstance that the Bible itself becomes just another matter of 'tittles . . . on the tattlepage' (212.30-6).

That, after all, is time's way: 'Wring out the clothes! Wring in the dew!' As the river flows toward the delta, getting wider with each mile (at 212.25 the washerwomen who could bump heads on the first page now have to send their soap back and forth by raft), the scope likewise becomes wider, more variegated, its vast chronicle levelling grievances. The incriminating red-on-white insignia of I/1's Waterloo are, in their last incarnation, a relic of some ancient rite of Hymen: 'I'll lay a few stones on the hostel sheets. A man and his bride embraced between them.' (Compare Joyce's letter to Nora of 7 August 1909.[3] Joyce and Nora first made love in a Zurich 'hostel'.) Dreaded Wellington on his 'big white harse' is now 'the great Finnleader', glimpsed atop a 'ghostwhite horse', a faraway phantom seen through the dusk. As the author-sponsored notes to the episode specify, beginning at 213.13, 'one woman is turned into a tree and the other into a stone'.[4] Shem-type and Shaun-type are still peering at the imposing white figure the initial sight of which brought about the blindness now descending. The white horse is also Lady Godiva's, seen by Peeping Tom as he goes blind. Yet at the same time we are able to measure how great a gulf now separates that witnessing from this one. At the beginning of life, we view the generative act with amazed dread; at the end, we look back at it with fond longing. It seems, in fact, that the 'immense shadow' of Book I has been among the usual other things the shadow of a man's life, beginning with the act of conception — the start of life for the begotten, the rite of passage into manhood for the begetter, the fall from innocence for the watchers, the 'beginning of all thisorder' (540.19) for the book — which since then has been passing down 'the gullies of the eras' (582.18), frequently echoing and doubling back to the mystery of its origin while drifting downstream.

The physical source of this 'tale of a tub' is Kate's cleaning, more and more water being slopped in a 'deluge' (214.07) from her bucket and making a 'marsh' (212.31), 'swamp' (213.02), and 'mere' (213.10) of the floor, mop strands 'hitherandthithering' through the wet, so that (as at 586.09-12) all signs of guilt are washed away. These pages diminish, even resolve, all conflicts, including the one between returning exile and native, which has been raging through the *Wake*'s pages since the invader of the first page 'rearrived'. In a pattern perhaps drawn from Irish history, Book I begins with a contested invasion, proceeds through various stages of uneasy assimilation, and ends with a diaspora. All the strenuously differentiated identities worked out in the middle chapters of the *Wake*'s first major movement, especially those murderous contraries Shem and Shaun, are dissolved and dispersed: 'Who were Shem and Shaun the living sons or daughters of?' Sons or *daughters*? Oblivion, the 'darkling adown surface of affluvial flowandflow' (404.01), has won out.

FOURTEEN

Book II, Chapter 1

AT THE start of I/3 we were told that 'in some future we shall presently here ... the mime mumming the mick and his nick miming their maggies', acting out the 'Eyrawyggla saga' whose major events had just been reviewed (48.09-16), and in II/1 HCE does mime the saga of his life out of the cues of the here and now. There are, I think, four main levels in this mime. First, taking up where we left off, is the central figure himself, still in a trance, gazing into the mirror: the 'entrancings' of the beginning (219.03) is a *double entendre* alerting us to the father-figure who at 240.29 is described as being 'Intrance' and who towards the end is still mesmerised by the sound of water (254.18-19), under 'a deep abuliousness' (255.27-8) from which we are cautioned not to 'erewaken' him (255.05). As Rose and O'Hanlon have shown,[1] throughout II/1 HCE is identified with Emanuel Swedenborg, the visionary who talked, while in a trance, with the kinds of spirits, angels, who are the mime's main characters.

Second, there is a tea party going on downstairs in the kitchen, complete with pot and kettle, cups and saucers, cream, honey, and various edibles.

Third is a sexualised children's charade, usually taking the form of 'the game we used to call Angels and Devils or colours', described by Joyce: 'The Angels, girls, are grouped behind the Angel, Shaun, and the Devil has to come over three times and ask for a colour. If the colour he asks for has been chosen by any girl she has to run and he tries to catch her.'[2] The game *'we'* used to play: the tea-party charade does indeed seem to rekindle childhood memories in HCE, as it did in his author.

The children evoked by these memories (and II/1 is full

of magical evocations)³ in turn act out what Joyce's main sources for the games of II/1 said many children's games do act out, their parents' mating rituals. Hence the fourth level of this chapter: a dramatic enactment of that story sounded on the book's first page, the story of elopement, return, jealous rivalry, and woman's choice. Mrs Glasheen has observed astutely that the four chapters of Book II go through four ages, from childhood to senility⁴ — as if one life were being lived through — but at the same time all four phases relate to one momentous period in HCE's life, the period of his alliance with ALP and the act of sexual creation which resulted: even in the 'senility' chapter, II/4, the four old men of the piece are watching two young lovers in a departing boat's honeymoon cabin.

219.01-222.20: At the start we also get a capsule biography. First is (as 'GLUGG') the Shem-type of HCE's earliest, basest impulses. ('Glugg' (cf. 345.16-25) is the mime-sound of a bottle being poured — or kettle pouring water for tea — glug-glugging out the 'combarative embottled history' (140.33) written/compounded/brewed by Shem, stoppered up with him and cast on the waters; as always, the biographical story starts with Shemian memories.) Then come the young 'FLORAS' who, since they are said to have 'divorced' Glugg, must once have married him. Then 'IZOD', the prize among them, their distillation, who turns from Glugg to the more grown-up 'CHUFF' (Shaun), a muscular Christian whose 'chalk and sanguine pictograph on the safety drop' reveals traces of the father's scarlet-on-white stigmata. Next is 'ANN', 'mother of the house', 'Izod' grown up and tied down. Then 'HUMP', the mountainous HCE, 'studding sail once more' on a voyage which turns out (he changes in a trice from captain to 'supercargo', a kind of seagoing grocer) to have as its destination not new horizons but his establishment. Then that establishment's *habituées*, 'THE CUSTOMERS', 'Grown-up Gentlemen' and 'civics'. Then 'SAUNDERSON', drunk and horizontal, and 'KATE', here as elsewhere the dregs of a female life lived in Ireland. Such, from defiant youth to defeated old age, will be the life lived out in the four chapters of Book II, the *Wake*'s 'Big Storey' (219.20-1).

222.21-227.18: To follow these four levels thoroughly

would require a chapter longer than the original. Instead, I
will trace them, one at a time, through the first five pages
following the introduction, and after that sketch in their
main coordinates.

1. Trance: As he was before, HCE stands mesmerised before the fireplace (Issy wishes he wouldn't 'only gawk'
(225.18)), with its fading fire, mirror, elopement fan, mantelpiece picture of good versus evil (here Mick/George against
Nick/dragon) listening to 'the spirit's whispers in his magical
helmet' (220.25-6), that seductive whispering from upstairs,
as described in II/2:

> But Bruto and Cassio are ware only of trifid tongues[3] the
> whispered wilfulness, ('tis demonal!) and shadows shadows
> multiplicating (il folsoletto nel falsoletto col fazzolotto dal
> fuzzolezzo),[4] totients quotients, they tackle their quarrel
> ...What if she love Sieger less though she leave Ruhm
> moan?...Enten eller, either or. (281.15-23) [footnotes in
> text]

As footnote 3 to this passage confirms, the cause of this
Cassius-Othello quarrel is both Desdemona's *fazzoletto*, her
handkerchief, and the falsetto of her whispering voice, initiating a rivalry between two brothers, sparking the 'demonal'
conflict of II/1, which is in fact arranged according to 'trifid
tongues', that is three separate provocative 'Tipatonguing[s]
...in pigeony linguish' (584.03-4; cf. 232.12-13), to which
HCE-as-Shem thrice tries to respond satisfactorily. The
'shadows shadows multiplicating' have their origin in the
falling dusk, as a result of which the oil lamp on the table
(559.14; cf. *Ulysses* 736) casts its shimmering rings on the
walls and ceilings behind HCE's back — 'with waverings that
made shimmershake rather...all the duskcended airs and
shylit beaconings from shehind hims back' (222.34-6).

Three-pronged firefork in hand (222.29), tormented and
lured by the wind-whistling (223.09-11) 'brividies from exist-
ers' (222.27-8), HCE lunges forward ('Up he stulped') up
against his mirror reflection ('And they are met, face a facing')
who, opposing him, becomes a heroic knight defending the
menaced maiden with a 'trifle [trefoil — shamrock] from the
grass [glass — mirror]' which is the reflection of the three-

pronged weapon. Foiled as a 'feinder' — fiend, fireplace's fender, fender of the HCE-cad encounter of Book I, German for 'enemy' — he stares at the 'fireshield', sighs, looks 'upon the bloomingrund' flowers, and listens — 'listed' — again, vainly, for the voice from on high, then sinks into a 'subnesciousness' which is also the Shem/Sackerson kitchen beneath the bedroom: 'he sod down with the roust of the meast'. 224.09-21 bitterly recalls the primal scene[5] — the last time the sight and sound of a woman bothered him this way.

Sinking down through the chimney flue, he is given a 'hinder sight' of the flower-girls' drawers imagined above, and the prospect of engaging in one of those children's guessing-games where one party tries to name the colour of the other's drawers is enough to bring him popping back up, as through a 'trapadour', to guess. His first guess, moonstone, is on the right track towards 'heliotrope', stone of the sun, but the infernal associations of the fireplace deflect him: moonstone mixes with brimstone as 'monbreamstone'; a pearl is a 'Van Diemen's coral pearl'; something — perhaps 'diamond' — becomes 'Hellfeuersteyn', fireflint. As light-rings the girls whirl merrily around the glowing Chuff; as flowers they droop and wilt sadly; Issy, especially, 'avoice from afire', is now a coal in the fireplace, still glowing but 'fading out'. Like the recently invoked 'Cinderynelly [who] angled her slipper' to lure a 'groom' (224.30-1), she shrinks into the ashes but looks forward to the splendour of her 'new fiancy' and fancy clothes, no sooner wished for than (226.24-9) provided. The reverse-rainbow passage which follows (226.30-227.18) owes much to the Cinderella story — riches turning to rags at midnight — just called forth by the image of Issy-in-fireplace-ashes.

2. Tea party: One reason for Shem's infernal preoccupations is that he begins this section as a spluttering, whistling tea kettle, hanging, like a condemned felon, over the kitchen fire by the pothook which 119.29 has called 'the family gibbet': 'He was sbuffing and sputing, tussing like anisine, whipping his eyesoult and gnatsching his teats' (222.26-7). In this incarnation, his agonising about his parents as 'his old fontmouther' and 'colline born janitor' takes the form of repudi-

ation of the water inside him, coming from the mother's font
and the father's Wicklow 'collines', (from which, of course,
all Dublin tap water comes), a repudiation which he expresses
by angrily blowing out (compare *Ulysses*, 62, 63) plumes of
steam (two of them, one from each side of the covered top)
and spitting out drops of scalding water — 'With that hehry
antlets on him and the baublelight bulching out of his sockets'
(224.12-13) — after which he sinks into his 'limbopool' and
broods over the primal scene and attendant outrages in tea-
kettlese (224.18-20). (The girls mock his form of self-expres-
sion: 'Ni, he . . . play with esteem' (225.06-7).)

On this level the brother battle becomes a case of 'Ket's
rebollions cooling the Popes back' (151.14-15) or, alternatively, 'a pfan coalding the keddle mickwhite' (596.32).
'Arrest thee, scaldbrother!' says the intercepting Shaun-type,
one stuck-out spout mirroring the other, after which, 'buzzling is brains', the kettle (Shem will later report of this meeting that 'he was ambothed upon by the very spit of himself'
(230.02)) is confused about which is which — because, I
think, like blood-brothers they have just gone through a
ritual transfer of fluid, some of the kettle's water going into
the pot: at 223.32 the kettle is taken back to the 'beckline'
('beck' as in 'stream') for more water, then (224.07-8) hung
back near the fire, after which it starts hissing again. (It is
also being rehung on the gallows: at 224.25 it will pop back
up through a 'trapadour'.)

The girls, as the seven cups of a tea-set, may have exalted
aspirations to what, as flowers, they will later call the 'mus-
caline pistil' (237.03) of Shaun's spout, but even here the
obvious overtone of a phallic 'pistol' reminds us of how improper, how Shemian, are the impulses it represents. Here,
for instance, is that pot's contents being poured, from the
spout, into the seven cups, in a sequence which sounds about
all the forbidden associations — violent, scatological, and
erotic, both homosexual and heterosexual — of protuberance-
inserted-in-vessel:

He dove his head into Wat Murrey, gave Stewart Ryall
a puck on the plexus, wrestled a hurry-come-union with
the Gillie Beg, wiped all his sinses, martial and menial, out

of Shrove Sundy MacFearsome, excremuncted as freely as any frothblower into MacIsaac, had a belting bout, chaste to chaste, with McAdoo about nothing and ... imbretellated himself for any time untellable with what hung over to the Machonochie Middle from the MacSiccaries of the Breeks. (227.29-228.02)

The girls also double as tea leaves (e.g. 225.35-6); Issy's guessing-game hints are also queries about what flavour tea Shem would like (223.05-8; see also 226.10-13). Issy is also a tea-party hostess frustrated by Shem's perverse unwillingness to understand the social rituals: when the subject of muffins and such arises, she, having made her overtures from beside the marmalade jar (223.08), offers him syrup and jam, only to have him, spouting and hissing, reject the fare as bread and cursed water, and run off to 'topheetuck', a teapot's Tophet (225.09-14). On this level, the reversed-rainbow sequence is the fortune-telling by 'teaput tosspot' (P. W. Joyce: 'Cup-tossing: reading fortunes from tea-leaves thrown out ... from the tea-cup or teapot')[6] promised from Kate at 221.13; none of the girls has much to look forward to.

3. Angels and Devils: Devil/dog/wolf/Ethiope Shem, seeking the sun, tries to guess Issy's secret of 'heliotrope', but, being challenged by 'Mick', sulks, and, being distracted by the girls, guesses wrong, after which he runs away. Technically, having won, Issy should be happy, but of course winning isn't the point of such games; Issy's gloom at her lonely triumph is natural enough.

4. Courtship: Cued by the 'elopement fan' before him and the whispering from above, HCE relives the early days when, like the twenty-two year old Joyce, he courted the woman he loved and won her from his Shaunian rival. The guessing game is a mating ritual in which the young 'trapadour' attempts to find out what kind of stone to give his beloved in order to win her heart: moonstone, diamond, and pearl are obvious choices (cf. Shaun's later charge to beware Shem's 'perals' (433.06) and hold out for a diamond (433.14-15), his reference to Shem's 'moonshane' (489.27)), but all wrong. To Issy the escape that Shem-as-suitor offers is both liberating ('To part from these, my corsets . . .') and frighten-

ing ('. . . is into overlusting fear'), and she is, as they say, of two minds about it, torn between the dangerous 'woolf' and the angelic 'Arck', between (226.09-10) exile's Paris and home-dweller's Ireland. At the end of this passage she plays it safe and chooses Shaun, getting nuptially 'noosed' in an 'unmerried' marriage complete with ring and rice, but even the wedding tune — a French song, bitterly enough (226.34-227.02) — sadly 'waters the fleurettes of novembrance', and the reversed-rainbow vista of widows and priest-ridden biddies is, this time around, a ghastly prophecy of the life she has just chosen.

Of these four levels, the first and last will continue through Book II. The trance will deepen and eventually lapse into sleep; the Nick figure who initiates the mime also starts the recurring story of disruptive suitor rearriving in Ireland to take the woman away from his domestic rival.

227.19-234.05: The suitor tries again: the tea-drinker/tea-kettle is stimulated by, in the case of the drinker, the caffeine in his 'Shina' tea, his 'mouthfull of ecstasy (for Shing-Yung-Thing in Shina' (231.09-10)) and, in the case of the kettle, by being returned to 'anger arbour' of the fireplace, where he heats up again (at 228.06 he threatens to start squealing), into day-dreaming a typical revenge-fantasy: he will become a famous Byronic poet-prophet, 'eagelly plumed' with those two jets of steam that were spurting out of the kettle at 224.12, lionised by the Lyons tea-shop English set and their 'satiety of arthurs', advancing a programme of free tea leaves for everybody! and no more scaldings! (228.35-6), paying back his father the kettle by revealing that 'he too had a great big oh in the megafundum of his tomashunders' — kettles do have big holes — and his mother the stream by revealing her origin in the 'gap as down low', and imperiously spurning (cf. *Portrait* 63) the woman who has just spurned him.

In short, the 'reminiscensitive' middle-aged HCE is recalling, and sentimentalising, the 'grand carreiro' of, roughly, Joyce's early years, moving backwards from *Ulysses* (229.13-16) to (231.05-8) 'sentimental poetry of what I actually wrote at the age of nine',[7] when the artist as a young man was preparing to take the world by storm. Alas, the 'mouthfull of ecstasy' turns out to be too hot for our 'temporary chewer', whose resulting torment reminds him of what was in fact the upshot of the young Joyce's bohemian days in Paris — poverty, hunger, and the 'Hunger toothache' Stephen Dedalus associates with Paris (*Ulysses* 42) — and brings him down to the reality of his plodding toothless present, from Pegasus flight to 'pucking Pugases', where as Issy later tells us he 'hasn't the teath nor the grits to choo' (270. fn.2).) At 231.23-7 he 'rehad himself' by energetically inserting his dentures with 'esercizism', an adjustment which allows him to feel youthfully-toothily aggressive once more, to the point of becoming a dog, complete with 'canines' (a.k.a. 'eye teeth'), who even when rejected again brags that 'he could ciappacioppachew upon a skarp snakk of pure undefallen engelsk' (233.32-3).

This latter stage of his return is also encouraged by — again — Issy's 'voice from afire', as the fading coal 'in the lost of the gleamens' (232.06-7) flares up, sending out a spurt of fire and a telegraph-like crackle (cf. 244.13: 'tinct, tint') which, though it signals that 'she's marrid', is plaintive enough to lure him 'back to errind' from his fantasised exile. So he becomes a returned suitor/sailor, his pot-kettle spout a tar's pigtail (his picture resembles a 'pitcher'), answering her 'pip!' 'pet!' telegraph message with a 'bolderdash' which leads to the second guessing-game series of questions. In these questions we can discern a request for three medicinal plants, juniper, marjoram, and nannyberries, the first the distinctive ingredient of that sailor's friend gin, the second a folk remedy for both toothache and insanity, the third recommended as stimulants.[8] Anyway, he doesn't get any of them, or the girl either, and sails off, 'to join the armada' — which is to say that he will come once again, to England as invader, to Ireland as shipwrecked refugee.

234.06-243.36: Back to the tea party. Shaun (cf. 163.03-4) is the tea set's honey pitcher, with 'his smile likequid glue', dispensing 'swinginging hopops so goholden' from his lip to what ALP will later describe as 'all the chippy young cuppinjars cluttering round us' (621.15-16). Thus honeyed, the girls respond with a chanted tribute envisioning their high-society high-tea home together in language that is, in a word, sweet, indeed mainly a confectionery catalogue (235.32-236.18). Tea served, it's time for cakes and jam.

Soon they become flowers turning their calyx cups to Shaun (the calendar picture pose is also recalled) as golden sun/pitcher/honeybee, waiting to catch 'his elixir'. As the sun Shaun is setting, 'ebbing wasteward', withdrawing more of its golden influence with every minute, the voices of the girls accordingly take on a yearning tone modulating into seduction.

The drama has come perilously close to home, to the originary situation of far-off daughter's voice whispering to her forbidden paternal paramour, and HCE is roused accordingly: 'Daurdour!' (Daughter!) That explains, I think, why at 238.25-6 we can catch the voices of the accusing soldiers, those regular spics on HCE's guilt, and why we wind up (239.16-27) with a celebration of sexual licence.[9] Issy has roused the beast in her listener, who, having earlier been put back to boil in the fireplace, demands our attention now from his 'wherebus', where he is 'foulend up' — splattering steam-spurting anus-like hole at the top of the kettle's dome — by making 'a belchybubhub and a hellabelow', thus fulfilling the programme's promise (221.36-222.01) of an 'interjection (Buckley!) by the firement in the pit'. He 'rises' now 'with his spittyful eyes' and 'tumescinquinance', tumescent (and *inquinans*, befouling) penis, rising up (240.05-10),[10] the Shemian 'memory schemado' aroused by Issy's words changing him from Mick into Nick, from honey pitcher into kettle.

The difficult three pages which follow (up to 243.36) combine the spluttering, 'rather incoherend' (242.15) pidgin characteristic of Shem's overheated monologues with the convoluted strain of HCE's self-defence. As Campbell and Robinson put it, 'instead of confessing his own sins, the young scamp is reciting the story of his father's'.[11] The character described is both blacksmith-forged kettle, 'born of thug tribe into brood blackmail', and pottery pot, 'weedhearted [that is, full of tea] boy of potter and mudder', 'shape of hegoat' under 'sheep of herrgott', dismissing the charges against the father as a fiction staged by actors and actresses more interested in winning Oscars, those false laurels, than in the truth.

The picture he then paints of himself merges Shem-type and Shaun-type: he is both old (eighty-one) and infantile ('with a daarlingt babyboy bucktooth' — which, since 'the arc

of his drive was forty full and his stumps were pulled at eighty'
(129.32-3), probably tells us that the life cycle has started
again), the favourite of both grandfather and youthful gun
fodder, both crime and prime ministers, dressed in black like
Shem and 'blanking' like Shaun, like Shem masturbating with
his 'theopot' and like Shaun a model little tea-party server;
towards the end of this section the Shemian self aroused by
the sound of a girl's whispers is domesticated, Shaun-ised
once again, by an alliance of Suffragettes, matrons, and — the
last word — 'widders'. In this phase of the courtship story,
the recently married woman has settled down with bourgeois
hubby, first spiting the outcast Shemian 'Envyeyes' (235.24)
but soon, in an access of *bovarisme*, calling him back, stimulating him into imagining marriage to her.

244.01-253.32: The mime's programme promised that
there would be 'animal variations amid everglaning mangrove-
mazes' (221.19-20), in other words as things got swampier,
darker, and mazier, and sure enough the animal acts begin
now, as dusk 'darkles', the shore 'is visited by the tide', and
'Hound through the maize has fled'. HCE sinks more deeply
into his trance. The animal acts come from familiar stuff: the
remembered stone-throwing attacker is a fishy 'Gill'[12] in the
basin, his trail of missiles a watery wake of melting 'rocksdrops'; mantelpiece dragon becomes 'dragonfly'; bear is bearskin rug; the father who fiercely inserted his dentures to
retrieve his wild youth is now an old elephant who will 'rest
him from tusker toils' after singing a paean to his tusks,
'Great is Eliphas Magistrodontos'.

'Hopopodorme' tells us that, like Leopold Bloom at dusk,
the elephantine hippopotamine HCE has dropped off (cf.
255.05). The mood is subdued; even Glugg's third and final
return — drawn, as always, by the alluring sound of 'Icy-la-
Belle!' — is at first relatively peaceful. This time he is no wolf
or fang-baring dog but a 'chastenot coulter' galloping home,
repenting the 'loss of reason' which made him 'chastenot' —
repenting, in a word, '(secs)'. On the 'Teapotty' (247.15)
level he is 'simmering', rather than 'sbuffing and sputing',
weeping for the loss of childish innocence and the high-tea
sweets being served, especially Issy's 'wee tart'. For one thing,
like the the young exiled Joyce, he is experiencing that most

efficacious of spirit-breakers, hunger, and is consequently eager to join the tea party.

Sweet Issy has other ideas. Her black and white nun's habit turns out to be in the eye of the colour-blind observer (248.21-2). In fact Glugg, whose 'Envyeyes' were earlier spying with binoculars at Issy's high-society wedding from 'our garden rare' (235.24-6), is goaded into resuming his decidedly chromatic peeping, to guess the colour of her drawers, for instance, or unpuzzle this highly eroticised 'heliotrope' hint:

> My top it was brought Achill's low, my middle I ope before you, my bottom's a vulser if ever there valsed and my whole the flower that stars the day and is solly well worth your pilger's fahrt. (248.11-14).

(Achilles) Heel-I-O-trope (as in dance turn), of course, but the 'top' that brought Achilles low was also, as we know from *Doctor Faustus*, Helen's face, cause of the war that killed him, the waltzing bottom is some temptress's dancing feet, and the place in between, the 'middle I ope before you', is obviously the vagina, here belonging to Io, one of the young women for whom the old father falls.

So as usual Issy is both virgin and temptress, her voice a siren-song pretending to be a hymn, and indeed up to Glugg's third and final guess, at 249.25-250.02. Issy and her companions goad their swain mercilessly, under colour of showing 'Her reverence'; the 'house of breathings', in particular (249.06-20), with its roof in the grape-against-jasper colours of the heliotrope stone, is a pleasure palace presented as a temple.

It may also be, less grandly, a high-class boutique or millinery shop in which, Issy hints (248.30-6), Glugg, if he really wants to 'land her', might get her something nice. In his third try at the guessing game Glugg, like a salesman dealing with an imperious customer, tries desperately to meet her wishes: Would you like some red ribbons? Are you certain that it's an unshorn style? Can you choose a fresh item?[13] He mimes various proverbially lowly types, in the process becoming a Sackerson, a 'piebold nig' (250.36), a Hunnish barbarian (251.03), 'An oaf, no more' (251.21). (He is 'piebold' where earlier he was a 'chastenot coulter' because it has started sprinkling outside, covering him with spots (see also 251.16-17, 26-7): a flash of lightning (250.23-6) lights up the water drops which glitter in the 'flares' as 'diamondinah's' and bring out the 'scent' of the flowers.) On the tea-party level, he is also at the bottom of the social scale, here in the kitchen utensil set — a 'stockpot leaden', giving off (253.17) one final plaintive 'tootle' after a last brother-battle (252.04-18) between 'Metellus and Ametallikos ... obscindgemeinded biekerers', metal kettle versus non-metal pot. Glugg still has a shot at Issy, though the price is the breaking of his spirit, a 'natural rejection' of all he once stood for: 'Creedless croonless hangs his haughty. There end no moe red devil in the white of his eye.' Morosely mooning over his congenitally lowly lot, the lot which as the Mookse told us (159.01-2) is destined for his kind in all generations (from great-great-great-grandmother to great-great-great-grandson) and climes (from Russia to Peru), he is told that his half-hearted try was another flop: he *should* have done the decent thing and offered a comfortable marriage, but instead came out with the usual 'come into the garner mauve' of the aging roué. Even as a clerk/tailor he has failed: Issy is 'wearing none of the three'.

253.33-259.10: The dozing HCE half-contemplates — as one can, in a hypnagogic state — rousing himself and coming fully awake. There are brave comparisons to the returns of those buried heroes Finn and Arthur, but in fact the incarnation that 'all come[s] aft to you, puritysnooper' is Sackerson, 'old Joe, the Java Jane, older even than Odam Costollo'. 'Why wilt thou erewaken him from his earth, O summonorother ...?' Why indeed: there is no point in waking up to such a fate. The 'producer (Mr John Baptister Vickar)' sends himself back under, and the job of calling the children in out of the rain to studies and bed falls to the wife, a hen gathering in her chicks.

Under her aegis we get a clichéd family portrait: beaten-down husband — 'henpecked', in a word — seeking oblivion in a household of disrespectful children (257.10-24) and a harridan who lets him know that 'Fionia is fed up with Fidge Fudgesons' (257.36), that she is tired of his loutish ways: ALP's bellow of 'Uplouderamain', Gaelic for 'lazy idler', is directed at the father as much as anybody. Let him here ask that standard question of the resurgent Finnegan, 'didits dinkun's dud?' and the answer comes back unequivocally: 'Yip! Yup!' His roving days are done for good: even Ishmael is repatriated and renamed 'Ismael', and the last prayer of his children is that they may not follow the disreputable example of his early days, that they 'not gomeet madhowiatrees'. Such is the end of the returning-rover story just mimed. When we next encounter the story, in II/2, it will be, as they say, academic, conned in textbooks about

> what happened to our eleven in thirtytwo antepostdating the Valgur Eire [the era of vulgar Earwicker] . . . and why was Sindat sitthing on him sitbom like a saildior [Sinbad the sailor, seething soldier, salesman, sitting like a tailor: Shem] . . . where G.P.O. is zentrum [General Post Office: Shaun, staying put] and D.U.T.C. are radients [Dublin United Tramways Company plus Flying *Dutch*man: Shem, circling around] . . . (256.21-30)

So on to the night lessons.

FIFTEEN

Book II, Chapter 2

II/2 is the crossroads of *Finnegans Wake*. Intersections are everywhere: incarnation, transubstantiation, lightning, intercourse, the 'square imposed on the triangle' which is 'the Aristotelian symbol for unified body and soul',[1] the descent of the Kabbala's Ain-Soph into matter, the 'interloopings' circles of the geometry lesson, the crossed utensils of the final footnote, and so on. Like *Ulysses*' 'Wandering Rocks', in which Leo Knuth has found a wealth of similar insignia,[2] II/2 is the tenth chapter of its book, or, as some write it, Chapter X — a designation which may remind us of the tradition that the cross is itself a symbol of one reality's intersection with another. The diagram on page 293 is, as many have said, the book's formal centre, introduced with the 'lapis'[3] or philosopher's stone for transmuting one element into another. It is poised (approximately) in the middle of Book II as Book II is poised between past and future, between Shem-dominated vision and Shaun-dominated vision, and in fact just before it appears we hear that 'a poor soul is between shift and shift ere the death he has lived through becomes the life he is to die into' (293.02-5). The chapter is a multi-layered chronicle reviewing private and universal history (it begins with an A and ends with an O), culminating in a moment of sexual, generative, and eucharistic transformation, of intersection and crossing-over.

This movement occurs on many levels. We will concentrate on two. The first is, again, the trance. Sheldon Brivic observes of the format that it 'may be seen as presenting an interaction between parts', and argues that in this it resembles the letter, which is elsewhere described as, one, a collaboration of different hands (118.24-6) and, two, a 'trancedone boyscript', put together by Shem and Shaun, 'with tittivits', tittering footnotes, by Issy (374.03-4).[4] I am going to suggest that this be taken literally. II/2 is the record of an entranced mind whose reverie incorporates the external presences impinging on it. Specifically, it records the trance of a man — the same one who had 'a deep abuliousness . . . descend upon' him near the end of II/1 (255.27-8) — staring at himself in the mantelpiece mirror noted before. To his left, in the picture above the mirror, is a Shem-type (hence one set of marginal notes); opposite it, to the right, is a Shaun-type (hence the other set); coming from below, 'from his beelyingplace below the tightmark' (262. fn.1) is Issy's whispering (hence the tittering footnotes). Before him, in the mirror, is his face, the subject of Shem's first note: *'With his broad and hairy face, to Ireland a disgrace'*, and, especially, that face's most prominent feature, as remarked in III/1 — a 'self-tinted . . . ruddled' (403.07-8) nose which fixes his attention — as we find out when one brother thanks the other for waking him from the daze induced by staring at a 'red mass' (304.05-11).

The red mass is, roughly, triangular; ask a child to draw such a nose (and the chapter's geometry lesson is also an introductory art lesson, in which students are taught to break up face and body into Euclidian polygons) and you will likely get an upright red triangle. Of course the triangle of 293 is also a representation of the mother's pubic delta, which, as it happens, is evidently red as well: the first sight of her *Mons Veneris* is of a 'Grand Mons Injun' (HCE's red nose is a 'becco of wild hindigan' (403.13)); Issy's birth is intermittently recalled as an expulsion from a fiery, red-hot place, here called her 'bluishing refluction' (299.17-18).

Then there is the matter of Joyce's reference, in one of his notorious letters, to the supposed redness of Nora's vagina,[5] a reference probably echoed in this chapter's allusion to the woman's 'redtangles' (298.25), which in turn are later remembered as 'her bosky old delltangle'. So it seems we need only appeal to elementary visual association to understand how a man staring at his nose in a mirror can wind up evoking the *Wake*'s premier symbol of origins — beginning of life and (as riverbed delta) civilisations, first problem in Euclid, centre of the primal scene, even, so the Bass Ale Company assures us, the oldest trademark in existence. And speaking of that label, it is the focus of the analogous scene in *Ulysses*, where Leopold Bloom, staring at the 'rubied triangle' on the bottle before him, goes into a trance, his soul 'wafted over regions of cycles of cycles of generations,' which evokes visions of wife and daughter (*Ulysses* 414).

260.01-268.06: The second level is, roughly, proleptically autobiographical — following the narrative of rearriving exile and the troubles accompanying his return which was sounded on the book's first page, mimed in II/1, and which will be narrated in II/3. The entranced HCE, staring at his double in the mirror, imagines himself as an older version of the returning sailor of II/1, a returning ghost haunting the scenes of his former life. Where are we? asks the narrator in the first line, beginning the homing-in that will take him to 'that pint of porter place'. The homecoming ocean voyage — 'Hencetaking tides we haply return, trumpeted by prawns and ensigned with seakale, to befinding ourself' — also turns out to reprise that earlier return of I/1. As there, the 'other' we encounter is Sackerson, this time beside Kate, and the two of them together seem, disconcertingly, to be ('to befinding ourself') the new proprietors, the reincarnated HCE and ALP, as well as the usual welter of other 'archetypt[s]' (263.30). As in I/1 we halt at the front door — 'And that simmelk steed still in the groundloftfan' (262.22-3) — and (262.06) 'Knock', this time to no avail.

Looking through the window (and mirror: footnote 2 tells us to 'kool in the salg', look in the glass, spelled in mirror-hand) we see some of the old crew, as if grown older, and miss the presence of others (263.01-12). The homecoming becomes sentimental, mourning the noble dead — 'A phantom city, phaked of philim pholk', etc. — but Shem's and Issy's notes undercut the mood: 'All be dood', sums up Issy, mocking the returner's come-down from dreams of 'wealth in marble arch' to the reality of 'pool beg slowe'. Balked at the door, our re-arriving spirit now flies 'hickerwards the thicker' (the tree by her window) 'Which assoars us from the murk . . . to the clarience of the childlight in the studiorum upsturts'. 266.20-267.07 is, accordingly, largely a celebration of Issy-as-cynosure, flame to moth, charmer 'under the branches of the elms', though as Brivic points out the phrase 'ondrawer of our unconscionable, flickerflapper fore our underdrugged' also casts her as a flirting flapper unconscionably drawing HCE by appealing to his Freudian *unterdruckt*, repressed unconscious.[6] (Also the fire in the fireplace, flickering to his lower half.)

268.07-272.08: He and we peer at Issy in her room. She is knitting and meditating on the 'inbourne' womanly wisdom learned from her 'Gramma' and mother. The lesson is that she must play her cards right with men, leading them on up to a point, being careful not to wind up either with a Shem-type (268. fn.6 accuses 'gramma' of having made that mistake herself) or as a 'wallflower', choosing a Shaun. Such a policy is the origin of all property conflicts (the imperial fracas over Cleopatra is adduced) of, as Shaun in the right-hand margin puts it, 'EARLY NOTIONS OF ACQUIRED RIGHTS', hence the cause of the wars to follow. It is also an explicit rejection of the retrograde father whose spirit lurks about Issy's window, whose body is by the fireplace underneath, hissing up the chimney: 'Beware how in that hist subtaile of schlangder[2] lies liaison to tease oreilles!' (The footnote to this sentence cruelly fingers the toothless old father.)

272.09-278.06: This difficult passage begins by tracing the consequences of Issy's Eve-like interference in things. At 271.24-5 we were hailing a 'Heva' who, revising *Genesis*, was coaxing her flabbily serpentine father to 'chatters'; 272.09 gives us a striking metaphor for Original Sin ('Dark ages clasp the daisy roots') and begins a trip over into the bedroom of the boys ('stepplease') who will illustrate what that means. The 'PANOPTICAL PURVIEW OF POLITICAL PROGRESS AND THE FUTURE PRESENTATION OF THE PAST' which follows resembles the scene in *Paradise Lost* in which the Archangel Michael shows Adam vistas from the future history his fall has just brought about. The dozing twins are roused to act out the cyclical struggles of civilisation in a panorama whose disorderliness may be due to the befogged state of those two boys just taking their heads out of 'Lough Murph'; in any case someone or other is, according to 274.17-18, 'with frayed nerves wondering', and like the earlier re-arriver of 263.01-7 in need of information about how things have or haven't changed, how house, tree, and father still stand, how stars still shimmer and shoot. Conveying this information, the guidebook voice returns to reintroduce us to the house's inhabitants, sketching a scene of a late-evening pastoral wherein Shaunian shepherd, after the recent broils, sits down with goatish Shemian 'Becchus'.

Speaking of Bacchus, the pub's business is now going strong. Customers are arriving; the seven-coloured outfit of the server is sooted with darkness; drinks are being poured. HCE's hail-fellow publican side is in its eminence, though Shem sniggers that his throne and sceptre are really just an umbrella stand and a stick. The conformist moral is clear: '. . . who wants to cheat the choker's got to learn to chew the cud'; as if to illustrate the alternative, Shem is reduced (278. fn.1) to a 'felon' and (278.L1) consigned to torturer and executioner. But even here there are stirrings of discontent with this bovine existence: 'We drames our dreams tell Bappy returns', says a voice apparently speaking for 'Anna', longing for her 'redbanked profanian with his bakset of yosters', of yesteryears.

278.07-281.36: 'INTERCIPIT INTERMISSIO' reads the right-hand margin, as Issy-sound arrests the entranced HCE's attention and works as a further 'spellbinder' on his thoughts. HCE notices her plink-plunking water sound as it might be heard by different listeners — nuns hearing it as sighs echoing their own denied longings, a coalman as a 'Coalmansbell', a wren as a bird's pecking, a postman as a post office's packing of mail, the lilting Issy herself (278. fn.3) as the tinkling of a piano. He strains to hear more distinctly ('A halt for hearsake'), to make out her voice in continuous monologue.

That voice returns us to what was hinted at the end of the previous section: the roused young woman ruing her boring marriage and sending to her dream lover a conflicting message. On the one hand she calls to him; on the other, she tells him what Issy tells the returning sailor of II/1's mime, that 'she's marrid'. (Upstairs, Issy is washing — hence the plink-plunk — and congratulating herself on her appearance in the mirror; hence the allusions to how nice she looks.)

As a message from woman to man seeking to revive his old self, this is a type of the *Wake*'s letter, and so at 278.07-24 we have a run-through of letter motifs, culminating in HCE's answering desire to 'raise a ladder' like Parnell climbing up the ladder to Kitty O'Shea, and the inevitable consequence, that the father's followers 'wend to raze a leader'. HCE bends to Issy's 'rainstones ringing', her sound of 'Pot price pon patrilinear plop', and is told (279. fn.1) what he wants to hear, that Issy is 'throne away' on her callow 'Jr', that she longs to be wooed by a real man like her 'Sr'.

This 'liquick music' 'from cinder Christinette' is also an incitement to war between the brothers, between rearriving James-type and entrenched John-type. The limpid Quinet sentence of 281.04-13 ends on '*batailles*', looking forward to the brothers' battles for Issy-flowers, as Shaun seems to comprehend in a note about 'BELLETRISTICKS'; there follows a tableau from *Othello*, that monument of jealousy, with Issy goading on the antagonists from underneath. The issue is summed up neatly at the end:

| And! | INTERROGATION |
| Nay, rather! | EXCLAMATION |

A choice must be made, and that's the trouble.

282.01-286.18: In the *Wake*'s scheme, the origin of jealousy is the Oedipal drama of childhood, the beginning of the fall into corruption. The infant who begins his Freudian 'education to reality' here is both Shem and Shaun, both 'laird' and 'boor', the two hands on which he counts his fingers as always a symbol of (temporary) brotherly reconciliation. Those fingers, counted at different stages in his education as he grows up, oscillate symbolically between one stage and the other: first infantile innocence (beginning, like *Portrait*, with a 'boko', a 'moocow'), then, with 'pickpocket' etc., a lapse into mischievous ways, though 'pickpocket promise' (ring finger) and 'upwithem' (little finger, extended with ostentatious gentility while drinking tea) show that at the end of this phase he is becoming 'civilised', then a repressive religious training seeking 'to pin the tenners, thumbs down', so effective that for a while he names his fingers after cardinals, then a backslide into 'Ace, deuce, tricks, quarts, quims', plus loafing and comedy, and, worse yet, on to the ingrained vices of (283. fn.2) the father, 'his deed', to 'sexes, suppers, oglers, novels, and dice'. (Among other things, he has learned to use his fingers to masturbate.)

The abstractions of geometry are more difficult. The dismay he feels at the geometry lesson corresponds to that of the little boy at the primal scene, watching his mother and unable to touch her, feeling for the first time that he has lost his hold on her. As the Thompsons note,[7] the geometry problem introduced at 283.32 recalls that primal scene; we may add that the illustrative 'Tullagrove pole . . . at a septain inclinaison' recalls the propagating tree which so riles Professor Jones in I/6 (159.31-160.15). The usual 'rainborne pamtomomium' consequences follow, culminating in publication of the father's shame after the witnessed outrage, here as a 'pictorial' (284.28-30) in the usual red-on-white scheme (286.04-18).

286.19-292.32: The 'Problem ye ferst, construct ann aquilittoral dryankle Probe loom' of the next stage in the lesson is both sexual — how can two make a triangular third? How are babies made? — and exploratory: among other things, 'Dolph' and 'Kev' are sailor-navigators triangulating their way by 'coastmap' into the Dublin littoral, geometry fusing with geography.[8] The father who is dreaming them both is, as we find out at 293.01-15, entering into the deepest phase of his trance, returning to an earlier moment 'of times lost or strayed' (292.16). That moment is the last memorable time when he went into a trance — the meeting with ALP, near Trinity College, when he was her sailor and she was his 'Goldilocks' (see 290.11 in conjunction with footnote 4).

He was also a figure containing, *in potentia*, both Shem and Shaun, both adventurer and bourgeois, and the character who emerges now — along with the others, all invaders: Patrick, Strongbow, Tristan — is Sir Thomas Lipton, known affectionately as 'Sir Tea', sailor and grocer, whose revolutionary harnessing of mass communications to convert the public to tea-drinking is throughout 287.28-292.32 paralleled with Patrick's conversion of the native Irish to his own sign of the T, the cross, and Tristan's telegraphing of his signatory 'T' to Iseult.

This one-sentence fugue keeps recurring to the theme of the returning sailor/invader/suitor, both as founder and as disrupter, entering and seeking to either colonise or usurp the colonisations of others on the river's banks. Very roughly, it follows HCE-as-disrupter's career from youth to his present age, first as Dolph-like corrupter of university youth, teaching them a perverted version of the facts of life, then as the young invader of Dolph's stories, a 'coxswain' winning 'the pretty Lady Elisabbess', then, having deserted her, 'doubling back' to win her again, though this time, 'his craft ebbing', he is becoming a disreputable old man interested in the daughter, 'foundling a nelliza the second', then a Mark-like micher of 'insensible virility and . . . gaulish moustaches', 'circling toward' us yet again, finally an 'illwinded goodfornobody', with 'switftshut scareyss', buzzling over past and fantasising future in the 'pupilteachertaut duplex' of his 'cerebralised saucepan'. As at the outset of I/1, the interjections of affected French remind us that the re-arrival has two coordinates, Paris and Dublin; as McHugh points out, the Latin at the beginning describes us as 'beholding in fact the site of Paris'. The passage begins with the news that 'a spirit spires' and a suggestion that we revolve (*revolvamus*') things in our minds, along with a picture of a 'recurrently' revolutionary Dolph, so it should not surprise us that at the end of the sentence's manifold turnings-around the positions of the marginal notes have been reversed. Literally, what has happened is that the rapt HCE has (292.25) closed his eyes (that's why the marginal notes, visually cued, disappear for the duration, while the footnotes, audibly cued, do not), subsiding into memories both personal and racial which by degrees bring him up to the present time, at which point he more or less comes to as one who has passed with 'Ellis threw his cookingclass' (294.08), through the looking-glass.

293.01-308.25: Hold a finger before your face, focus on it, and any object behind it is doubled. Opening his eyes to stare at his own nose with his 'doubleviewed seeds' (296.01), HCE sees everything out of its plane as double, notably the transparent outline of his own 'roundhead' (4.34) which now appears as a 'twain of doubling bicirculars' that 'dunloop into eath the ocher' (295.30-3). He is seeing himself, a fact that seems to be acknowledged when one mirror-twin says to the other that both he and the diagram he has drawn are 'Match of a matchness, like your Bigdud dadder' (294.17).

With some tinkering — drawing a dotted-line inverted triangle to match the upright triangle, forming a 'bluishing refluction below' (299.17-18), making the diagram symmetrical on both a horizontal and a vertical axis — the illustration represents: 1. The mother's vagina (the doubled circles are probably, as several have remarked, her buttocks) desired by two rival lovers for the receptacle of their 'seeds'; 2. Dublin bay, scene of battle between two rival claimants for sovereignty, being approached by an invading/settling sailor who at 294.05 drops 'anchore' and proclaims 'Another grand discobely'. 3. A magical inscription for the calling of spirits. 4. A dirty picture, used as Exhibit A in Shem's masturbation lesson, a lesson which succeeds at 297.04-5 and leaves Shaun with a 'languil pennant' (298.06-7), a diminished 'Doll the laziest' changed from 'Doll the fiercest' (298.09-11). In all cases it represents a return to the source, *'Sarga, or the path of outgoing'* (294. L1). Shem's sex-lesson in particular recalls Molly Bloom's observation about men, that 'theyre all mad to get in there where they come out of' (*Ulysses* 760), and sure enough its revelation is also a return to the moment of childbirth: 'And this is what you'll say.[2] Waaaaaa. Tch! Sluice! Pla!'

So the multiple layered backwards journey of 287.18-292.32 continues, as a Yeatsian 'dreaming back' — the diagram is also a meditator's mandala — taking HCE back. He returns to the pre-existent realm where earthly identities are exchanged, to the moment of reincarnation, conception, and gestation — here of Jacob and Esau, with their 'interplay of bones in the Womb'. Behind the lesson we can hear a dialogue from the *Wake*'s main version of the conflict between domestic John and returned-exile James, the story of Jacob's filching of the birthright from Esau, his trickery of Isaac.

All this begins with our speaker attempting to re-orient himself after the six-page reverie just passed. As student he is shown the diagram; as traveller his attention is focused on the rediscovered 'Modder ilond'; as entranced revenant he is congratulated in Yeatsian language — 'One recalls Byzantium' — for his 'Straorbinaire' memory of the *Anima Mundi*; as Esau, revolving in the womb with his brother — 'Gyre O, gyre

O, gyrotundo!' — he is tricked twice by his brother, with results that 295. L2 ('*The haves and the havenots: a distinction.*') predicts. First trick: Jacob persuades him to take the upper region of the womb (under the navel: his brother takes the lower triangle), so that he will not be the first-born after all. Second trick: the 'modest mock Pie' is the mess of pottage ('pi' = 'P' = pea = lentils) Esau traded for his birthright. After some pedagogical/magical razzle-dazzle the sexual/algebraic point of which seems to be that the greatest of things, all of life, comes from the least of things, a hole, a point, a 'base anything', the triumphant usurper chides his brother for 'gaping up the wrong palce' and directs him to, so to speak, the point. Shaun realises that he has been out-foxed, that his brother has worked a 'hoax', and, thanks to the hoax, is now 'topsawyer', and strikes back. Shaun's marginal note reads '*Primanouriture and Ultimogeniture*', stating the issue even while, typically, getting it mixed up with questions of food. At the same time, the conflict is one of sons against father, who is here remembered at his most frightening, during the primal scene, the 'juggaleer's veins' of his neck and erection (and nose) standing out horribly as he rides the mother (the language describing this is marginally incoherent, the language of panic).

There follows a combination writing-lesson (the letter being written expresses bereavement for the lost mother, a wish to besiege the father) and argument. Shem is the teacher, offering examples — 'Steal', 'Barke', 'Starn', 'Swhipt', 'Wiles', 'Pshaw', — whose subversive import Shaun can't quite grasp, but which works to convert the battle from brother-against-brother to brothers-against-father. At first the two brothers of *Hamlet*, one murdering the other in the garden ('WITH EBONISER' — Claudio's poison is 'ebona'), the other hoping to repay the favour by proxy with 'a toxis', they soon join to frame the son's fight — 'let us be singulfied' — against the 'salubrated sickenagiaour' who is their common enemy. The anti-father alliance, which will dominate the next chapter, is forged, and the two join in studies, preparing to write a historical work on subjects almost all of which relate to the father's life and disgrace. The following chapter, II/3, will be largely a historian/story-teller's indictment of the father,

delivered by attackers who have now completed their prep-
arations, who have done their homework and got the goods
on their man.

SIXTEEN

Book II, Chapter 3

II/3 continues the story first mimed and then studied in the previous two chapters. The rearriving rogue who haunted at the window of the study and repeatedly washed ashore during the trance-within-a-trance monologue of 287.18-292.32 now, as the Norwegian captain, comes ashore for good, woos and wins the disputed woman and, after some dickering, marries her. He becomes fat and established (his story will later be summarised as 'Goes Tory'), in 'his grossery baseness' (367.02), and so imperious that when the natives take their revenge against him, it is by blasting a Russian General, alternatively 'the Saur of all the Haurousians' (344.33). Thus deposed, he becomes a harried and executed king, then a ghostly pretender haunting his old realm, and finally, once again, an exile, beginning the voyage down river which will continue until the end of the book, where he will be ready for the 'recirculation' of the first page.

As always, these transformations occur inside the head. In *A Portrait of the Artist as a Young Man* (p. 116), the narrator had said of Stephen that 'the foul memories condensed within his brain', and here as well the brain is a 'harmonic condenser enginium' (310.01), gathering, focusing, and transforming external sights and sounds. Especially sounds: as Margaret Solomon was the first to suggest,[1] the radio introduced at the start of the chapter is also the sleeper's head and trunk, his cranium ('a howdrocephalous enlargement'), brain ('harmonic condenser enginium'), mouth ('vitaltone speaker'), eyes ('circumcentric megacycles'), heart ('magazine battery'), arteries ('twintriodic singulvalvulous pipelines'), front and back ('up his corpular fruent and down his reuctionary buckling') — and the most prominent feature is the ears, the

'umbrella antennas for distance getting' (309.17-18), leading
to 'a meatous conch'. This 'conch' is 'culpable of cunduncing
Naul and Santry' (310.12-13; cf. 598.15-16: 'In that european
end meets Ind'), the synthesis of all and sundry beginning
with internalisation of what is heard ('We just are upsidedown singing what ever the dimkims mummur allalilty she
pulls inner out heads' (373.33-5)) mixed with memory to
produce an internal mummery — 'the mummery of whose
deed, a lur of Nur, immerges a mirage in a merror' (310.23-4).

Lying in his bed — he goes from vertical to horizontal,
probably at 314.06-9 — HCE runs through the myth of his
own life (we get a preliminary account of it at 309.02-10:
primal scene, meeting with woman, elopement, wake, resurrection) while absorbing the pub's noise, especially from
downstairs. To an extent the noise breaking into his thoughts
constitutes an assault — hence 'culpable' — especially considering its parricidal overtones. In the previous chapter, I
noted the allusion to the 'ebona' poured into the King
Hamlet's ear by his brother. We remember the effects of that
poison:

> And a most instant tetter barked about
> Most-lazar-like with vile and loathsome crust
> All my smooth body. (*Hamlet*, I.v.71-3)

'*Barked about*': and here HCE's muttering assailants 'arbor-
ised around, up his corpular fruent and down his reuctionary
buckling'; in Book III HCE will become a barrel, bound with
staves of wood, and at 503.30 a tree.

309.01-325.12: Like King Hamlet he will be assassinated
in this chapter, but at the outset he is, along with the tide
(309.03-4), at 'the height of his life'. (When the tide falls, so
will he.) For now he identifies with the invader rather than
the invaded, and the Norwegian captain story being told
downstairs is transformed in his 'melegoturny marygoraumd'
into a fable of his youthful triumph against the forces of
native conservatism personified in the tailor.

As throughout the chapter, the broadcast of the downstairs
radio makes a contribution as well. The narrative up to 325.12
is to some extent a function of the programme in the background, as reviewed at the end of the sequence:

Am. Dg.

Welter focussed.

Wind from the nordth. Warmer towards muffinbell, Lull.

As our revelant Colunnfiller predicted in last mount's chattiry sermon, the allexpected depression over Schiumdinebbia, a bygger muster of veirying precipitation and haralded by faugh sicknells, (hear kokkenhovens ekstras!) and umwalloped in an unusuable suite of clouds, having filthered through the middelhav of the same gorgers' kennel on its wage wealthwards and incursioned a sotten retch of low pleasure, missed in some parts but with lucal drizzles, the outlook for tomarry (Streamstress Mandig) beamed brider, his ability good.

What hopends to they?

Giant crash in Aden. Birdflights confirm abbroaching nubtials. Burial of Lifetenant-Groevener Hatchett, R.I.D. Devine's Previdence.

Ls. De. (324.23-325.03)

In fact there are two main broadcasts being recalled here, often overlapping — a result of the reception's 'wandering' from frequency to frequency and the interference which is especially bad at night, when, as Shaun's inquisitors later say, anybody with a wireless can 'peck up bostoons' (489.36-490.01). (The radio does in fact get signals from Norway and Czechoslovakia.) Here, the two main programmes are the weather forecast/focus and a chatty 'charity' sermon intended to drive home the message of the Quinquagesima service (celebrated last month, repeated over the air this last moment) that, in the words of the Collect, 'all our doings without charity are nothing worth'. It is delivered by means of an exemplum about a dog-in-the-manger type who lived his life selfishly and died unmourned, a burgermeister gorging filthily and acquiring wealth in the pursuit of 'low pleasure', depressing all with whom he comes in contact, now as predicted struck down by divine providence and buried, missed in few places and there with only luke-warm tears, leaving the world a brighter place for his absence.

Mingling with this narrative is the weather report — wind

from the north, originating in Scandinavia, has filtered into the sleeper's room (the gorger's kennel) through the window and culminated in a 'Giant crash', which as we shall see occurs as the windowboards are blown open. Clearly, the Norwegian captain who keeps blowing into Dublin bay owes much to this Scandinavian wind. Along with that is the story being told downstairs of

> a hunchbacked Norwegian captain who ordered a suit from a Dublin tailor, J. H. Kerse of 34 Upper Sackville Street. The finished suit did not fit him, and the captain berated the tailor for being unable to sew, whereupon the irate tailor denounced him for being impossible to fit.[2]

And recalled by *that* story is the memory of the 'welsher' (322.08) or 'aleconner' (319.04) who repeatedly finagles free drinks from the bartending manservant, which story, as I have argued, is one of the main determinants of the 'prank-quean' fairy-tale of I/1.

Keeping in mind as many as possible of the shaping influences — shifting broadcast, weather, memory of elopement days, welsher story, Norwegian captain story, public house raillery — we will run through the events after our introductory tour around the listener's anatomy. To begin with, that radio/body 'donated' to the dreamer recalls the glass coffin (and submarine, and bottle) in which he was stoppered and submerged in Lough Neagh (76.10-32), and from which he is now released: 'under the foamer dispensation when he pullupped the turfeycork by the greats of gobble out of Lougk Neagk' (310.33-4).

The cork is also a plug being pulled from the basin by the bottle-washer Sackerson, who, as in II/2, now mans the premises downstairs, serving drinks and collecting payment, and who alternately opposes and blends with the landlord: his beerpull, for instance, is generally the captain's tiller. The story beginning about his troubles with the good-for-nothing welsher blends easily with the sermon, which opens with prayers for the Pope and thanks for Catholic emancipation (310.35-311.02). There is an invocation (311.11-14), a public speaker's customary glass of water (311.15-20), and then the narrative begins.

The tale is of negotiation between opposites carried on by intermediary agents — the ship's husband (the crew's provisions-purchaser when on land, a link between the world of roving and the world of landlubber commerce) for the sailor, 'Kersse' for the tailor. Each agent is, to a degree, an extension of his master: the captain will become a husband; the tailor will do a lot of cursing. That the sailor should send someone named a 'husband' to negotiate his 'suit' indicates that the tailor's daughter, the young ALP, is the object of the negotiation. The price the captain offers is his vow of marriage, a vow which he may not honour: the eloper of this story debauches the daughter (312.05-12) and is called (compare: 'Taffy was a Welshman, Taffy was a thief' — the welsher has stolen his first drink) a 'tief'.

As callous seducer, he is identified with the sermon's malefactor, taking his low pleasure. He is also the blustery weather later recalled by the weatherman, wreaking havoc in home and harbour: 'And the tides made, veer and haul, and the times marred, rear and fall, and, holey bucket, dinned he raign!' (312.10-12) There follows (312.17-313.03) an ecumenical passage from the sermon, after which a customer turns up the volume (formerly at 'low frequency amplification' (312.33)) and the tone changes from soft-spoken conciliation to its tub-thumping opposite (313.04-6). The indignant Kersse re-enters, flinging his curse to the accompaniment of the rising wind, both oratorical and meteorological: 'following pnomoneya [Greek 'pneumata'] he is consistently blown to Adams' (313.12). Against this background the ensuing look back at the till-minding server doubles as a portrait of the sermon's 'foully fallen dissentant' (313.33) going to the dogs with gambling and drink, and when at 314.08-9 the windowboards of the dreamer's room succumb to the storm and burst open, the noise is also the sound of the wastrel's collapse.

This irruption of weather into the sleeper's room brings with it the tree's branches, whipping around in the wind — in which capacity tree and flapping blind will be anthropomorphised as, for example, 'the flappernooser, master of the good lifebark *Ulivengrene* of Onslought' (329.05-6), remembered as a 'teerm [tree; see the immediately previous lines] that blows in all the vallums to signify majestate [ALP/Issy's kingly lover]' (478.11-12), and the reason that the Oedipally resented father was earlier identified as '*Meistral* Wikingson [my italics], furframed Noordwogen's kampften . . . fanned by ozeone brisees' (241.18-20).

The 'vallums', originating in the curtains bellying in the wind, now configure the captain's return — 'threw the sheets in the wind . . . his rubmelucky truss rehorsing the pouffed skirts of his overhawl' (315.14-16). The sleeper's obsessions work their usual changes: 'That's all mighty fine but what about another [drink]' becomes a 'sissed' 'That's all murtagh purtagh but whad ababs his dopter' (314.30-1), and something, perhaps just a branch, becomes a highwayman's phallic 'stickup' (315.17), a 'pokeway paw' (315.34-5) sticking through the window. The wind has prevailed 'against our aerian insulation resistance, two boards that beached ast one' and in the process 'spluiced' an obviously hymeneal 'menbrace' (316.02-9). (This may be the point when the curtains are blown down.) Nonetheless the 'low pleasure' in which the captain will specialise this time is gluttony, a vice probably prompted by the rotund-appearing curtains bellying in the breeze as the 'pouffed skirts' and 'bellows pockets fulled of potchtatos' of the tailor's 'goragorridgorballyed' antagonist (223.16-17). A feast is laid for him, ominously beginning with the aphrodisiacal oyster.

The oil-on-fire sound of static — 'they plied him behaste on the fare. Say wehrn!' — signals that someone is turning the dial (and pouring a drink), looking for something else; the programme chosen is presenting either a re-enactment of Daniel O'Connell's ('old damn ukonnen' (323.26)) career or coverage of a speech given in the Dáil by one of his many descendants. As Mrs Glasheen notes,[3] O'Connell here doubles with the O'Connor Power, a politician who evidently specialised in 'premonitory' alarms. Bits of this broadcast have been picked up before, especially in the sermoniser's reference to Catholic emancipation.

O'Connell's is the voice of a ghost, embittered by the disdain of the rising generation, remembering the brave words of his heyday, penitent about what proved to be the uncertain trumpet of his 'ersewild aleconner' self (319.03-8), seeking solace with his well-remembered indulgences in drink,

food, and women. He is thus continuous with the bingeing
figure of the sermon, and with the returning gorbellied captain who now faces, simultaneously (317.32-3), the Head of
Howth (he is entering the bay) and the head of his host (he
is being fed), both calling him home. The latter tries to get
him to make good on his marriage promise, and is answered
with a politician's rigmarole. We are also hearing about the
welsher's cadging of his second drink: Sackerson pours it and
chalks it up (319.10-15), asks for payment in vain, and curses
the trickster. Welsher-captain levants once again, the cold
and hot climes of his travels (Africa and Bering Sea, sun and
snow) originating in the cold and hot taps of the servant's
bottle-washing (320.25-31).

Back momentarily, on the 'infernal machinery' of the
radio, to the sermon, where, the exemplary malefactor having
been 'suitably punished', we learn of Christ's forgiveness, a
'poor fish . . . upholding a lampthorne . . . to all men in bona-
fay' and — indeed this seems to have been the main point of
the sermon — we are asked to give charitably, forgetting
thoughts of personal property: 'He cupped his years to catch
me's to you in what's yours as minest to hissent'. This unwelcome appeal moves someone to change stations yet again,
and this time we pick up the horse race news which will return
later and be reviewed at 341.18-342.32; under its influence
the curse/Kersse figure is a diminutive (hence Chinese) jockey,
dressed in the traditional flashy colors, arriving from 'the
Boildawl stuumplecheats' (also 'dail' — interference from the
political/historical broadcast), telling one and all 'how the
whole blazy raze acurraghed'.

Then — more static, oil-on-fire (322.22-323.24) — back
to the O'Connor broadcast, with a xenophobic tirade modelled
after 'Circe's' fantasised address of Lord Mayor Bloom (cf.
Ulysses 479) against the foreign captain/lover/welsher, 'a
wenchman . . . coming from a beach of promisck', then one
more change, back to the ('beforetime') horses, 'that bunch
of palers on their round', who as we rejoin them are heading
for the home stretch. Apparently the race ends unsatisfactorily
for someone (324.13-14), who demands angrily that they
'change that whole set. Shut down and shet up'. The finish
of the winning horse, with the sound of the crowd's cheers

in the background, becomes the captain's third and final rearrival, this time 'hailed . . . cheeringly', and the crackly static becomes (besides a drinker's toast) a welcoming huzzah: 'Scaald!' There follows the aforementioned weather report review, then an advertisement for tea, news of yet another 'dyrby' coming up, and previews of future programmes, especially a string quartet; all these become parts of the marriage to 'Anna Lynchya Pourable' which – the race over, sermon finished, captain home for the final time – we are ready to celebrate.

325.13-342.32: The race may be over, but the summary at the end of this next section tells us that, courtesy of *The Irish Race and World*, we are about to get a dramatic reprise of the kind given the Gold Cup in *Ulysses* (pp. 415-16), what will eventually be called a '*saggind spurts flash*' (342.34-5). A simplified narrative of that account goes as follows (see 341.18-342.32): sounds of noisy merriment; conversation of one definite and one dubious race-going priest (descended from 38.25-36.13) exchanging tips and confessional secrets; begging orphans; a cardsharp, a sot, and various other regulars; a startling noise of some sort, at first taken, incorrectly, for the start of the race; the start of the race; a lot of excitement as '*Emancipator, the Creman Hunter*' owned by '*Major Hermyn C. Entwhistle*', defeats three geldings but loses to two young fillies, who show him their rears. As usual, the broadcast cues much of the action, which begins ('Comither, a*horace*' – my italics) with noisy merriment and ends with a reprise of HCE's exposure-and-insult, here obviously coinciding with the disposition of those horses. The 'ships gospfather' (325.18) of the wedding owes a lot to that clerical conversation (with overtones from the sermon); near the end of his talk we can detect one of the pair telling the other, his 'truest patrions good founter,' to 'better your tooblue prodestind arson' on a certain tip and see 'Horuse . . . crihump over his enemy', adding tipster's details ('Fuss his farther was the norse norse east and Muss his mother was a gluepot') about breeding. (The father loses his bet: 432.12-14 will have him offering 'mass for a coppall of geldings' – the gelding *coppal* (Gaelic for 'horse') who loses the race – and complaining about the muddy conditions.)

These influences are assimilated to the listening dreamer's aroused memory of that period, when the forces of religion, prudence, and domestic comfort began to 'beat his barge into a battering pram', following the wild 'Norwegian captain' days of his elopement. James and John, sailor and tailor, the returning lover and the rivals who, like Penelope's suitors, were originally waiting to ambush him (316.22-5) are reconciled, and the scamp who at the beginning of the story was, like the young Joyce meeting the young Nora, 'beggin' (311.31), is granted the girl on the condition that he be baptised and join the church. During the festivities which follow the groom begins to assume two heroic roles — first as bear, hence Russian (329.19-20; remember that he first called his wife 'Goldilocks'), second, doubling with one of the riders getting ready for the race, as the mounted hunter of the calendar picture (329.27-8).

At 330.20 something crucial happens: 'Rolloraped.' It is the sound of the roller blind, probably jolted by the recent blasts from outside, unfurling over the window (it is still 'drawn' at 559.05), thus making possible the shadow-show which will soon give us the television programme of Butt and Taff on the *'bairdboard bombardment screen'* of *'tastefully taut guranium satin'* (349.08-9), the *'verbicovisual present- ment'* of the horse race against a *'curkscraw bind'* (341.18), and, here, the 'pictures motion'. The first moving pictures shown against it are inspired by the children, in turn evoked by those orphans at the racetrack, pantomiming in silhouettes ('The threelegged man and the tulippied dewydress') the story of their missing parents; in the HCE-ALP chronicle, the children (announced at 330.30-3) have arrived to make trouble for the father. The blind flaps loudly enough in the wind ('Pappappappa . . . macmacmacwhack . . .') to make for one of the *Wake*'s thunderwords (and, possibly, the unex- pected noise of the racetrack account (342.10-11), reviving the story of what followed: primal scene, encounter with cad (332.25) and all that ensued; the cad is also inspired by the various low-lifes described at the track, especially *'Slippery Sam'* (341.36-342.09).

The 'Enterruption' which breaks in at 332.36 derives from interference from a Czech station; this being the thirties, it brings ominous political news, of troops (presumably German — Field Marshal von Moltke is cited at 333.13) marching through the 'danzing corridor'. That 'clopping' is also, after the manner of radio drama sound effects, the clopping of the horse's hooves at the track. Most overtly, it signals Kate's arrival downstairs to convey ALP's request to her husband that he come up and join her in bed. Within the sleeper's room, it seems to signal ALP's arrival — she knocked at 330.30-2, opens the door at 333.01-4, closes it behind her at 334.28-30, leaving momentary silence in her wake — on her usual business of attempting to rouse her husband, 'in her amnest plein language', here with news that everyone else is getting up. She also brings him a reviving drink, a 'cure for . . . lethurgies', hailed at 334.20-1 as reviving 'rum'.

It works. The succeeding pages are full of the sounds and sights of resurrection. The customers turn their attention to the calendar picture of the resplendent mounted hunter (334.31-6), the turbulent weather crashes outside — the race was/will be won by a mudder, a 'moder of moders' (330.36) — and the sleeper begins to imagine himself re-enacting his one foray of the day, the trip to the privy outside. Beginning at 335.17 he is once again in his imagination a 'Wullingthund' who, having washed, gets dressed and takes us back to the 'gartener's' garden where it all began — 'We are once amore as babes awondering in a wold made fresh where with the hen in the storyaboot we start from scratch' (336.16-18) — for a 'second wreathing' of his story of crime and triumph.

As it often does, the scene comes accompanied with the voices of the watching soldiers (336.21-32) discussing his 'peckadillies', recalling and hence reviving the event in the privy and the event which it recalled. We are ready for the 'Butt And Taff' re-enactment of the sin of the father, here incarnated as the Russian general because HCE, with his 'goldilocks', was a 'bear', because the recent Czech broadcast has introduced allusions (333.04) to Russian politics and history (like the tide, we seem to be drifting east: Ireland — Norway — Czechoslovakia — Russia; Shaun in the next book will take us to America), and because the story probably being told downstairs so perfectly matches the father's own remembered situation:

Buckley, he [Joyce] explained, was an Irish soldier in the
Crimean War who drew a bead on a Russian General, but
when he observed his splendid epaulettes and decorations,
he could not bring himself to shoot. After a moment, alive
to his duty, he raised his rifle again, but just then the
general let down his pants to defecate. The sight of the
enemy in so helpless and human a plight was too much for
Buckley, who again lowered his gun. But when the general
prepared to finish the operation with a piece of grassy turf,
Buckley lost all respect for him and fired.[4]

When he came to the piece of turf, Beckett remarked,
'Another insult to Ireland.'[5]

The ensuing cross-talk owes most to that story, to the
memory of the scene in the privy and the primal scene revived by it (along with the Mutt and Jute dialogue which
followed), to the recently remarked calendar picture, and,
especially up to 341.17, to those two race-going clerics on
the radio. In fact 'Butt' and 'Taff' — 'ffat ttub' backwards,
so as before in I/1 HCE of the 'big white harse' is being spied
on by his mirror-image[6] — begin as variants of the clerics, as
'a smart boy, of the peat freers' and a *'mottledged youth,
clergical appealance'*, introduced just as the race gets under-
way, standing at the rail and watching the horses take off.
Butt is apparently the one with the watcher's binoculars; for
his part Taff looks warily up at the rain — its drops account
for the *'mottledged'*, *'pied'* appearance of his clothes — and
around at the wetness that will determine the outcome, the
victory of the mudder. As reported, the backed horse loses
out to two fillies, though the race is close enough to end in a
photo finish which recalls the 'shutter' snapshot of HCE's
sin; as always the 'snapper' is in red ink (341.05-6).

Taking place against the screen of the window's blind, the
exchange also recalls (339.12-13; 339.28-30) the recent
invasion of wind and tree figuring the Norwegian captain,
of whom the general is an older version, a later incarnation
of the father who in marrying moved from sea to land, from
ocean-going brigand to continental imperialist. Many of the
shapes and gestures of the ensuing *Son et Lumière* can be
accounted for if the reader will envision an erratically flaring

fire on one side of a dark room, an occasionally flapping and twisting screen on the other, various objects (bedposts, stool, bearskin rug with head propped up) silhouetted in between, and on the edge of the action, a one-eyed observer listening to noises from below and without, all the while, like Taff, '*strangling . . . to merumber*' (339.31), to '*regulect all the straggles for wive in the rut of the past*' (340.13-14). As usual, these conjurations take on lives of their own and beget their own visions, as when Butt shines a lantern in Taff's eyes, dazzling him and making his '*bulgeglarying stargapers razzle-dazzlingly full of eyes, full of balls, full of holes, full of buttons, full of stains, full of medals, full of blickblackblobs*' which become the decorations, buttons, etc on the general's uniform, then, fading, the gold coins which, Zeus-like, he showers, then the great constellations (340.30) among which the general is Ursa Major. The multiple image conjured is of bear, of bearish father 'humping' the mother,[7] of general, of disgraced father, of feared master, of horse trailing fillies, and of Norwegian captain: 'Bernesson Mac Mahahon [Gaelic 'bear'] from Osro [Oslo] bearing nose easger for sweeth prolettas on his swooth prowl!' (340.17-18)[8]

This section concludes with the radio racetrack account whose reverberations we have just traced.

342.33-346.13: While the noise of revelry below and storm without grows louder, the radio broadcasts a roundup of 'society' news which contributes to the narrative as follows:

1. (345.35-346.02; cf. 343.13-19) The fashionplates at the race are forced by the weather to spoil the effect of their new clothes by putting on mackintoshes. It being the start of spring, the fashionable world are leaving off their heavy furs and wearing mackintoshes. They are also weakening themselves and spoiling their figures by eating cream tarts and '*muckinstushes*', whatever those are. Compare the Butt introduced in this section, '*slinking his squad muttons shoulder so as to loop more life the jauntlyman*' after the hail starts falling, complaining about his, and his father's, spoiled proportions (343.05-19).

2. (346.02-7; cf. 343.19-344.07) More high-society hijinks, this time centred on the arrival of the fashionable *Ballet Russe* — '*the second coming of antigreenst*'; red is the

opposite of green — which from 1932 to 1938 was in fact revived for its 'second coming'. '*The neatschknee Novgolosh*'
is probably Rimsky-Korsakov, whose first composition was
an opera about that prototypical Russian patriarch, Ivan the
Great: the cadence is resounded at 344.14 as 'nitshnykopf-
goknob', though Joyce takes the liberty of changing Ivan the
Great into Ivan the 'tourrible' (344.13). '*The Arumbian
Knives Riders axecutes devilances round the jehumispheure*'
conveys the characteristic high-kicking Russian dance. Compare, as described by Butt and Taff, the arrival of the Russian
general, 'with his sabaothsopolettes . . . legging boldylugged',
then singing in his 'grandoper' way.

3. (346.07-12; cf. 345.10-25) '*Old Yales boys*' make '*rebo-
lutions for the cunning New Yirls*': Yale keys resolve to un-
lock 'cunning' locks (compare 626.30-1); America's gilded
youth goes to New York where the boys heat up and seduce
the girls; as always the father (an 'old boy', as in alumnus)
leches after the new girl. Worse yet, there is a whiff of chic
androgyny in the goings-on, since the old boys are also
making revolutions and becoming new girls. Compare Butt,
who like Bloom in 'Circe' knuckles down and simultaneously
becomes a girl as 'my bill it forsooks allegiance'. This transformation is partially cued as he '*chancegors induniforms*' to
green, white and brown, the colours of the (feminine) gowns
hanging on the door. Thus near the end of his 344.08-345.03
speech Butt lapses into the idiom of ALP, remembering with
fear (344.35-345.03) the wedding night when, as she recalls
later, HCE 'showed me his propendiculous loadpoker' (493.10).
There also seems to be some radio report about the making
of New Year's resolutions (the night of 21 March is, in the
old calendar, New Year's Eve) which produces Butt's forswear-
ing of tobacco (345.14-15).

4. (346.12-13; cf. 345.16-33) The programme concludes
with a laxative commercial, which with typical extravagance
promises resurrection. Compare the end of the cross-talk act
leading up to this latest broadcast summary, in which Taff
hands 'this scup', '*the communion of sense*', to Butt so that
he will be 'bladdy orafferteed', and Butt testifies that it is
indeed improving his 'foerses of nature'.

This section concludes with the radio newscast whose
reverberations we have just traced.

346.14-359.30: In this section the sound of '*bealting pots*' from below grows louder, bell chimes signalling the time come over the radio, and the bedded HCE comes out with a spectacular fart whose '*spectracular mephiticism*' produces both the evacuation of the Russian general — just handed his cup of laxative, after all — and the notoriously anal Oscar Wilde.

As Russian general the father drops his pants, relieves himself, and is shot, a sequence influenced by the radio broadcast described at 359.22-6:

> You have jest (a ham) beamed listening through (a ham pig) his haulted excerpt from John Whiston's fiveaxled production, *The Coach With The Six Insides*, from the Tales of Yore of the times gone by before there was a hofdking or a hoovthing or a pinginapoke in Oreland, all sould. Goes Tory by Eeric Whigs . . .

As McHugh notes, the phrase 'six insides' comes from Carlyle's account of Louis XVI's flight from Paris ending in Varennes, where he was recognised — he had been disguised as the steward ('last of the stewards peut-être' (41.36)) — and captured, a debacle which led directly to his execution. Under its influence, the mutating fatherfigure who was (328.33) 'the oversear of the seize', keened at 16.33 as 'Louee, louee!', and will soon be the last high king of Ireland ('steward' to 'Stewart' to Charles Stewart Parnell, Ireland's uncrowned king, to Rory O'Connor, Ireland's last crowned king), becomes the last king of the *ancien régime*, the weak, uxorious ('her handpicked hunsbend' — 364.36), all-too-human huntsman-monarch, Louis XVI.

Like many such productions, the drama is presented as a series of reminiscences by veterans, given in monologues probably influenced ('how the thickens they come back to one to rust!') by the famous opening of *A Tale of Two Cities*. We get reminiscences first from one of the soldiers ('Hittit was of another time . . .' (346.36-347.01)), then from a chorus of participants (354.22-3), and finally — this is where the tale begins to be the ghost story promised — from the king himself (356.16-17).

The first speaker is an erstwhile loyalist soldier, of 'the loyal leibsters' (351.06), who turns on his king when he sees him making his royal exit, his 'exitous erseroyal', 'rolland allover ourloud's lande' in the coach of Carlyle's account (353.15-18). He begins his reverie with a nostalgic memory of his days as a student/soldier, when he was with a gang of 'thurkmen three' similar to those royalist champions the Three Musketeers, with their toasts to 'our royal devouts' and to 'those khakireinettes, our miladies in their toileries' — their own *mademoiselles*, plus the queen in the *Tuileries*, from which Louis and his queen escaped.

Under the influence of the dreamer's flatulence the father becomes a Wildean pederast, eager to have a lad '*elter his mehind*', his role as great white caterpillar deriving from the fire-cast '*metenergic reglow of beaming Batt*' on the blind, its '*heliotropical*' glimmer returning in Wilde's '*sunflawered beautonhole*'. His speech from 350.15 to 352.15 first imitates the prosecuted father, like Wilde on trial '*at Oldbally Court*', then comes round to joining those who 'insurrectioned' and 'shuttm' — shot him and shuttered him, in camera, *in camera*, and in the escaping carriage, the 'wendowed courage' he was spotted 'jiggilyjugging about in' (351.10-11, 352.13-15). (And, of course, shat: father's sin is son's sin; when Butt talks about letting down his 'culonelle' (351.30-3) he is also the father letting down his pants; when he shoots him it is with a patriarch's 'crozzier'.) At the moment of attack there is another fragrant report from the dreamer (353.22-32), and the sons join in an assault on him.

The scene is shifting to the backyard 'gadden', where we are to re-enact the father's post-purgative promenade of I/1, where the post-hibernation bear has unstoppered himself of his mythical 'fecal plug', and where Louis stands exposed. The father, having completed his act, has stood up and hitched mohair pants back up to join woollen shirt, rejoining Shem-garment and Shaun-garment, 'Bruni Lanno's woollies on Brani Lonni's hairyparts' (373.16-17) in one '*magisquammy-thical mulattomilitiaman*', both black and white.

The sons argue about what they should do with the cap-tured king, who speaking in his own defence consoles him-self that 'whole men is lepers' in the eyes of God, that in the

end all are overthrown, and so on, and for the return journey
sinks back into memories of his childhood. These combine
with other images — of the trip to the privy (simultaneously a
'purgative' spell in a confessional by this most pious of the
Bourbons: see especially 357.20-358.16 *passim*) with its
Beardsley pornography (also, on the confessional level, a
king's illuminated missal) and, especially, the desperate carriage journey just arrested, as experienced by a traveller looking through the windows at the passing landscape (356.31-
357.01). At the end of his confessional reminiscence we hear
— shades of the Norwegian captain[9] — that 'win again was in
again. Flying the Perseoroyal' (358.19-20), accompanied by
his family. There follows a report of the revolutionary tribunal's deliberation over the king's fate (358.36-359.20)
which also details seven points of Pelagian doctrine as presented in a heresy trial.[10] (Revolutionaries are often in effect
Pelagians, denying original sin; the Pelagians were prominent
among Patrick's antagonists and accusers.) The gist is that
since Adam's sin is not our own we can dissociate ourselves
from that archetypal father-offender — an argument pleasing
to a regicide, one would think, and indeed the six points
make the verdict, and the rationale for it, sufficiently clear:
1. he has to die; 2. he's done it to himself; 3. he's our sacrificial pelican; he's a hunter (Louis loved to hunt) who's taken
human life and foresaken his children; 4. he is like an antediluvian (as in, *'après nous, le déluge'*) sinner damned by
God; he was too cautious for us revolutionaries; 5. he could
and should have been better; 6. boiled down, he's just another
parasitic aristocrat, a member of the 'baubleclass'.

359.30-366.30: Although this bird-call interruption is
plausible, such intervals having been popular on the radio of
the time, the 359.31-360.16 sequence is partly determined
by the voice of Issy, 'decoying more nesters to fall down the
flue' (28.09), coming from the chimney. Traces of her
'dewfolded song of the naughtingels' came through the end
of the tribunal sequence (359.18-19). The adaptation of the
French children's song *'Alouette, gentil Alouette'* which
follows (359.28) synthesises associations of France, birds,
and girl. (Considering that it is about plucking a bird, it is
also ominous.) The following evocation of Issy as Egyptian

sky goddess Nut, her voice hypnotising the 'nossowl buzzard' from on high, derives from the same cause.

When the drama resumes at 361.35 a standard *Wake* sequence — temptation by girls, then accusation by soldiers — repeats in a setting influenced by the historical narrative. The indictment continues, charging the king with (like the young Joyce) abandoning his native land; the dreary prospect of 362.23-35 can be taken for the most part as an Irish ill-wisher's version of the Grub Street life awaiting Joyce. The indictment ends with the usual charges. In his answering defence (363.20-366.30) the accused admits to having taken his 'friends [French] leave' with/from his 'bonnick lass' (363.18-19) along with other sins, but pleads for tolerance on the nominally revolutionary grounds that all are 'fellows culpows'. 'No mum has the rod to pud a stub to the lurch of amotion', he argues (365.26-7), acting the king whose outward motion was stopped at Varennes (and, of course, another, Irish, 'king'). He tries to use his influence as 'their kin' (364.04-14), but when that and his efforts 'in stay of execution' (366.16-17) fail, he awakens to his proper dignity and assumes the mantel of Caesar ('czar', as Ó hEithir notes,[11] is derivative of 'Caesar') against his 'brutals' 'paysecurers': 'thit thides or marse makes a good dayle to be shattat'.

366.31-373-12: Shot, decapitated, or simply fallen ('And dong wonged Magongty till the bombtomb of the warr'), the father is now gone, it is thought, for good, and immediately becomes an occasion for grief and 'Synopticked' mythologising by 'Our four avunculusts'. They appear (368.24-6) as four jowly old jobbers in on the secret that their established religion is a 'ruse', exploiting the tragedy of a replaceable martyr, the 'faller'. As apostles, preaching the second coming of their lord, they are participants in an ironic drama which Joyce might have borrowed, though I doubt he did, from the famous 'Grand Inquisitor' chapter of *The Brothers Karamazov*: the 'Jukoleon' of whom they preach returns and beholds a post-deluge, still-deluded land, prime among the deluders being those four 'Wringlings' preaching 'wronglings' to 'dodos' and 'dupes', 'blowing great' and promulgating all kinds of prohibitions with the support ('Guns') of the state (367.15-368.23); eventually this returning figure will be told to die again or go away.

This figure is the ghost of the murdered king, haunting his persecutors, doubling as the dauphin whose supposed escape from Louis's killers was long the basis for claims to the French throne. (Remember the 'Dauphin' of *Huckleberry Finn*? 367.18 quotes a phrase — 'The duke done it' — from the page on which he reveals 'the secret of his birth'.) Heralded by the usual downstairs speculation about a 'rudrik kingcomed to an inn court' (a vision prompted by the calendar picture (369.18-22)), he appears first as 'polisignstunter. The Sockerson boy' (370.30-2).

The main source of this avenging apparition is of course Sackerson, that perennial 'other', as in I/1 encountered on the return from the privy. Also, the figure lying in the bedroom has had enough of the weather coming in through the blown-open windowboards and has called for him, who had 'hord from fard a piping' (371.05) to come close them up. Meanwhile the roistering of the cast-out customers bodes ill for the would-be returner/haunter: they are overheard from outside 'marshalsing', martially singing the *Marseillaise*, a 'lyncheon partyng' (372.30) to put an end to his similarly returning reincarnation, to lunch on his remains, and to turn him around, launch him on his final 'parting' exile — 'To speed the bogre's barque away' (373.10).

373.13-380.5: 'The dumb he shoots the shopper rope. And they all pour forth' (372.05-6) indicates that far from closing the shutters the oafish Sackerson made things worse — perhaps he heard 'shut them up' as 'shutter open'. In the boisterous paragraph from 373.13 to 380.05, shouting master and servant are trying to make themselves understood to one another over the noisy weather, and things don't start to quiet down until, with a 'BENK! . . . BINK . . . BUNK . . . BENK BANK BONK' (379.27-30), the servant finally succeeds in slamming (or hammering — the sound echoes Christ's being nailed to the cross) the windowboards shut, after which comes the chapter's relatively peaceful last pages. The scene is also an encounter between the haunting spectre of an old king — Louis XVI, Odysseus, the ghost of Hamlet's father, the Christ of the second coming, 'Wholehunting the pairk on a methylogical mission' (373.20-1) — and those who have devoted themselves to his apotheosised memory, and now wish he would go away or (as Finn, Finnegan, Arthur) lie back down. At first they claim (373.13-17) that, like the spurious 'Dauphins' who surfaced after the revolution, he is a pretender in both senses of the word. But eventually he is recognised for himself and urged to disguise himself (377.09-11) and 'Abedicate' (379.19), abdicate and lie back in bed. Mainly, he is asked, politely, to die. That red corduroy surcoat, hanging on the door opposite the bed, next to the 'casement', becomes the figure of a hanged martyr and hanged god: 'Isn't it great he is swaying above us for his good and ours . . . He's doorknobs dead!' (377.36-378.02) HCE sees himself when he looks at it this time; he has been thinking of putting it on, with his servant's help, as protection against the weather: 'Never mind your gibbous. Slip on your ropen collar and draw the noosebag on your head' (377.07-9). (At the beginning of Book III he will in fact be wearing it.)

Roughly, 373.13-380.05 passes through the following stages. First HCE is told that the red-on-white insignia of his sin have become the red letters of the gospel, being cited in a 'postoral lector', with overtones of communion bread and wine (373.36-374.24). Then he is told that he will be tried by twelve jurors (descended from his erstwhile apostles) with results that, like James Joyce's devotion to *Finnegans Wake*, can only damage his reputation: 'You'll have loss of fame from Wimmegame's fake' (375.17-376.11). Then, in a passage crammed with allusions to Finn McCool and especially to the Diarmuid and Gráinne saga[12] he is told that his sons and daughter are growing up in his absence, that the daughter has fallen in love, that despite his jealousy it is time for him to sink into the background like the displaced Finn (374.23-375.29). Then he is told that, having put on a lot of weight (376.14-15), he is welcome to attend the wedding, with the understanding that his body will supply the feast and, as a kind of pinata-like version of Zurich's sacrificial ogre the Bogge, being whacked by the guests and exploding out favours for everyone's amusement, the entertainment (376.15-378.21).[13] Then he is told that this is his last chance to deliver his message because various commentators are eager to work their will on his words, and won't be imposed on much longer (378.21-379.06). Finally, he is told to get up on the cross, down in ground, back in the coffin (Louis's coach-and-four has returned at 377.23-5, this time as a horse-drawn coffin), back out to sea and under the water (the Titanic is recalled (379.31-2)), to blot out one by one the seven orifices of his 'nodsloddledome' and the rainbow thoughts inside it, in sum to give his would-be beneficiaries whatever he has to give and go away (379.06-380.05).

380.06-382.30: And he does go away. In his last incarnation he becomes old Rory O'Connor, last high king of Ireland, beaten, beaten down, and, at the very end, sailing off for 'Nattenlaender', as Scandinavian 'Land of night' the ultimate end of the Norwegian captain whose onslaught began this chapter's sequence of tales. It is the end predicted: 'First you were Nomad, next you were Namar [Hebrew for 'tiger'], now you're Numah [as in *pneuma*, spirit] and it's soon you'll be Nomon [a no-man, a baffling gnomon]' (374.22-3).

His final subsidence occurs on three main levels. Down-stairs (where he came after returning from the privy), he drinks up the customers' spilled or unfinished liquor. Up-stairs, he is a 'waterproof monarch' lying 'under the grass quilt' of his 'pallyass' (380.25), above the puddles on the floor. Finally, as Rory O'Connor he is all those supplanted patriarchs to which the chapter's chronicle of captain, general, and king has been leading.

Shortly before delivering the *coup de grâce*, his persecutors had predicted that 'he'll Shonny Bhoy be', with 'he bares sobs conscious inklings shadowed on soulskin' (377.26-8). And in Book III he will return, as the buoyed-up Sonny-Boy Shaun, a barrel ('Wear anartful of outer nocense!' — 378.32-3) full of the brew identified — 'I'm enormously full of that foreigner, I'll say I am!' (463.14-15) — with Shem and his writings, both of which are throughout the *Wake* represented as deriving from the leavings of others, the 'winespilth' just soaked up by the old king. Which is to say he will be a type of the *Wake*'s bottle, containing the letter with its inky shadows of the subconscious, washing ashore and being retrieved by 'a hin'. The vessel that departs at the end of II/3 and carries the four old men throughout the next chapter, III/4, sails into Book III.

SEVENTEEN

Book II, Chapter 4

IN A posture which will be mirrored in III/3 by his descendant Shaun, the prostrate HCE lies in his bed beneath the four bedposts, and in communing with them communes with his past, in four parts. They appear as old men, their bald heads the bed-knobs, because that is what he feels like. Communing with his past, he calls up images of his youth, and the old men become voyeurs peering through windows at a newlyweds' wedding-night (395.07-396.02). Having begun Book II with the infantile miming of a romance, we now conclude in II/4 with the senescent observation of it; having begun on the stage, acting, we conclude in the balcony, watching; having begun as children looking forward to adulthood, we conclude as codgers looking back at youth.

'The big event of the Mamalujo chapter [II/4] is Joyce's love for Nora', says Thomas A. Cowan,[1] to which we may add Roland McHugh's observation that Trinity College is probably its 'primary location', that the chapter is full of the names of places and landmarks from that area.[2] It is the scene of the first meeting of this book's lovers, as it was of James and Nora's first meeting; the 'history' studied by the epicene professor of history Joyce identified with the narrator[3] has that meeting as its epochal event, as studied at Trinity. Like the children of II/2, only from the other direction, the professor studies that event and its consequences, one of which may have been ('I beg your pardon, Goldilocks, my heaven on earth, but you'd have a lovely face for a pantomime') the mime with which Book II began.

As Ian MacArthur says,[4] the four old men appear in counter-clockwise order, from Johnny (west) to Mark (south) to Luke (east) to Matthew (north), the right direction, after all, for a chapter given over to re-tracing the past, and one which finishes with the hour-hand pointing to twelve, the hour at which Book III begins. Then too, in another retrograde movement, the tide is going out, bearing the vessel to the ocean whose 'wet windwhistling' (506.21-2), as heard by the four old men 'spraining their ears, luistening and listening to the oceans of kissening' (384.18-19), permeates the writing. The sounds originate in the storm just shut out and, since the elopement (cf. 312.05-12) was also a stormy affair, help to conjure the 'Gaelic champion' and 'colleen bawn' (384.21-33) on their ocean voyage.

   383.01-386.11: As I have written elsewhere,[5] there is another noisy presence — Issy's cat, which enters through the door left open by the manservant and, against the background noise of the 'rockbysuckerassousyoceanal sea' (384.03-4), begins squawking, so it seems, about its *idée fixe*, birds. When last heard from it was being addressed by the bird-luring Issy whose chimney-filtered voice seemed to be calling the father 'a nossowl buzzard' (361.16); now here it is back calling HCE, among other things, an *'old buzzard'* (383.05). The abusive 'shrillgleescreaming' probably carries traces of the taunting song being sung by the customers as they weaved away; certainly the opening ditty encapsulates the charges recently revived there. The following scene re-enacts the watchers' schooldays, when, prophetically, they attended a production of Boucicault's *Arrah-na-Pogue*, all about a 'big kuss' (383.18). With ocean noise in the background, the memory of this romantic comedy, viewed from a distance, intersects with HCE's memory of the elopement, recalled from afar. Inevitably, signs of the troublesome passion sanitised out seep through: that the play's hero should be 'bunnyhugging' his girl (384.21) seems innocent enough until we learn later that the sound of the primal scene was of 'a hopper behidin the door slappin his feet in a pool of bran' (486.30-2); the list of lessons (for instance 385.10-3) is full of obvious *double entendre*.

   Introduced as a 'circling' 'wildcaps', the cat helps account, I think, for a number of the turns that this sequence takes: the rousing call of 384.05, the diet of fish, the Egyptian interlude (385.04-6), a running parallel between the students at the theatre and a cat or cats watching either a goldfish in a fishbowl or, like Elizabethans at a bearpit, a dog, 'the mad dane ating his vitals' (385.16-17). Towards the end the students fade back into the old men, back into 'wishening' for the young lovers of 'the wald times'.

386.12-388.09: During Johnny's monologue, Issy's cat, prancing up and down the bed along the length of HCE's mountainous body with its tail on high, takes on the role of a show horse at a *dressage* demonstration, another entertainment remembered from the Trinity days. Our observer is thinking of horses because he is thinking of father-figures — types of himself, especially the mounted 'Willingdone' who at Waterloo (10.07-9) picked up half a hat from the filth, here the 'half a tall hat' worn by an 'old determined despot' whose 'fathomglasses', boring through the dark like the cat's green eyes to 'remembore' the past, recall Willingdone's 'tallowscoop'. This figure, introduced as 'the old Merquus of Pawerschoof' (of Powerscourt House, on S. *William* Street) goes through several patriarchal incarnations before ending as King Mark, being drowned and supplanted in the time when 'Fair Margrate waited Swede Villem' (a 'goldilocks' wedded a Viking; II/3's last of the Stewarts is supplanted by William and Mary). At 387.33-5 we can see the drowned father's widow 'wreathing' — reading, writing, twining together — her 'murmoirs' into the scene which will become the almanac picture downstairs. The Tristan-and-Iseult account which follows (387.36-388.06) reflects her interpretation of that picture: old husband, the inn-keeper of the picture, coming out through the 'darras'; interesting wonderful weapon-bearing hunter entering the yard; young servant-woman tumbling for him; matronly wife wishing she could do the same: intimations of divorce.

388.10-390.33: The sea adventure of Johnny's monologue becomes, in Marcus' section, emblematic of Ireland's history of invasions and the resulting troubles; the history lesson is now on 'the matther of Erryn', and the 'gynecollege' story which emerges is the old one of Eve, Eva McMurrough, and Helen, the story of the woman who caused all the trouble. The 'gouty old galahat' whose 'deepseepeepers gazed and sazed and dazecrazemazed into her dullokbloon rodolling olosheen eyenbowls' is both our nauseous hero being sick into bedside bowl (or chamberpot) and archetypal lover being bewitched by his woman's eyes. I think that after this experience HCE violates one of the pub's ordinances (586.05) — by standing up and urinating, clumsily, into the fireplace, in the process 'making wind and water, and . . . a Neptune's mess of all of himself' (391.17-18), drenching floor (390.21-2) and, as 'poor Dion Cassius Poosycomb, all drowned too' (391.23), cat. That he should be getting up to leave the bed he shares with his wife perhaps accounts for the last page's intimations of separation; in any case, he here sees himself more as wronged husband than as usurping lover, and weeps and moans accordingly.

390.34-392.13: Lucas's miserable and remorseful monologue resurrects the father's failings, especially with women, by whom he is haled before 'the Married Male Familyman's Auctioneer's court' to make a confession (391.30-1). Feeling at his lowest, with 'his old age coming over him', HCE is doing his best to make his way across the 'stamped bronnanoleum' (391.21) of the floor and get himself dressed so he can go downstairs and feed himself. 'Sculling over the giamond's courseway' of the wet floor, he goes to 'the rim of the rom', apologetically engaging in some 'hunnish familiarities' (392.05) with the lady's garments spread out on the chair when he sits down on them, and fiddles befuddledly with sleeves and buttons.

392.14-396.33: 'Matt Emeritus' continues Lucas's abasement, 'sitting there . . . for an expiatory rite', like patience on a monument (392.21-5), feeling miserable, hearing in the sound of the weather the 'rattle of hailstorms' (392.28) which had earlier signalled HCE's attacker of I/3. That objectionable fellow had called for HCE's execution (70.19-27); here the listener volunteers 'to blow his brains' out himself (392.30). Thus beset, he departs for the kitchen downstairs, spurred on, 'his mouth watering', by thoughts of food — 'brown loaf and dilisk', finnan haddies and mock turtle soup, porridge and bouillon. (Compare 'Lestrygonians', where the hungry Bloom for example perceives the Liffey as 'treacly'; here for example Dublin becomes 'Hungerford-on-Mudway'.) III/3 will later recall this meal as 'that buel of gruel he gobed at bedgo' (441.28-9). The cat, as cats do, follows him, hoping for its share of the goods. At times during these pages man and cat become virtually identified with one another: the recollections of childhood are also recollections of kittenhood (393.34-394.09 in particular gives an anthropomorphised account of the cat's infancy); like its master the cat has been reliving its past 'in dreams of yore' (cf. *Ulysses* 694). Following him now with 'night tentacles', the eyes reaching out like underwater appendages through the darkness, 'dooing a dunloop' around him as he heads for the kitchen, correctly reading his signals that 'left no doubt in his minder' that he is going to come across with 'their passion grand, that one fresh from the cow' — milk — and jumping up his leg in anticipation as he pours it into a bowl, the cat becomes an ecstatic worshipper, awaiting and then receiving a communion of the Milky Way in theological language recalling (245.11-13) the earlier fish discussion of whale-god and infinite pebbles and 'the poissission of the hoghly course': its milk

> exteriorises on this ourherenow plane [the dish on the floor] in disunited solod, likeward, and gushious bodies [it seems to have become somewhat separated] with (science, say!) perilwhitened passionpanting pugnoplangent intuitions of reunited selfdom (murky whey, abstrew adim!) [it is lapped up, its constituents reunited in the process] in the higherdimissional selfless Allself [and swallowed] ... (394.34-395.02)

The cat's frenzied behaviour, open mouth and associations with Issy result in the sexual dimension of this scene and the chapter's climax (395.26-396.03), which literally describes HCE tossing a sausage,[6] a 'greased pigskin' into the gaping 'gullet'.

396.34-399.34: In this final section the four old men come together as they have once before (141.04-7) to sing, like a chorus of cats yowling from an alley, like a gang of ghosts joining in a ghastly charivari, like Michael Furey moaning outside the room of his beloved and her husband, like wind whining through the tree outside the window, in 'community singing', serenading the just-consummated pair. As quarterings of the moribund HCE whose soul is about to drift off into new regions of sleep they recall the arrival earlier this day of old days bottled, preserved, waiting to be unstoppered — the 'capitaletter' from 'Mrs Shemans', sure to 'regul their reves by incubation' — and indeed the Shaun of Book III will be regaled, and beset, by memories of the buried and bottled Shem.

The song they are to sing is more than once compared to *Auld Lang Syne*, appropriate for a chorus on the verge of midnight, 'now in the future' (398.07). At the end it is one last appeal of ghosts to living, old age to new: 'Hear, O hear' (Compare the ghost in *Hamlet*: 'List, list, O list!'). Like the imagined Michael Furey of *The Dead*, each of the four makes one last appeal to the woman to leave her living lover and come with him, each taking a tack considered racy of the soil: promise of money from the north (398.31-399.02), sweet-talking blarney from the south (399.03-10), finicking barter-talk and legalisms from the east (399.11-19), from the west the compelling voice of Nora Barnacle's first lover, the '*lad*' from '*Bohermore*' who enjoyed her, so Joyce feared, '*long before anyone*'. All together, they can be taken as the voice of the Irish, calling not to Patrick but to the Nora whose last name is given at 399.10, asking her to stay in their world of the dead, to hold back from taking the sea-voyage she in fact took.

EIGHTEEN

Book III, Chapter 1

RETURNED to his room, HCE goes to sleep and has his own dream, of Shaun, vision of the future of his son, who will fulfil the ambitions denied the father. Shaun is a type of John McCormack, the alter ego whose career the tenor Joyce observed with overt disdain and transparent envy, probably since the day his inability to read music cost him a victory in the *Feis Cheoil*, which had recently launched McCormack's spectacular career. (Shaun/McCormack will get ridiculed in the next chapter for being unable to read anything *but* music. Joyce nursed grudges.) 562.29-30 suggests that Joyce had hopes that his son Giorgio, another tenor, might imitate McCormack's success. In contrast to such brilliant prospects, the ruined old sot of the end of Book II becomes an abject ass (405.06), watching his golden boy follow McCormack's route of fame in the east (Europe) followed by fortune in the west (America). It is as if the 'last pre-electric king of Ireland' (380.12-13) who 'took to his pallyass' (380.25) and sank to the floor while 'allocutioning in bellcantos' to himself (381.18), and who exited II/4 with a 'Haw!' (399.30), has now come to the pass those scenes foretold: a miserable ass, dreaming his escapist *'Dreans of Ergen Adams'* (381.19) about the singing son who will not make his mistakes. The dreamer intensifies the degradation by contrasting it with Shaun's angelic splendour, thus framing a melodramatic tableau: dissolute father, chief of the 'undesireable parents', lectured and spurned by enterprising son.

403.01-407.25: Derived from HCE's 'lower' past, the ass is often identified with Shem[1] – which is why, I think, the Shemian Butt breaks out into a 'haw haw' (347.32-3) and why Shaun attacks his brother as 'Isaac Egari's Ass' (408.26) and addresses the ass as 'broather brooher' (425.30-1); for its part the ass replies by calling him 'mine bruder' (427.19).[2] Both Shem and ass belong to 'the country of the old', 'the humbler classes' (427.26-7) being left behind in 'Samoanesia', a soon-to-be forgotten land of primitive emotions. Thus at 624.16-17 ALP admonishes her husband to repress his 'stunts of Donachie's yeards agoad', his exploits from donkey's years ago, and of the donkey years.

III/1 opens with that figure in the final two stages of the book's autobiographical seven-stage sequence, the phase of glaucoma, review, self-examination, and self-reproach. The speaker is a translated sleepwalker, looking down on himself next to his wife in bed, through the green-to-grey (407.11-12)-to-rainbow (403.06-15)[3] distortion of glaucoma. The male figure — himself — 'wobiling befear my remembrandts' is first distinguished by his glaring green glaucoma-smitten eyes, then by other frightening features which taken together remind him of 'Gugurtha! Gugurtha!' — Jugurtha, symbol of the unappeased and lowering ('wild hindigan') primitive.[4] The woman appears to be practising fellatio (405.15-17) on him, though probably what is going on is simply a variant of the head-to-foot sleeping posture adopted by the Blooms, and Joyces, as overseen by a watcher whose perception of such sights is conditioned by memories of the primal scene. The associations account for the 'Black! Switch out!' that follows: as always, a forbidden sight leads to blacking-out and shutting-in (eye is blinded, camera's shutter comes down), and denial.

Especially denial: the horrifying 'remembrandts' is instantly prettified into a Sunday-supplement pastoral accompanied by church bells striking midnight (heard at 403.01-4), then transformed into a heartening, pious version of the future: First the observer makes out the still-wet floor glistening in firelight and lamplight — like the river outdoors, he decides, and the bedclothes are therefore 'laundry reposing', left in the river by the washerwomen. Crackling fire accordingly becomes 'the creepers and the gliders and flivvers of the earth breath and the dancetongues of the woodfires and the hummers in their ground', 'echoating' along the banks of the river, and their chant is the name of that future self he is primed to

evoke: 'Shaun! Shaun! Post the post!' The bedside lamp becomes the lamp of a watchman — on the river? He must be
floating, then. He must be — ah! — a barrel, a perception perhaps suggested by the corduroy coat donned earlier, the
garment's ribs, belt and collar becoming the barrel's staves
and hoops. The sleeper is, after all, rotund, like a barrel, and
recently filled with liquor. The coat is 'a classy mac Frieze
o'coat', like the 'enormous frieze overcoats' of Guinness
delivery men.[5] Very well, then, a floating barrel of Guinness,
like that bottle with the letter — a letter-carrier then, like
Boucicault's Shaun the Post, with the disc at his base becoming 'hammered' 'iron heels' (404.20-1), his 'popular choker'
(404.25-6) recasting the 'ropen collar' donned by the king
of II/3. In his genesis, Shaun is a product of repression, a
picture made to screen out another picture; his Freudian slips
and outbursts will give glimpses of the impulses he is made
to deny.

406.26-409.07: First he must get established. As the barrel, half-filled with the porter which like the cad of 38.04-8
he tries to pass off as 'shampain in his head' (407.31), he
floats, half-submerged, to a bank covered with 'virgin bush',
where he comes to rest propped upright. The do-re-mi of his
first words (407.27-8) probably originates in the glug-glug
sound of bubbles coming from his bunghole; when he reaches
the bank he is 'winded', 'utterly spent', almost too heavy to
go on floating (408.04-7). Thus made conscious of how
bulky and 'unwordy' he appears, he introduces himself with
a blandly self-deprecatory speech.

409.08-30: The ass, now a plaintive 'we', joins with the
'echoating' voice of the Irish (404.07) to ask Shaun 'who out
of symphony gave you the permit' — what symphonic powers-
that-be made him the musical king of the hill, what official
authorised him to be the prophetic message-bearer? (A question about a 'permit' also challenges the pub-keeper's authority.) Shaun's answer to this first question will be, typically,
that the office and the message devolve on him 'from on
high' (410.01) — from the moon's control of the tide, from
the Issyan Cinderella-like 'Miss Enders' (412.23) originating
on high from heaven via a carrier pigeon/dove (cf. 232.12).
Anxieties show through in the gratuitous references to 'a

pair of men out of glasshouses [i.e. stone-throwers] . . . named MacBlacks' or 'MacBlakes'. They are the father-attacking duo from Book I, the king-killing Macbeth of Book II, the unpredictable rival prophet Blake, the black-sheep brother Shem, and the blacksmiths hammering out the iron of Shaun-the-barrel's hoops and nails a mere 'fortnichts' ago, as such a reminder of lowly origins; in all these capacities they are to be feared and appeased, here with politician's promises (409.24-6).

409.31-411.21: In response to the second question, also about the empowering 'order', Shaun complains about the strenuousness of his river-to-bay-and-back route which he is just beginning, 'circulating' as far as Lambay Island (410.13). The third question (the words 'a whisper reaches us' should be added at 410.21, after 'limricked')[6] introduces the old *casus belli*, woman, especially the mother (Emania is a Shakespearian mother): 'Speak to us of Emailia'. To the extent that the ass is Shem, he now threatens Shaun's exclusive claims to the mother's affection. The fourth question next addresses Shaun as a whimpering 'beg little big moreboy', and sure enough he lapses into a mama's boy; at the end, as eater, communicant, and 'mothersmothered' (191.25) child, he sticks out his tongue to receive host and food, to insult his questioner and continue the scandalous love-play intimated earlier, and to declare defiantly, 'Her's me hongue!': Here's my tongue; her — mommy — is my honey.

411.22-414.13: Shaun's gesture reminds his interlocutor of a prize 'dogmestic' dog at a show, displaying its tongue, whence Shaun's reference to the lamp-bearing Diogenes. (Because Diogenese = Cynic = 'dog-like'.) He also seems to be reminded of wolves (as I have pointed out elsewhere[7] in heraldry a wolf is distinguished from a dog by a protruding tongue), thus of the story of the wolf and Little Red Riding Hood, who becomes 'wearing greenridinghued' because our glaucoma-smitten examiner sees everything as green; in fact Shaun soon lapses into the indignant brother-smiter, whose blow causes the eye condition of which greenness is the most distinctive symptom. The cause of dispute remains 'O murder mere'.

I do not understand much of the sixth answer or the question; it seems that as usual, the most sensitive subjects (here, the mother), are the most obscured. Joyce seems aware of the reader's difficulty: he introduces a fable, and the last time he did that it was because of Professor Jones's sense that 'my explanations here are probably above your understandings' (152.04-5).

414.14-419.10: The fable opens with a throat-clearing hacking-coughing-spitting thunderword which may also be the sound of the barrel grinding against the shore. (The source is doubtless the sleeper's influenza cough, first mentioned at 26.26-7.) Shaun-barrel is 'Ondt', Shem-Gracehoper the beer or porter within — 'that wandervogl wail withyin! . . . [that] goes down the friskly shortiest like treacling tumtim' (419.13-15). Much of the story turns on the barrel's denying that it is a mere container for the brew 'withyin'. The Ondt is, as they say, the wooden, 'chairmanlooking' figure 'making spaces' in himself when dispensing beer. The Gracehoper is the rotten brew, supplying drinks for one and all, causing merriment followed (416.13-7) by hangover, circulating through the body and wreaking havoc with 'the lustres' — again, the suspected connection between Joyce's alcoholism and his eye troubles — and various organs, eventually being voided in 'an irritant, penetrant, siphonopterous spuk' (416.36-417.01) into a river, from which he hopes to return to his old home, presumably after the cycle of evaporation, condensation, rain and brewing. The Ondt is solid, fixed, and the 'spatialist' philosophy he exemplifies is, almost literally, the creed of the empty-headed. As wooden container he is the house left by the prodigal son, who true to form runs off, has fun, ruins himself, and then tries to return, thus re-enacting once again the *Wake*'s John and James story: 'Let him be *Art*alone the Weeps with his *paris*ites peeling off him' (418.01-2; my italics) says the Ondt about the home-coming wretch. The Gracehoper by contrast is experience, fermentation, metamorphosis, the fizzy, overdetermined Wakean mutations from which all life arises, to which all descend nightly in dreams, and which the Ondt is determined to deny at all costs. In doing that the Ondt is also denying part of his own origins, a point made emphatically in the Gracehoper's concluding poem.

419.11-424.13: That the next question (number nine)

should single out Shaun's farflung vocabulary and 'wander-vogl wail' for praise only rubs this point in. In reaction, Shaun reasserts his own separateness and superiority. At 419.20-2 the question about whether he could 'read' Shem's odd writing is apparently taken as a challenge to 'reed' (compare 18.18) something of his own; in answer he grabs his reed, his 'cinnamon quistoquill', and insists that, like someone in a session of automatic writing, he could do it with his eyes closed. The account of Shem's letter's fate, with its list of Dublin-area addresses all once occupied by Joyce (420.17-421.14), is also a mordant survey of the ruinous destiny awaiting a Joyce-like writer who stays in Ireland or heeds the call to 'Come Baked to Auld Aireen'; his final reward will be an ironic 'Here's the Bayleaffs' — the bailiffs at his door.

Question and answer number ten continue the indictment, explicitly fusing father and brother, those two rivals for the mother. Question number eleven then elicits (422.23-424.13) what is probably the *Wake*'s most frankly autobiographical, and hostile, treatment of the John-James rivalry. Shaun recalls Shem's unwelcome debut in the nursery he once had all to himself: he remembers his mother 'for two days . . . squealing down for noisy priors and bawling out to her jameymock farceson in Shemish', remembers her prophetically Shemian cry eventually blending with that of the noisome 'cribibber' who was to show up in the nursery, and then traces the Joycean career of this 'Childe Horrid' through the experiences with literature, religion and women, especially a woman named Barnacle (423.22). The Shem described here is a mess, prone to every failing and infirmity of the flesh, and Shaun's statement that 'he prediseased me' is a comment on Shem/James' diseased realm of the living as seen from the ethereal Ondt-ish realm of the deceased, the young John Joyce's comment on his supplanter in the world he has left or is leaving behind.

424.14-428.27: Addressed recently as 'the gracious one', Shaun blesses himself, makes an 'act of oblivion', and in the last of the *Wake*'s ten thunderwords blows himself up with 'a crawsbomb'. Since the source of this noise is evidently the 'crickcrackcruck' (426.05) of the barrel losing its under-pinning and the 'pebils' (424.27) giving way under it, Shaun has cause to look to his last end; as John Scarry has observed he is falling into the Liffey,[8] and shortly after he does that he will begin to fill with water and sink. In fact the 'aller-grossest transfusiasm' of the 'blood donor beginning to work ... disseminating the foul emanation' (425.10-15) is the Liffey itself, beginning to seep through bunghole and cracks; under its debilitating Shemian and maternal influence — the booze-soaked Shem/Gracehoper was voided into the river; the mother is always identified with the river — Shaun breaks 'down on the mooherhead, getting quite jerry over her' (426.08). That is why his parting tirade is increasingly sub-verted by Shemian interjections (for instance at 425.14) from the 'transfusiasm' overtaking him. As we would expect at such a moment, the Esau and Jacob story of brotherly usurp-ation figures prominently: Shaun is a 'hairyman' offering to eat 'a chickerow of beans', alternately at war and at one with his 'soamheis brother'. Ready or not, the current is about to take him. Amid splashes and gulps of the river (426.14-16) he slops around in the weedy water along the bank until 'the dreamskhwindel necklassoed him' and, collapsing onto his side, he 'rolled buoyantly backwards' out of the viewer's sight, trailing a wake of bubbles and taking his lamp with him, keened by the presiding ass.

NINETEEN

Book III, Chapter 2

AFTER floating some distance downstream, Shaun-the-barrel has come to rest once again, this time against a bankside pile speaking in a language which is called 'his Dutchener's native' but is in fact a sodden Scandinavian. We may speculate that Scandinavian and Dutch are the languages of two sea-oriented peoples, one proverbially adventurous, the other proverbially phlegmatic, that the difference between the two might be seen as the difference between stormy and stagnant water, and that a once-roguish sailor now sunk in sleep and liquor might appropriately be subsiding from one to the other. In any case the pile is identified as Sackerson, an 'exsearfaceman' now 'tumbled slumbersomely on sleep', embodiment of the submerged past. Behind this figure is the sleeping HCE, snoring in a 'Slops hospodch' (620.32) way and talking in his sleep (467.08-9), resembling his servant because of the catarrhal wheeze of his snore and the 'butterblond' (429.18) light cast on his hair by bedside lamp, which at 430.06 turns him into 'the first human yellowstone landmark'.

That lamp has gone through changes of its own. As Shaun-the-watchman's 'belted lamp' (404.13), it guttered, glowed, and flared, fading to 'dall and youllow' (427.15-18). It casts a yellow glow throughout III/2, especially after being 'amply altered for the brighter' (429.12). Under its influence the snoring sleep-talking HCE becomes the murmuring blonde Sackerson, going on about his 'Dotter' — that daughter whom HCE covets, and whom he suspects his servant of having fathered. As elsewhere Sackerson is the lower self, from which Shaun/Jaun must awake and ascend, then to look back 'by rintrospection' at himself sleeping 'far away on the pillow' (445.29-30).

429.01-431.20: Also as elsewhere, this figure can menace. Its location is a clue. The barrel has floated as far as 'Lazar's Walk' (429.05), once the tidal south bank of the Liffey and site of the Danish landing near where the invaders erected the Steyne, a pillar celebrating the *Wake*'s archetypal act of military usurpation.[1] The submerged pile Sackerson is also that pillar, and his location at 'Lazar's Walk' hints that he may not be as permanently moribund as he seems. In fact a good deal of Jaun's indignation, directed at one point against a 'sukinsin of a vitch' (437.29-30), can be traced to such hints; the Norwegian captain may return. Even now that figure is able to exercise some of its old powers over the disputed Issy, or at least over her entourage. The 'twentynine hedge daughters' introduced at 430.01 enter as the leaves of a riverside hedge, dipping severally into the water near the barrel's resting-place, 'under its tree' — most likely the 'Crampton's Pear Tree' that, as Mink notes, Joyce apparently confused with Crampton's Monument, which occupied the old site of the Steyne.[2] That is, the girls first appear as gathered around that upright monolith of which the invader's Steyne is one version, the tree another, and Sackerson another, and although they later affect a proper revulsion at 'the snores of [yet another manifestation] the log', still as cygnets/iron filings/cyclists, they are first 'attracted', magnetically, to the 'yellowstone landmark' of that tree/magnet/sight.

So once again, we begin with a scandalous attraction, which must be wished away. At 430.17, Shaun starts to do his stuff: the golden lampglow which has just mutated to Sackerson's 'treasure trove for the crown' becomes the 'reinforced crown' of a (presumably straw) hat doffed by jaunty Jaun as he bows to the girls, who thus encouraged put on their 'best beehiviour' and rush 'sowarmly for the post as buzzy as sie could bie', bees to golden honey. The barrel has lurched over, tipping toward the hedge and in the process knocking loose its top disk (it will come off altogether at 471.12-13), and the 'nice perfumios' escaping through the resulting aperture is the smell of beer attracting drinkers, the smell of sweetness attracting bees (Joyce evidently knew that some beers are made from treacle — see 474.10), and the smell of bottled-up semen efflorescing through the celibate priest's pores and attracting women, who as in *Ulysses* 375 'buzz round it like flies round treacle'. Everything is sweetened: Jaun's scrotum becomes a bag of jellybeans (430.30-1); the inflammatory red stockings — leggings — of Waterloo are 'read Irish legginds', and so on. But Shaun's equanimity is disturbed by the disputed leap-year girl (signalled by a doubled water-sound, 'her waves of splabashing'), enough to prompt Jaun to address his sermon to 'Sister dearest'.

431.21-439.14: 'I speak from inspiration' Shaun will say about this sermon (436.21) — and indeed in this chapter and the next he will be a 'medium' for 'spirts' (439.22) other than his own. The first spirit is the defunct Father Michael (432.07), whose words come 'From above' (432.19) bringing the usual priestly chatter about the horse race: we hear once again of the unlucky 'effusion' which affected the outcome, of the 'coppal of geldings' which the father backed, and for which he said a futile mass. It all seems digressive, and yet the sermon which follows, based on Father Michael's 'advice', might be said to back the gelding contingent against rivals of either sex. Shaun/Michael speaks for the sterile and static — especially the infant John Joyce, the *'jeune premier'* (430.22) who preceded James — in urging Issy and her friends to slow down, stay put, remain landlocked. All movement is taboo, ocean travel especially, above all elopement with an arriviste adventurer whose resemblance to the young James Joyce is pretty clear.

439.15-446.26: Brave words notwithstanding, Shaun-as-barrel is unsteady and leaky — 'I feel spirts of itchery outching out from all over me', he says, thinking nostalgically of the 'sludgehummer's force' of the blacksmith who fashioned his hoops and the cooper who fastened them, back when he was young and continent (439.22-5) — even letting out an embarrassing 'Poof!' from submerged bunghole. This last indiscretion is brazened out as music, as proof of enduring lung power, as the source of sprightly bubbles that may 'tingle' the lucky girls (439.29), and so on; that the music is 'topnoted' (439.19) tells us that the barrel is nearly filled up, the tones blown from it therefore vibrating in the 'upperotic rogister' (439.25-6), like the sound of a 'highly strong' (441.27) chord.

A barrel filling up is a barrel about to sink, and Shaun's

sense of his impending demise, his 'perfect leave' (439.26), contributes to the urgency of his sermon as he attacks his supplanter with growing fervour. In this mood he becomes — what else? — a barrel organ (441.24-7), blasting a tabernacled audience with its/his swelling message. The organ is the ventriloquist of instruments, and in fact the speaker who while feeling those 'spirts of itchery' likened himself to a stage ventriloquist (439.17.18)[3] seems to find it harder and harder to distinguish his own voice from the 'outsider's' (442.23): 'We'll he'll burst our his mouth . . .' (442.29). At times the roles of the two brothers become reversed or, perhaps, merged: Shaun throughout this passage is the voyager who will return; Shem is the singer with his seductive 'songs of Arupee' (442.25); the union Shaun proposes with Issy is described (446.08-9) in the imagery of the Claddagh ring, that symbol of brotherly reconciliation. This part of the sermon is remarkable for its mixture of vindictiveness and pathos, for its envious hostility to the degenerate (both as brother and, at 443.21-444.05, father) who will be left among the living, who even now is encroaching, and for its appeal to Issy to wait for Shaun's highly problematical return, to at least remember him.

446.27-452.07: It turns out that Shaun is in 'no violent hurry' (449.05) to leave the living. For one thing, as Tindall remarks, 'Joining the king up there . . . means replacement by a young successor down here';[4] James waits in the wings. In fact Shaun's Bloomian programme (446.27-448.33) of 'Meliorism in massquantities' (447.02-3) is evidence that given the chance he means to stay around for a while, reconciling the disparity between heaven and earth by bringing the former down to the latter, with predictably comic results.

He is most reluctant to leave Issy, that paragon of mutable beauty. The two-beat sound he hears at 448.34-449.06 (449.24-5 says it is the church clock striking two) is taken as one of Issy's doubled signals. Following a complicated associative sequence explained by Stuart Gilbert with the author's collaboration,[5] he becomes in turn a hunter's retriever (449.06-9, 449.20-2) pointing out the sound he has picked up and a happy dweller 'in the birds' lodging, me pheasants among' (449.17-18; Issy's birdcalls are remembered), thence a hunter in his shelter, peering up through his 'upfielded neviewscope', thence a 'dapping' fisherman, all the while expressing affection for 'the finny ones, those happy greppies in their minnowahaw' (450.04-5). (Joyce called this 'the paragraph about poaching and fishing'.)[6]

Both birds (e.g. 359.31-360.16) and fish (e.g. 524.19-525.05) are frequent incarnations of Issy and her friends, for whose favour Shaun is, so to speak, angling. Beneath the hunter (in reeds, at water's edge) and fisherman (at water's edge) is our old friend the barrel, at water's edge, escorted by those 'finny ones'. He has a 'rent in my riverside' (450.02-3) — presumably the bunghole — and speaks ominously of 'sink[ing] it sumtotal' (450.36), of 'drink[ing] annyblack water' (451.15). His serenade is now in the high voice — variously compared to a piccolo (450.19) and flute (451.08) — of the sort we would expect an almost-full barrel to give off. He is also the barrelly tenor McCormack, at 466.31-2 making a mess of a Latin phrase — 'that's uval lavguage for you!' he comments, apparently not recognising the tongue — and even requiring to have the standard do-re-mi translated into English (450.20-1).[7] (As the *Wake* reminds us, his rival Joyce may not have been able to read the music at the *Feis Ceoil*, but was a wizard with other languages.) A philistine, he reserves his most impassioned lyricism for the subject of making money. (McCormack made a mint. Joyce resented it.) Near the end of this section the barrel's escaping bubbles, which were formerly 'ropes of pearls for gamey girls' (446.26), crown a new-rich tycoon's cup of champagne (451.23-5), luring Issy to 'uxoriously furnished compartments'.

452.08-457.24: That cup evokes the parting cup of the calendar picture, the *Wake*'s standard emblem for leave-takings of this sort. Shaun-hunter becomes a dashing huntsman bidding adieu to his lass with a toast (453.35-454.03). It is time for him to leave, both because the tide, just past flood, is about to bear him away[8] and because he is about to sink. The nutriment with which he gorges himself before being off 'on my usual rounds' (456.25) is the Liffey-water and sewage filling him up, displacing the large air bubble that 'hopped out of his woolly's throat' in a laugh 'of a side-pslitting nature' (454.08-12); that his tea is 'a taste tooth psalty'

(456.04) reminds us that Lazar's Walk is within the Liffey's tidal — hence salty — reaches.

Filling with the female element, Shaun becomes womanly, declaring himself 'half '*Nora*wain' (452.36; my italics), referring to 'my poor primmafore's wake' (453.03), being identified as 'Ann Posht the Shorn' (454.06-7). The hunting trip Shaun-as-gallant is taking, the ascent to 'Johannisburg's' (453.33) heaven which Shaun-John-as-levitating-angel is beginning, is a forerunner of ALP's final visit 'to meet a king' (452.26), return to her father's arms — both manly setting-out and womanly home-coming.

About to sink, Shaun is a waterlogged barrel caught in a spell of rain ('yon clouds' have returned and have not yet 'dissipated'), a 'forty years shower' (453.30-1), his nails and hoops catching the same light glistering on the surface as he rolls about ('. . . all of them . . . were just starting to spladher splodher . . . when suddenly . . . swifter as mercury he wheels right round starnly on the Rizzies suddenly, with his gimlets blazing rather sternish . . .' (454.13-23)), his bubble a 'sigh', the raindrops the girls' tears (454.23-5), mingling his lament with theirs.

457.25-461.32: In fact it is a commentary on Shaun's address that it should glide so easily into Issy's saccharine reply — should, indeed, merge with it. In its last paragraph (457.05-24), Shaun's speech overlaps the overheard words coming as usual from that 'focus' (Latin 'fireplace') at which he was 'picking up airs from th'other over th'ether'. Thus 'Shaun's' 'drawhure deelish' (457.15) derives in part from Issy's 'drawher nearest' (457.26), and other Issy cues show through:

> Devil a curly hair I care! If any lightfoot Clod Dewvale [famous highwayman] was to hold me up, dicksturping me [another one, Dick Turpin] and marauding me of my rights to my onus, yan, tyan, tethera, methera, pimp, I'd let him have my best pair of galloper's heels in the cream-sourer. (457.10-14).

This may be Shaun pre-emptively rebuking a Shem-type; it is certainly Issy fantasising lasciviously about the romantic outlaw she is forever dreaming of: we note, for instance, a marauding 'dick', her own yoni, and a promised reward of those inflammatory 'read Irish legginds' for the brute who is man enough to take her away.

457.25-468.19: As earlier, then, the voice of Issy intercepts the dreamer's thoughts, 'to flusther sweet nunsongs in his quickturned ear' (457.28-9). Given the hour, she is probably 'sleepytalking' (327.21), dreaming as usual of her 'dicksturping' demon lover; indeed most of her overheard address is a coy message to this figure. The message is typically ambivalent. The siren-songs are also 'nunsongs' (457.29), the love-letter a 'veronique' (458.14) offered to Jesus on his *Via Crucis*. Coyness can go no further. Given such conflicting cues, Shaun reacts with a typically Wakean exercise in self-induced schizophrenia. He divides himself in two, into Jonathan (himself) and David — the Biblical David being a notorious lady's man — and overtly repudiates the part of whom that snoring log/servant/dreamer is a noisome reminder: 'Talk of wolf in a stomach by all that's verminous!' (462.26-7). The skinny 'Dave' to whom he here consigns Issy is, as E. L. Epstein demonstrates, his newly-aroused penis,[9] as well as that disreputable peeping deadbeat from I/1, the welshing Welshman.[10] The beginning of his reply offers a neat glimpse of the self-censoring process at work: Issy's concluding 'ah ah ah ah' (461.32) is probably the sound of a woman's orgasm and certainly the enthusiastic response of someone being taught how to 'tumble' (461.31), but Shaun's emphatic 'MEN!' (461.33) converts it into the conclusion of a prayer — lid clamped on libido at the last minute. Likewise the seducer's champagne recalled from 451.23-5 becomes the 'chalished drink' of the Eucharist (461.35, 462.01). Preparing to raise his vantage to a higher world, Shaun seeks to sanctify that masturbatory self-distancing from experience for which Joyce mostly blamed the church. The saint is also a voyeur, observing (and urging: 465.11-12) couplings from afar, prominent among them the remembered primal scene (466.01).

The contrast between the rivals is one of experience versus innocence. Dave is the world traveller (464.25-36), fluent in the French which Shaun, remembering the compromising position of the couple on the bed, thinks of as the scandalous language of Tintagel, a land where a woman is likely to invite you to 'languish to scandal in her bosky old delltangle' (465.02-3). Shaun is by contrast resolutely monolingual — seems, in fact, to take pride in the way he (as McCormack) butchers *'Miserere me in miseribilibus'* as 'Mr R. E. Meehan is in misery with his billyboots' (466.31-4). His attitude towards the vaunted worldliness of the figure arriving 'after his French evolution' (462.34) is similarly jaundiced. Perhaps recalling Stephen Dedalus's remark that 'A brother is as easily forgotten as an umbrella', he enjoys comparing his replacement to a 'penumbrella' (462.21) — to, that is, a crook-shaped 'Crozier' (464.03), a 'spatton spit' (464.11) 'that saved manny a poor sinker from water on the grave' (463.20) and whose sole nourishment apart from rain comes from pigeon droppings (463.27-8) — an umbrella being, after all, a traveller of sorts.

468.20-473.25: The barrel is ready to sink, as Issy predicted Shaun would now, at 'the end of your chapter' (460.36-461.01). It washes up against the bank a few more times, bobs, spins around, and loses its top disk at 471.12-14, thus becoming a bucket (471.14) which fills with water and sinks; the bubbles trailing after it, the narrative informs us, will supply matter for the sermons of the country's friars (472.02-4).

Unaccountably, to Shaun anyway, the departure is in the wrong direction — down rather than up. The barrel bobbing up and sinking down is also a would-be saint in the fireplace trying to ascend up the chimney, Santa Claus-like, to the room overhead, and instead, after blessing his undertaking with 'Bennydick hotfoots onimpudent stayers!' (469.23-4), crashing down to the room underneath, a comical Dante/Romeo aspiring to his Beatrice/Juliet and falling to the perdition below; the 'posse of tossing hankerwaves' which bids him goodbye is among the usual other things — girls' waving handkerchiefs, trees' fluttering leaves, water's waves — the flickering flames of the fire, as in *Portrait*, p. 26: 'The fire rose and fell on the wall. It was like waves.'

The bedside lamp gutters again, prompting first the 'meednight sunflower' to which the girls pray (470.07), then the 'familiar yellow label'/stamp which Shaun as merchant/postman slaps on the barrel/package in preparation for the final departure (470.26-7). Their 'Maronite' blessing[11] probably originates, like 'Sackerson's' mumbling of 471.33-4, in the sleeper's snoring: its six verses (470.15-20) all begin emphatically and then trail off in sibilants, like the 'snort! psssssssss!' of farcical stage snorers. Like the other chapters of Book III, III/2 begins and ends with a glimpse of the dreamer beneath the pantomime, snoring away.

TWENTY

Book III, Chapter 3

III/3 is at times the least coherent chapter of *Finnegans Wake*. Part of the trouble comes from its 'seriously textually corrupt' manuscript,[1] compounding the confusion of what, given Joyce's purpose, was bound to be an especially difficult sequence. Functionally, III/3 is the book's summing-up chapter, a kind of dream-built peroration before the waking-up of III/4. Here are some of its 'levels':

1. Joyce was apparently aware of the intensification in dream activity shortly before waking, later documented by laboratory studies, and certainly aware of the phenomenon of the early-morning erection, 'when the morn hath razed out limpalove' (338.30-1). The sleeper whose lust was rekindled by Issy's appeal near the end of III/2, who begins this chapter by searching for 'my darling only one' (478.29-30), and who at 500.22 is still calling for 'I sold!', shortly thereafter exhibits an impressing 'Remounting . . . ouragan of spaces' (504.14), 'the fanest of our truefalluses' (506.17-18), sticking upright from his horizontal form, and concludes with a bravura re-enactment of his wedding-night debauch of the young (hence Issy-ish) ALP. III/3 feverishly relives the generative act and echoes with the voices which attend or follow from it, especially those of the 'nightmare' (583.09) inevitably accompanying such guilty secrets. The four old men who exit (554.10) with a chorus of whinnying *are* Shaun's nightmare, bringing with them seven names for 'fear' (474.24-475.02) — magi/disciples/crucifixioners seeking, summoning, recording, and persecuting the submerged *Ichthos* caught in their net.

2. Joyce also knew (see *Ulysses* 114) of the tradition that a drowning man's whole life flashes before him. The barrel

which sank at the end of III/2 (recalled at 510.17-18 and elsewhere), leaking streams of 'dulcitude' and giving out an occasional bubble, is also a man lying on the riverbed, looking up at the water surface above, and, as predicted (472.17-18) reviewing the figures of the life now coming to an end. The 'phosphor' (475.15) shimmer which surrounds him comes from the river's phosphorescent algae, the silvery fish swimming around him, and the light playing on the river's surface, as seen from above.

3. In one part of the dreamer's imagination the barrel sinks. In another it continues its tide-borne journey down river to the sea — going backwards, that is, and in the process retracing the landmarks passed earlier while going the other way. Joyce referred to the Shaun chapters as 'a description of a postman travelling backwards in the night through the events already narrated',[2] and sure enough, we can at times detect the figures and events of the book's first half, especially the inquisition of I/3, passing in reverse order.[3]

4. The Shaun of III/2 fell to the kitchen fireplace below, haunt of Sackerson and Kate. Repositories of 'downstairs' secrets, they are naturally part of the inquisition; indeed in the next chapter's trial Kate will report on HCE's 'blasphemously confessed' sins (572.28-9). Accordingly, we can sometimes catch the voices of the mannish (bearded) Kate and womanish (breasted) Sackerson, discussing the figure which has just fallen down before them, in the babble of the epicene inquisitors.

5. In this way the events of the chapter resemble the story of the song 'Finnegan's Wake' just before the resurrection — man and woman (Biddy O'Brien and Paddy McGee) disputing over the corpse, causing a 'row and a ruction' which awakens the body. (The locale is, after all, 'Lazar's Walk'.) The passing pageant is also the conflicting testimony of his memorialists; the autobiographical review is also a survey of past deeds similar to that undergone by the departed soul as prescribed by one of the chapter's major sources, *The Book of the Dead*.[4]

6. III/3 is, then, a ghost-raising, though one bedevilled by two sources of confusion. First, Shaun is still the ventriloquial conductor he was in the previous chapter, emitting a

welter of different voices. Second, the questioners, with different and often conflicting interests, are also projectors whose preconceptions constantly interfere: Shaun's ventriloquial 'drama parapolylogic' succeeds his earlier 'dream monologue' (474.04-5), for instance, precisely because multiple scrutinisers have succeeded a single scrutiniser. 'For he was ever their quarrel, the way they would see themselves, everybug his bodiment atop of annywom her notion' (475.19-21): they talk both to him and through the figure who, as one of them puts it, 'took the words out of my mouth' (480.25).

7. Shaun's barrel doubles as the letter-bearing bottle, and the scrutiny of its contents is also an examination of the letter. We are in the sixth stage of the book's architectonic seven-stage sequence, in which the principal is left 'to pay himself off in kind remembrances', to review the memories buried in that letter.

474.01-477.30: Common to the various dimensions of these first few pages is a supine unconscious subject being observed from on high by watchers who arrive and begin to question him in an inquisition which frequently lapses into an argument among themselves. 'Yawn's' latent multiplicity is indicated in his posture, lying at 'one *foule* stretch' (my italics), and in his status as 'the map of the souls' groupography' — 'souls", not 'soul's'. From the start the examination is a collective self-examination as well; indeed the initial salutations, calling him 'kid', 'Chirpy', and 'chap' (477.14-17), may remind us of the apostles' iconic identity with man, lion (missing here, but mentioned twenty lines later), ox, and eagle.

477.31-482.07: 'Y?', Shaun/Yawn's first utterance, among other things, asks for the Y-girl, Issy, whose whisperings recently roused him. 'You have your letters', says one of the questioners, a statement that Yawn takes as referring to the 'godsends' letters (compare 269.17, 446.05) exchanged between Issy and himself, but actually part of an inquiry into the alphabet of his 'malherbal Magis landeguage' (478.09-10; compare 119.10-123.10). So they start at cross-purposes, Yawn hoping to find Issy ('Y'), his inquisitors meaning to locate and call up the submerged 'fatherick' (478.28) whose 'letter' is here the Earwickerian ⊓, or 'M'. Perhaps in defence

against their aggressive pedantry, Yawn mutates into Patrick
— put-upon servant of four masters, re-arrived interloper
under the hostile scrutiny of natives, relatively unlettered
French-born innocent who nonetheless finds the 'cloover'
shamrock, *'la clee dang les champs'* (478.21) hidden from his
examiners, still looking for 'her' — Issy, here as Patrick's
kidnapped sister Lupita. (The name also traces to *pater*,
father, thus accommodating the questioners' purpose.)
Patrick/Yawn's bleat about 'The woods of fogloot' (Patrick's
Wood of Foclut) and 'padredges' then elicits one of this
chapter's misprisions: Johnny, typical Connachtian sporting
enthusiast that he is (see 140.36-141.04), takes 'cloover' and
'padredges' as plover and partridges being hunted in Yawn's
'woods', and becomes nostalgic about the joys of following
the hounds, back in 'my little grey home in the west'. The
reminiscence in turn terrifies Yawn, who has cause to suspect
that if any hunting is done he will be the quarry, and who
accordingly translates 'woods of fogloot' into 'The wolves
of Fochlut! . . . Do not flingamejig to the twolves!'

Luke reassures Yawn, and interprets his earlier mention of
a 'barrow' (echo of the submerged barrel, relic of Viking's
'barrow . . . burialbattell, the boat of millions of years' —
479.24-6) as testimony about an invader's ship; as Connacht's
idée fixe is hunting, so Leinster's is sea-going conquerors.
Under this influence Yawn's wolves become 'Wolfhound!
Wolf of the sea' (480.04) — the 'dynast of Leinster' who as
the mother's ravisher (202.23-4) personifies the sexually
menacing father. Next enters the authoritarian Ulster, 'Emania'
(480.21), to make fun of Yawn's yelping about wolves and
bring the confession back to HCE (481.01-3), 'Ouer Tad'
(481.20), 'Mushame, Mushame' (481.26) — that is, to the
Shemian father as O'Connell-like progenitor whose stallion-
like prowess traces to the primal scene, and who as 'piercey', a
variant of I/2's Persse O'Reilly, comprises both father and
brother.

482.08-486.31: Hot on the father's trail, the inquisitors turn
the subject to 'Keven', the saintly Shaunian antitype known
to be good at unearthing relics (110.31-5) such as 'the dogumen
number one' (482.20). After some bickering the 'Cork examiner' Luke introduces a 'suspicion' that 'The gist is the

gist of Shaum but the hand is the hand of Sameas' (483.03-4), that behind 'counterfeit Kevin' lies the old scandalous story. Yawn responds with an outburst denying all relation to 'Sameas', then asserting his purity and (485.05-6) noble origins, pretensions mocked by Luke. The me-no-spikka-de-English voice which Yawn next adopts suggests he is being deliberately obscure, and the vision next conjured up suggests why: the first upright, then sideways, then inverted 'initial T square' which Luke places against Yawn's temple, lips, and breast recalls three stages of the primal scene, mythified — arriving Tristan, reclining Iseult (arms reaching up, hair hanging down), a phallic emblem of intersection accompanied by the sound of 'a hopper behidin the door slappin his feet in a pool of bran.'[5] We are approaching *the* forbidden region.

486.32-491.26: Accordingly, these next few pages may well be the most jumbled of all. Having conjured up the primal scene, the questioners now ask Yawn to similarly envision, in his 'iberborealic imagination', the nature of his relationship to the brother with whom he observed it. The first questioner is evidently Matthew, his aggressive Protestantism bringing forth images of 'odinburgh' and 'orangery Saint Nessau Street'. Trying to testify under such scrutiny makes Yawn uncomfortable, both because he wants to forget Shem and because his doctrinal grounding in such relational mysteries as consubstantiality is not sufficiently firm to withstand the scrutiny of Matthew's Protestant dialectics; on this level 488.04-12 amounts to the lame statement that someone he knows explained it all just last week, followed by a muddled version of the explanation.

Beginning at 488.19, the nefarious, 'irismaimed' exile-brother ('Jake Jones' — 487.10) emerges as a Joycean type with numerous sins on his head, the first of which is 'looking at churches from behind' — that is, at their apses. He is 'The heart that wast our Graw McGree!', variant of the abhorred McGrath who 'ought to win that V. V. C. Fullgrapce' (488.36-489.04) — as McHugh notes, the Victoria Cross, but also, splicing the two V's to make 'W', the 'W.C.' or Waterloo Cup won, first, by the hound 'Mister Magrath', whose win over the English entry in the Waterloo Cup occasioned a patriotic song,[6] second ('Anna' means 'Grace'), by the father-as-demon-lover, winning over the woman at Waterloo. (As elsewhere, Shem and McGrath overlap.) In all these capacities he is traceable to the passionate HCE from before the days of his 'roung my middle ageing' (487.16), a self now recoverable only by 'Thinking young through the muddleage spread' (491.08).

The testimony has edged into the subject of the schism, thence to the exile that confirmed it: 490.03-5 draws on both an episode from Joyce's youth[7] and his encounter on Nassau Street with the 'parambolator', the sauntering Nora who 'merrily . . . rolled along' (615.21), for whom 'he's been failing . . . over sense', with whom he left father, brother, and country; most of the confusing 490.06-491.05 seems to concern this woman. By the end of this section the questioner has become Cork's Mark, under whose influence Yawn's testimony is about '*Marak*'.

491.26-497.03: With the Mark of 'Tristan and Iseult' in the picture, the examination is 'getting on to dadaddy again' (496.27-8), initially called forth as bellicose martyr. An incidental mention of 'Annie Delittle' is enough to evoke ALP, who describes HCE with his 'tummy . . . maladies', heroically — and sexually — revived by her ministrations: 494.15-26 features various bizarre representations of sexual congress, with HCE as Saturn, a prowling 'Ural Mount', and a 'giant sun in his emanence'. In her enthusiasm, ALP blasts her husband's enemies, especially the odious McGrath ally 'Sully', whom she offers to help execute by hanging with her handkerchief (495.11-14), or even worse: she will put him under her bed and press him to death (cf. *Troilus and Cressida* III.ii, 198-200) by making boisterous love with a rival. As elsewhere, there may be more than indignation behind ALP's animus. Her concluding boast about a respectable connection with 'a handsome sovereign' rings a little hollow, especially considering the exchange that follows, in which she is told she has been 'misled' and replies 'Alas for livings' *pledj*ures!' (My italics.) In any event, this sigh signals the withdrawal of support for the father, who becomes a 'humbugger . . . boycotted and girlcutted' by male and female. After reviewing one version of the scandalous story (there are even nursery rhymes (496.18-21) about it), the witness is requested, probably by Matthew, to again 'identify . . . with the him in you', to end the ALP voice and bring up the father.

497.04-501.06: Yawn obliges with a heroic portrait based on his own situation: like himself surrounded by inquisitors, like the sleeper surrounded by four bedposts and those bedroom articles that fall within the lamp's circle of light, the father is 'circumassembled' by 'tallows' and children, here as colonials bringing tribute to their sovereign. That the occasion should be his 'Imbandiment' (compare 8.34), that he should be sitting 'with his buttend up, expositoed for sale' (498.34-5), and hailed with cries (499.05-12) recalling *'merde'*, Waterloo's *mot de Cambronne* — all this recalls the outhouse pose of I/1 and its associations. The inquisition has reached down to the dreamer's most sensitive memories, signalled by the advent of 'an earthpresence' bearing 'all that's buried ofsins insince insensed insidesofme' (499.25-6). Playing Virgil to the inquisitors' Dante, it ushers them into a babel (499.30-501.05) testifying to the consequences of those sins — betrayal, war, civil and otherwise, various atrocities, including the modern press[8] — through which we hear the dreamer's longing cry for Issy, remembered as his 'Brinabride'.

501-06-506.08: The source of the repeating 'Zinzin' has apparently been the ticking watch ('Watch!' (499.29)) on the bedside table, heard dimly as the sleeper begins groping his way to consciousness; as always a pyrrhic is taken as a signal from Issy, rousing the sleeper further. The babel which greeted the inquisitors as they made their latest breakthrough (500.04-501.05) was a form of psychic defence, a static of 'interfairance' (504.18) thrown up to distract the examiners — and yet, swimming up towards the Issy-sound, the sleeper in effect moves towards them as well: while they continue to act like divers making 'soundings' (501.12), he is now ascending (501.27, 504.14). The stichomythic colloquy which follows the regaining of contact constitutes a rare example of cooperation between the two parties, sleeper and inquisitors joining to evoke a pastoral version of the morning's weather, the lusty activities of 'the sire season' (502.30-1), even the associated scandal ('Julie and Lulie at their parkiest' (502.24)), then together celebrating the triumphant 'sovereign beingstalk' (504.19) which signalises the dreamer's desire.

This tree is among the most overdetermined of the *Wake*'s symbols. For one thing as an 'overlisting eshtree' it is probably St Patrick's crozier, the *'baculus Iesu'* burnt in 1538 as an object of superstition,[9] hence a relic of Yawn-as-Patrick, from some pages back. It is definitely a version of the father-as-begetter, witnessed from a 'hidingplace' (504.08) in the act of 'germination' (505.12) with the 'sinsinsinning' (505.09-10) mother by a 'knickknaver' (505.34) who when spotted is 'thundered at' (506.07) and chased away. Depending on perspective, it is either 'exaltated' (505.14) or a 'shrub of libertine' (505.21), in either case the source of the whole story; 'are you derevatov of it yourself?' Yawn is asked, and the correct answer is yes, he is, as is the whole family of 'The wittold, the frausch and the dibble' (505.32) — the cuckold, the *frau* and the double(s). The green, black, and grey flag flying above it (503.22-5) forecasts the glaucoma which is as always visited on the witness.

506.09-514.29: The witnessing continues. Broached at 499.35-501.05, the critical moments of the dreamer's life flash before him at their most immediate and least mediated, mingled with the events of the past day. Introducing this section is that archetypal watcher (peeping) 'Thom', here his usual besotted self (506.34-507.12). The language is distinctly old-womanish, the appropriate idiom for a round of gossip; Kate is coming through once again, echoing the *Wake*'s prying biddies.

Watcher though he may be, 'Thom's' most conspicuous affinities at the outset are with the father witnessed in Waterloo's watercloset. He is a decrepit fifty-ish Protestant, a toothless 'old forker' (507.35-6) who in the company of 'subligate sisters' (508.22-3) 'outandouts his volimetangere and has a lightning consultation and he downadowns his pantoloogions and made a piece of first perpersonal puetry that staystale remains to be. Cleaned' (509.33-6). No sooner is this double scandal of defecation and copulation reviewed than it fades into a riotous wake/wedding, with guests 'from all lands' coming to 'his innwhite horse' (510.30) to bear witness, pay homage and raise hell.

The 'row and a ruction' is both the wake fracas and a dust-up at the HCE-ALP wedding, in the latter capacity reviving images from the HCE-cad encounter of Book I, that paradigm of rivalry and usurpation: 'Magraw', a 'wedding beastman' dressed in blue serge, appears with hammer while the bells ring twelve in the background, which sound joins with the remembered knocking at the gate to conjure a struggle between blue-clad hammerer and black-clad sexton; meanwhile various others are 'gickling his missus to gackles in the hall' (511.01-13). As with the cad encounter, the issue is the woman and, a major source of conflict, HCE's suspicions about Sackerson, who as pub handyman is its hammer-bearer, and who is here named, first abusively (511.20) by a male, then wistfully (512.28) by a female.

Amid the society-page report of the wedding (the bride's outfit recalls her 'serical' — silken — birthday gift of a gown; the groom's the almanac picture downstairs) are signs that the suitor-battle in the hall reflects the ambivalence of the bride, whose sex in general is said to 'hereditate a dark mien swart hairy' (511.22), whose choice involves a 'circumconver-sioning' from old truths and a 'caecodedition' to new ones (512.15-19), whose yielding to the man who will 'appierce' her is accompanied with 'Suilful' and 'sallowfoul' 'sigh' and 'moarning' (512.25-6). Nonetheless yield she does, beguiled as always by his 'glancefull coaxing' (512.09) and his sailor's 'Megalomagellan' (512.05) get-up, settling down with him by a hearth where burn brown Irish logs and black English coal, portents of the two sons ('Malkos' and a black foreigner) to follow, reminders of the two lovers past.

Sure enough, the celebrants assume the features of the Chapelizod establishment — 'Jorn', 'Jambs', 'Issabil', the 'quartet'. They are simultaneously the outcome of the 'marrage feats', attendants, and witnesses/reporters participat-ing in a raucous serenade outside the precincts (identified with both Nora's Finn's Hotel (514.18) and Bloom's Eccles St. (514.15)) of a boisterous wedding/honeymoon/birth/funeral.

514.30-519.14: With the funeral come 'funeral games' (515.23), the wake 'ruction' which the inquisitors recall when they press Yawn to 'Go to the end', retrieve the 'sup-pressions' of his memory. Obliging, Yawn calls up a Shem's-eye vision of the father at his most imperious, lording it over his 'plantagonist' — which since HCE is sometimes Henry Tudor can probably be translated as 'antagonistic forerunner'. As in our account of I/1's return from the privy, this 'sarsencruxer' 'plantagonist' is dreaming about drink (516.24-30); when he is roused by the master's knock the incident mutates into a psychomachia between brother and brother, vegetarian and meat-eater, Irishman and Dane, etc; by the end of the account it is Armageddon, the remembered bell-ringing doubling as both the angelus (517.05) and a 'clang houlish like Hull hopen for christmians' (518.35-6). One consequence is the infliction of glaucoma: 'Only it was turniphudded *dunce*, I beg your pardon, and he would jokes bowlderblow the betholder with his *black* masket off the bawling *green*' (517.08-9; my italics). The real issue, as always, is woman: '. . . if never he *looked* on *Leav*erholma's again' (517.19-20; my italics). As in I/4, the encounter becomes the subject of a trial in which the testimony — here about the antagonists rolling around 'togutter' in the 'Black Pig's Dyke' (517.13-15), earlier involving two brothers and a pig in a 'mudstorm' (86.12-20), covered with 'stucckomuck' (91.01-2) — recalls with the usual crazy embroidery the 'bluddle filth' of Waterloo/Clontarf ('like their caractacurs in an Irish Ruman to sorowbrate the expeltsion of the Danos' (518.22-3)) and its repercussions.

519.16-526.16: The stern Matthew emerges and like the judge of I/3 (cf. 87.33-88.07) demands to know how Yawn could have witnessed so much on what by his own testimony (519.03-10) was a stormy night. Yawn passes the buck back to his interrogators, whose conflicting interpretations he has after all been echoing: 'It was told me as an inspired statement [cf. the ventriloquial Shaun (436.21)] by a friend of myself', he begins (519.30-1), then implicates, under various guises, all four of his inquisitors in a mad narrative (519.30-520.21) the main story-line of which involves a sequence of clerics and one 'African man'. Mixed-up as this report may be — and Matthew for one (520.27) is completely lost — it does take the heat off. Perhaps incensed by all the talk of priests, Matthew so far forgets himself as to address his witness, acrimoniously, as 'R.C.' (520.35) and make accusations about which his Catholic colleagues feel sensitive; the result is a time out for civil war. The 'inspired' Yawn is now treated as a medium (522.20-4)[10] taking dictation from spirits, a psychiatric subject (522.27-36, 525.06-10) revealing repressed selves, a perjured 'third degree witness' (522.27) pretending to be someone else. The father's voice will eventually emerge from this ventriloquy; meantime we hear a stage Irishman (522.33-6), Sylvia Silence (cf. 61.01-11), a newspaper account (523.14-18), and those two star witnesses from Book I, Treacle Tom and 'my inmate friend, Frisky Shorty' (523.21-525.05).

These last two return us to the idiom of the pub gossipers, discussing the famous encounter. The 'fender, alias turfing iron' (518.15; cf. 63.07-11) of that meeting is now 'a piece of fire fittings' (524.08) — hardly a step in the direction of clearing matters up, and yet there is evidence that things are getting, literally, brighter: a questioner has just asked Yawn if the truth has 'become to dawn in you yet' (523.07), and the salient feature to emerge from 'Tom's' testimony is indeed an HCE-type named Coppinger (there are also signs of the submerged Shaun, looking up at the water surface) who discerns 'by yon socialist sun' a school of seductive 'gillybrighteners' (524.25-28). The sun, that is, is beginning to show itself, glimmering through the shutter's cracks in the room's window, to the northeast, lighting up the pile of 'argentine' in the 'casement', bringing thoughts of the licence above the window (523.34-524.06) with its engraved temptresses, of the park outside it and the park-sin-girls complex (524.04-525.05), and beyond that the bay, up which the father (who as horse was just described as standing 'at Bay (Dublin)') (533.17) will now, as salmon, swim. 'Coppinger's' interest in the little girl-fish is obviously 'absexed' (525.08), and so is that of *Our Human Conger Eel*' (525.26), 'The great fin may cumule' (525.31) 'plying the rape' (525.34). That is why, in part, the gossipers of 523.21-525.05 now fade back to the inquisitors-as-fishermen, netting, gaffing, and landing their *'spermin spunk'*-laden prey, accompanied by 'the fourth and final version of the rann' which always commemorates the father's disgrace.[11]

526.17-532.05: Yawn speaks in the voice of Connacht's John — 'Walker John Referent' (526.19) — the right province to comment on fishing and the great outdoors in general, for instance the park scene whose account here is influenced by the seal of Dublin now becoming visible, with its two 'Nircississies' girls, set in an Irish countryside of glens, streams, and the ponds in which the girls peer. Thus cued, Issy comes through next, at her mirror and (Pond's) 'coldcream' (527.13), teasing her double (and HCE and Shaun) for having gone 'in the dreemplace and at that time of the draym' (527.05-6) — for having gone sleepwalking, for having reached puberty, for having gone to the privy, for having dreamed all this; she then fades away with a sentimental evocation of the wedding (528.13). All her talk of translucencies and doublings has been too much for the hard-headed Matthew, who likes things definite: 'Is dads the thing in such or are tits the that?'

The Issy interlude is interrupted by a 'crackling' sound from the fireplace, which sound the over-reactive Matthew takes as radio interference from the 'Moonster firefly' Mark (528.08), sending harassing fire from the south: the 'skullabogue cheek' he attributes to Mark accommodates both '*scealbog*', kindling, and the rebel atrocity at Scullabogue. His indignation at this propels him into a long prosecutorial speech which reads in part like an anthology of the *Wake*'s conundrums, reviewed in a high dudgeon. With its hectoring rhetorical questions about matters anything but clear, Matthew's is the voice of the utilitarian north at its worst — descendant of the 'sharp Ulster voice' of the student in *Portrait* (p. 193) whose intellectual curiosity is confined to wondering what will be on the exam, Irish equivalent of the 'bright young chaps of the brandnew braintrust' (529.05) setting up their hot-shot bureaucracy in America, natural ally of the 'Heliopolitan constabulary' (530.16-17), Sackerson, now called to restore order.

It is the fate of such types to be let down by the native Irish, and indeed the 'Sickerson' who shows up now is his usual lewd and pickled self. His demented testimony, besides inciting a ribald outburst from one of Matthew's mates (530.25-30), is the prelude to Kate's even more vulgar revelations. She gives a scullery-maid's version of marital lovemaking: the scratched back, the kicking legs, the red-hot face, the man's practice of fantasising an encounter with a younger female while performing, all described in the language of kitchen work.

It is a dismal picture of relatively current reality; with it, we approach the intersection between the dreamer's store of memories, of 'buried ofsins insince insensed insidesofme' (499.25-6), and the here and now to which he has begun to climb. Matthew calls for a 'final ballot' and orders the subject to be 'Off with your persians' (cf. *King Lear*, III,vi, 77-80) — the bedclothes whose removal will of course leave the sleeper covered by a sheet. (On 533.24 we are reminded of the Ku Klux Klan.) Hence: 'Arise, sir ghostus!' (532.04) (Arise, Augustus — as in great Caesar's ghost? Joyce's middle name was 'Augusta', a name buried in the 'Augustanus' of 532.11.)

532.06-538.17: The distant signal comes through: the ghost is raised, the telegraph message is decoded (532.20-5), the 'ouija ouija' board (532.18) spells out its message, the radio's 'superstation' is amplified to the point that the BBC can be discerned through the static (533.29-534.07), most of all the dreamer, groping up into consciousness, recalls the guilt-inducing message sent by 'a youthful gigirl frifrif friend chirped Apples' and seeks to disentangle it from memories of his 'ripest littlums wifukie'. First, however, he assumes one last voice, that of Oscar Wilde. The young Joyce, writing of Wilde, had remarked his supposed 'epileptic tendency',[12] thus associating him with a neural condition which the medical science of the time saw, to quote from the *Encyclopedia Britannica* entry for 'Epilepsy', as a 'regression to the unconscious . . . comparable to existence before reality had become part of the mental demand'. Wilde's childish whining is one of many instances of regression in this passage — evidence of the infantile region which the excavation has reached. It opens with the invocation of a city, Amsterdam, which as Leo Knuth notes is 'often abbreviated to A'dam',[13] and proceeds to HCE's renunciation of his distinctively infantile sin in the garden with 'Apples', the 'unripe' girl distinguished from his 'ripest' wife. Referring questions about his character to the spiritual instructor of his childhood, adopting the sign-off routine of a radio programme, the subject tries to conclude by fading off in peace (533.29-534.02).

To no avail, of course: the inquisitors tune him back in, as a BBC announcer. Thus exposed, he stages a counterattack on the libellous figure who as elsewhere answers to the description of both Shem and Sackerson, plus, in this case, the Matthew of Ulster who has been leading the inquisition; the villain's 'fallse roude axehand' (534.20), for instance, combines Shem's perjury and one of the manservant's icons with Ulster's red hand. Like the 'Oscar Fingal O'Flahertie Wills Wilde' whom Joyce charged with denying his mutinous Irish nature — the O'Flahertie in him — HCE repudiates his Shem-past by boasting of his standing in the hierarchy, boasting of the time, in fact, he had the honour of making a presentation to the king. Later this episode will be recalled as a case of what Americans call ass-kissing (568.24), and here as well HCE has presented the king 'with my allbum's greethims' (535.10-11). Aping the Wilde who — Joyce supposed — would have disdained his own 'Ibscenest' writing, then denying the charges like a defendant breaking down on the stand (535.13-21), the speaker becomes a type of the the mother-dominated Wilde, calling for his 'Mudder'.

In response the inquisitors, now as 'his nephos and neberls', give an ostensibly sympathetic review of Wilde's last years undermined by their words: they call him 'Felix Culapert' and ask 'How's the buttes?'; the 'O rhyme us!' with which he responds conveys not only 'Oremus!' but 'O ream us!', reminder of the broken-down figure who turned to Catholicism but continued to hanker after stable-lads. Harsh as the portrait of this 'spirit' may be, there are clear similarities between one notorious Irish exile and another, one of whom began his literary career by naming himself after the first Christian martyr, one of whom finished his by naming himself after the most famous.

The dandified 'rinunciniation of pomps of heretofore' with which the speaker of 536.28-538.17 embraces 'Scripture' is mainly a renunciation of 'Deuterogamy' — the sin of sexual relations with two, *deux*, women, one of whom is the Deuter, daughter. He thus turns back the alluring call of 'milady's maid', the dark enchantress disguised as white-clad innocent, the 'niggeress' named 'Blanchette', with 'talc slopping over her cocoa contours', whose fireplace call precipitated his fall.

538.17-547.08: The image of Issy/Maggy as whited sepulchre, dark lady covered with talc, leads into the next section, in which the man leaving dreams for daylight comes increasingly to think in terms of dark inner in conflict with bright outer: 'The chort of Nicholas Within was my guide and I raised a dome on the wherewithouts of Michan' (541.04-5). We may reflect that using the chortling impulses of the Old Nick buried within to raise a doomy tome into Michael's daylight world typifies the kind of dialectic that has been producing this particular tome, and indeed one of these pages' main subjects is the construction of *Finnegans Wake*, but now as light begins to creep in the Nicholas element is mainly subject to repression and exorcism: 'in morgenattics litt I hope, in seralcellars louched I bleakmealers' (545.27). The snakes have been chased from Ireland (539.36-540.02), pirates and highwaymen exterminated by a squad of hangmen (540.26-541.16), the Danes expelled (541.17-23), both the stone-throwing antediluvian offensively gonadal Deucollion and the black Shemian Duke Ellington/alien, with his 'Gothamm chic' (538.29-33, cf. 176.33-4, 197.03, 437.28-34), suppressed by the Duke of Wellington, now coming back into his own after a cycle of abuse, and the 'bare idears' (538.18-19) of the daughter replaced with the homey charms of that woman who has been here all along (540.03-8).

The result in many ways resembles a re-telling of the Waterloo/Clontarf father-son conflict which figured so prominently in I/1 and the chapters thereafter, this time from the perspective of the father, who now need not be on the defensive (contrast 36.21-34) when he 'testif[ies] to my unclothed virtue by the longstone erectheion of our allfirst manhere' (539.02-4). Indeed one way of reading those first chapters — remembering that the book circles around — is as a rebellion against the claims made here. The establishment is in the ascendant, and since the sun is coming up that means seeing it whole, the good with the bad. The new order may be magnificent; it is also tyrannical and stultifying (its poets are 'Daunty, Gouty and Shopkeeper' (539.06)) and, like all empires, sordid in many of its details, a fact made clear by the two-page report (543.20-545.14) cataloguing the dwellings of some of its least sunlit subjects. Indeed this pitilessly detailed 'haunted, condemned and execrated' dwelling

(544.10-11) is one version of the reality towards which 'Struggling forlongs I have livramentoed, milles on milles' (545.24), towards which the dreamer is ascending. So be it: 'let them all come, they are my villeins' (545.13-14). For a certifying seal on his imperial pose, HCE turns, in thought anyway, to the sunlit east:

> These be my genteelician arms. At the crest, two young frish, etoiled, flappant, devoiled of their habiliments, vested sable, withdrewers argent. For the boss a coleopter, pondant, partifesswise, blazoned sinister, at the slough, proper. In the lower field a terce of lanciers, shaking unsheathed shafts, their arms crossed in saltire, embusked, sinople. Motto, in letters portent: *Hery Crass Evohodie.* (546.05-11)

It is, first, the Dublin coat of arms (being lit up over the window), with its two semi-draped young women, its three flame-spouting castles (see the etymology of 'lance' in the *OED*), its crass motto about how everybody should be obedient and happy; second a future self-portrait of a man with two blackened eyes, one blazing red nose, and an unsteady, stuttering but still dangerous — and forked — tongue; third a pirate flag of skull (two eye-holes, one mouth-hole) and crossbones, recalling the days when HCE was ALP's 'man megallant, with the bangled ears' (620.07-8); fourth an emblem of glaucoma's work, a blind man done in black ('sable'), grey ('argent') and green ('sinople'); fifth a diagram of the house, with its two youngsters upstairs, its 'boss' in between, its rebellious underlings in the 'lower' region; sixth a heraldic pastiche of the Joyce coat of arms ('an eagle gules volant in a field argent displayed' — *Ulysses* 572) atop the Earwicker coat of arms ('coleopter' means 'earwig') atop the Shakespeare coat of arms as it ought to be (shaking spears), all with bend sinister; seventh a sytlised memorial of the primal scene, especially as enacted at I/1's Waterloo: the two beckoning jinnies, the sinister boss, viewed 'partifesswise' while swinking at his 'slough' or 'Living Detch', the three soldiers brandishing their weapons in retaliation.

In sum, the substance of *Finnegans Wake* now being brought into daylight, a 'holocryptogam' still 'surrounded by obscurity', destined to be 'draggedasunder' by the likes of us, posterity (546.11-24), the ones Joyce once boasted would require a hundred years (see 547.13) to unpuzzle his works. Standing in for us, the four ask their last question, a question asked by many a reader when *Work in Progress* was still in progress: 'What is your numb?' Putting their last pennies in the slot to get one more play out of the old Wurlitzer, they elicit from him a seemingly unsought testimony on behalf of his wife's fidelity: her rejection of the two alternative 'louvers' of rumour (cf. 546.32-547.03 with 202.32-203.02), his assurance that his fair daughter, the Perdita-like 'that which was loost' (547.07; cf. *Ulysses* 195) is truly the daughter of himself and his 'faithful [blonde] Fulvia', finally his memory of that daughter's fateful begetting.

547.13-554.11: I remarked earlier that much of this speech resembled an imperious father's-eye Wellington-eye recounting of Waterloo, that debacle tracing back to the father's sexual possession of the mother. In his peroration, HCE defiantly reaffirms his pride of place at both that event and the elopement which made it possible. Lover and city-founder, he has made his sea-voyage in two directions, that of eloper leaving Dublin bay and invader entering it to seize and settle the land around it. About this moment with his wife he tells us, 'I did raft her flumingworthily' (547.16), did rapt her away as on a raft, carried toward the bay on the 'tiding down' current (547.17), then as now heading down to the sea (like the floating barrel as well), until the waters mingle, 'male-stream in shegulf' (547.32-3); at the same time this raft-tending is also an act of 'norsemanship' (547.26), by 'dint of strongbow' (547.31) battling back the natives, staking claims, cutting ribbons, building bridges. As at the primal scene 'I bade those polyfizzy*boi*sterous [my italics] seas to retire with hemselves from os (rookwards, thou seasea stamoror!)' (547.24-6): the father, who being all kings is Canute, commands the sea to retreat and the boys, those boisterous ever-doubling witnesses, to get out, cursing in particular (cf. 11.01-2) the one who 'seasea' saw, and who will henceforth be a blackened rook stammering its story. (Cf. Chaucer's 'The Manciple's Tale'.) As usual, this brave beginning fades into routine. HCE begins dressing his wife in 'lumineused luxories' (a glance at the birthday-gift gown) and other pretentious 'Parisian' fashions (548.17-33) and fattening her up (550.08-17); meanwhile the elopement's nuptial-couch bliss fades into dreary habit — 'I took my plowshure sadly, feeling pity for me sored' (549.27) — and the wife, supplied with 'carrycam' and 'mopsa's broom' (550.20-1), begins changing into Kate.

Daybreak exposes such prospects, but it also brightens. Evidence of the new day's dawning light is everywhere in these last pages — in ALP's 'lumineused luxories' (548.27), in the allusions to jewels, mirrors, lamps, windows, to things glittering, shimmering, shining and flashing, in the representation of the couple's wedding night as a solstitial light-emerging-from-darkness festival hailed ('Soll leve! Soll leve!') with a Latin-French approximation of 'The sun rises!' (549.01-21), finally with all the overlapping vistas of room, house, grounds, city, country and world, now illuminated and spread out, with which the chapter ends. With this light, and the sleeper's growing awareness of it, we have come to the edge of consciousness, and in fact the last half page illustrates one of those curious hypnagogic formulations which the mental science of Joyce's day was beginning to notice: the child's 'Cry off' from upstairs (559.30) penetrates the sleeper's reverie about his city's roads and is transformed to the whinnying of coach horses travelling those roads, penetrates further to the memory of his recent inquisition and becomes the hee-hawing ass of 'Mattahah! Marahah! Luahah! Joahana-hanahana!' (554.10), penetrates further into the cherished memory of the wedding night with his Anna and becomes the orgasmic cry of 'damsells softsidesaddled' being ridden 'covertly, covertly' by 'priccoping gents', penetrates further into the guilty preoccupation with Issy and becomes the cry of a schoolgirl being whipped (horsewhipped?), 'for her pleas-hadure', by her schoolmaster. Roads, city, inquisitors, ass, nightmare, daughter, mother, girl, guilt — in short, these are some of the most common fixtures of Book III, and especially of this longest and most troubling chapter. Their collective cry is also, perhaps, a plaintive farewell to Shaun/Juan/Yawn/HCE/Porter as, swimming upwards, he finally approaches the daylight above.

TWENTY-ONE

Book III, Chapter 4

LIKE THE corresponding 'Ithaca' of *Ulysses*, this penultimate chapter is a home-coming, and is accordingly characterised by moments of re-acquaintance, recognition, putting-in-perspective. Its main subject is the home – the house in Chapelizod, the establishment gathered within its walls, above all the marital bed in which the sexual union that has caused such trouble is acted out. Its style is of a fairy tale finally coming to an end, re-orienting its young listeners as at the end of the Alice books, told by an older narrator lulling children with a they-lived-happily-ever-after whose characters turn out (children love this trick) to be versions of the listeners' own family.

But then, a fairytale is no simple matter, as we discover if we try to fix on the identity of the narrator. Parent is talking to child, all right, but in so doing so successfully mimics the listener's idiom – as parental story-tellers are prone to do – that often it is the children themselves who seem to be telling the story, about their parents; parent-addressing-child lapses into child-reviewing-parent, retailing, like all the *Wake*'s fairytales, the primal scene which so traumatised both parties. Accordingly there are a number of variations on the theme of 'mirrorminded curiositease', of for instance a character being able 'to look on itself from beforehand' (576.23-4), along with a constant interpenetration between the chapter's two main levels, that of the children upstairs and that of the parents downstairs. On the opening page, for instance, the four bedposts of the main bedroom look down on the 'twinsbed' of the boys, upstairs; later on the 'cry off' is both a little boy's cry from upstairs, waking the mother, and the mother's love-making cry – heard at the end of the previous chapter — waking and frightening the boy, whose cry in turn wakes up the mother . . . and so on. III/4 is persistently stereoscopic in this way, with sometimes peculiar results, as when the father who is on one level visiting his daughter's room upstairs overhears (through the chimney) the mutterings of the father who is on the other level talking to himself downstairs. Sometimes it is deliberately misleading about what is going on where, as in the cunning use of 'without' to describe the boy(s) lying 'how they are without to see' (566.21), both without seeing and without, seeing.

What he/they are/aren't seeing is the coupling of HCE and ALP, which (again, on one level) is apparently in progress from the outset; that is why the couple is described as 'Discovered' at 559.21, and why the father is in such a wax about it. In this capacity they are, throughout the chapter, 'hodypoker and blazier' (558.30), phallic male and lamp-holding woman — poses which go through a number of variations and will eventually come around again at the Waterloo episode of I/1.

555.01-560.03: At the beginning there is a sense of things about to be revealed. With the exception of Sackerson (556.23-30), the sleepers are all waiting for something, mainly an escape from the spectres of 'those good old lousy days gone by' (555.05-6) that have (for Kate, literally (556.31-557.12)) been haunting the household. Behind those spectres is the old Sackersonian figure, in various guises. He is the stone-thrower amidst the 'leavethings from allpurgers' night' (556.28), the serpentine 'ghoosth' of the invading sailor, 'in his honeymoon trim' (557.06-12), whom the twelve customers anathematise as 'old wireless' (557.15), as such the sea-going signal-sender who has throughout been telegraphically seducing Issy with spondees of the sort ("twill be, win me, woo me, wed me' (556.21)) we have just heard again. Before leaving, he has one last office to fulfil: the 'glimmer of memory' of his brave days supplies the libidinal charge for the coupling. The anaphrodisiac daylit world of 'half morning' (566.07), with its 'coverlets of cowardice' (558.27), forces both partners to hold and cherish what shreds they can from the fleeing dream-images (she imagines him as 'Magrath'

(584.05); he imagines her as 'like a maiden wellheld') in order to complete the act; the climax, dispelling these last shreds, is announced with a cock-crow (584.27) proclaiming day's triumph over the retreating spectre.

Before that dispersal, 'a cry off' (558.32) wakens us to the 'Ordinary bedroom set' catalogued on 558.35-559.16. The wife leaves to see to the child, taking the lamp with her (in the process leaving a temporary 'Blackout' behind, which blackout is also a self-censoring on the part of the witness; cf. 403.17), creating a 'Circus' of light that follows her down the hall as she bears her lamp aloft. The many conceits here on chess and similar games derive from the 'chequered staircase' under her feet. She is followed by the husband. (My references here and hereafter to 'wife' and 'husband' refer to emanations or doubles; on one level they remain below, being observed by children hearing this chapter's story.)

560.04-563.36: The illumination of stairways and corridors becomes the occasion for a survey of the house and its inhabitants: the camera, having been set in motion, pans back. The narrator accompanies the parents to the daughter's room — it isn't clear whether they actually enter or just remember the interior — and in imagery partly borrowed from the downstairs calendar picture describes her holding up her 'gracecup fulled of bitterness' as 'handmade' to her master (the alluring 'plikaplak' continues dripping in the background); s/he concludes — no doubt gratifying her female listener — with remarks on how much better Issy is than her little friends. The next stop is the boy(s)' room, source (563.01) of the 'cry off'. They/he bear traces of the recent submarine dreamscape (Shaun still blows bubbles, Shem is chewing 'sweets fished out of the muck'); Shem/Jerry in parìcular continues to be haunted by memories of the ordeal just undergone. The arse-side of this figure, we are told, resembles (on the other level, is) the rotund father of the present (562.33-5), the penis the skinny rogue of younger days.

564.01-570.13: Awake, the son sees the father's backside, which, doubling with the downstairs scene, fades into a vista of the father's-rear-as-Phoenix-Park, a sight which inevitably recalls the primal scene 'where anciently first murders were

wanted to take root' (564.29-30), as witnessed, first, by
'Jeminy', the twins (564.01), then 'with one snaked's eyes'
(564.34). The memory so alarms the boy(s) that the mother
reassuringly promises that the picture is just imaginary and
that the 'bad bold faathern' will soon be going away to Dublin,
an assurance which she reinforces with slapping sound-effects
imitating the trotting of his horses. The sun, she says, is rising,
shining on that top-of-the-morning travelling coach. There is
an interlude in which the household, waiting for the arrival of
this royal coach, becomes a court in 'waiting', in the 'half
morning' of near-dawn (566.07-25). Then back to the fear-
some sight of the father's rear etc., instantly mythified/
prettified into the landscape through which the coach is rolling; when the father turns, his erection becomes the centre-
piece of the almanac picture whose figures — dogs, horses,
rider, young woman ('Squintina plies favours') making her
offering — populate the festive homecoming scene which now
emerges. Pages 566.28-570.13 mainly relate this homecoming
and the celebrations surrounding it — bell-ringings, acrobatics,
fireworks, etc. — with typical Wakean exuberance; behind it
all is recognisable the fat Earwicker, 'restrained by chain of
hands from pinchgut', making the fealty to 'your grace's
majers' (arriving in his royal coach) which as in I/2 earns him
his name and title.

570.14-576.17: We tiptoe towards Issy's room, with its
northeast-facing 'sceneries' (the yard, the privy, the park,
Dublin bay), its elm brushing against the outside of the
window, its conduits — fireplace and water pipes — for sending and receiving secret messages by tree bark and leaf,
water and fire, shameful tricklings and whisperings: 'Listen,
listen! I am doing it. Hear more to those voices! Always I am
hearing them' (571.24-5). We seem to hear (what Issy, like
the 'Nymph' of *Ulysses* — p. 546 — has heard many times)
the semi-conscious muttering of the father coming up through
the chimney from down below. He is, in this account, recalling
the day of his elopement and marriage and the legal right of
'Accesstopartnuzz' he assumed at that time, held against the
'netherworld's bosomfoes'. Curious, and wishing to hear
more clearly, we open the door to her room (572.08-10),
and pick up the hypnagogic monologue which follows, about

the complications which have followed from that 'Access-topartnuzz'.

There follows a droning, legalistic account of HCE's fall and its consequences. As 'Honuphrius' the father has invoked *'droit d'oreiller'* with his daughter Felicia, violating her through the ear (Issy is at times the Virgin Mary, and HCE is forever sending out doves) with his muttered chimney-borne solicitations. His guilty secret has come to be known by the gossip Kate, here the too-loud 'Fortissa'. The vision of 'Magravius' (McGrath) he conjures to 'solicit the chastity of Anita' (ALP) combines manservant ('Mauritius' – the name comes from 'Moor', as in 'Othello' – said to be urging Magravius on) and HCE's own youth: McGrath is also 'emulous of Honuphrius'. Fortissa and Mauritius have some 'illegitimate children' – unnamed, but we have elsewhere seen signs that HCE fears the worst, fears that Sackerson is Issy's father. And that projected impulse 'Magravius' has a 'schismatical wife' of his own – 'Gillia', the 'Lilly Kinsella' of the book, as leader of the seven rainbow girls (572.36-573.01) this account's equivalent of Issy's looking-glass double, Lilith to her Eve, the one who yields to Issy's demon lover. Sure enough, 'Gillia' is here Magrath's wife, but 'visited by Barnabas, the advocate of Honuphrius, an immoral person', and 'tenderly debauched . . . by Honuphrius'.

The account goes on to explore the complications raised by the presence of the sons, the customers, the four old men, ALP's former lovers, and others – the whole nest of intrigue and thwarted desire into which HCE entered years ago when, with his Felicia-Anita, he became a family man. The transcript which follows considers some of the issues arising from that act. The difference between HCE's Protestantism and ALP's Catholicism (a difference which itself began as a marital dispute, 'Hal Kilbride *v* Una Bellina' (576.06)) comes up;[1] a parallel dispute over a 'debt' (574.10) has to do with the proverbial 'marriage debt' owed (and about to be paid) by ALP to her husband; there is a good deal of laboured *double-entendre* on this score. As elsewhere the testimony comes from Kate, who literally sings on the witness stand. The 'whew whewwhew whew' with which the passage ends turns out to be the whistle of HCE's resigned snorer's sigh

(576.10; cf. 577.36-578.02). It is the signal to return 'To bed'.

576.18-580.22: Back down the stairs and to the bedroom now, completing the circuit. This passage is largely a prayer (cued by the mother's prayer for her sleeping child — 576.14-16), for husband and wife in two manifestations — as travellers, returning 'down the scales, the way they went up', and as progenitors, returning to the marriage bed. Another return is temporal — 'eskipping the clock back' to the young 'bull-seaboob and rivishy divil' who once begot their brood in that bed and who are now being reincarnated in it through lust in part kindled by whispering memories of that 'rivishy divil', 'flispering . . . to Finnegan, to sin again' (580.19-20).

The couple is making love, reaffirming their sheltered intimacy ('Bolt the grinden. Cave and can em.' (579.08)), excluding rivals among whom ironically is a variant of that love-struck petitioner who first greeted the young ALP with the words 'I beg' ('Beggards outdoor. Goat to the Endth, thou slowguard!' (579.12)), producing the traumatic result ('I'm sorry to say I saw!' (581.24-5)). At the beginning of the journey, they were adults looking at incarnations of their young selves. Now the process is reversed: we are looking at 'some king of the yeast, in his chrismy greyed brunzewig, with the snow in his mouth and the caspian asthma, so bulk of build' (578.03-5). So is the stage set for the final occurrence of the primal scene, of young self spying on old self.

580.23-586.19: The 'cop' (Sackerson) is watching the swaying lamplight from outside, ready to report it to the mob, in whose custody the rumour fades into a boozy toast to 'the huskiest coaxing experimenter' (582.03) and his posterity, larded with sententious 'philosophical' talk, then dissipates (582.21-6) into the fragments of legend. The male figure of the coupling is pre-eminently a horseman, an identity inherited from the calendar picture, from Waterloo, and most recently from 554.08-9. He is a number of other male figures as well — Jupiter (both planet and god), because of his rotundity and flushed ('Redspot') face (582.31), Noah and Cain, being witnessed and marked, and various illustrious cricketers. All are represented as objects of wanted or unwanted attention, being seen 'when, keek ['peep', via the P/K split of Gaelic], the hen in the doran's shantyqueer began in a kikkery [cf. 314.04 and 348.17, where 'kick' suggests the Norwegian for 'peep'] key [recall the welter of anxieties surrounding the room's keyhole] to laugh it off, yeigh, yeigh, [cf. the jinnies' cry at Waterloo, to irritate the father: 'Yaw, yaw, yaw!' (9.04)] neigh, neigh [cf. 554.07-10] '. As always, the event will be publicised, by the policeman outside the window and others, 'Photoflashing it far too wide' (583.15-16). The language prophesies both the infamous photograph and Lucia/Issy, the fair-haired 'fiery quean' (328.31) conceived: 'Here's the flood and the flaxen flood that's to come over helpless Irryland' (583.19-20). After the climax, the couple sinks into torpid 'oldun' age (586.19) compounded by post-orgasmic dumps: 584.28-585.21 draws heavily on those 'acknowledgments' which often conclude some amateur theatrical or pantomime, signalling that the show's over, and the page that follows largely amounts to a catalogue of commonplace prohibitions and the gossip which day will bring.

586.20-590.30: The presence of the eavesdropping Sackerson starts a sequence of reports which leads to the final summing-up of his master. Because it is Tuesday, his day off, he is hanging around to collect his salary before departing. The computation of 586.21-5 does not, *pace* Louis Mink and Clive Hart,[2] indicate a time of either 2:57 or 3:57 (as we will soon hear, it is now 'Dawn' (590.25), an assertion confirmed by references to the morning trolley, the milkman, the rooster), but rather a prospective reckoning of Sackerson's wages, taken from the 'argentine' now sparkling in its pile in the sun-streaked 'casement'. Sackerson would like to 'sammel up all wood's haypence and riviers argent (half back from three gangs ['gang' — Middle English for 'currency'] multaplussed on a twentylot add allto a fiver with the deuce or roamer's numbers ell a fee and do little ones' (586.23-5) while — killing two birds with one stone — making sure that the window-boards are shut good and tight, completely closing out the sun: 'he would mac siccar of inket goodsforetombed ereshiningem of light turkling eitheranny of thuncle's windopes' (586.29-31).

Waiting in the outer precincts, he becomes, inevitably, the prototypical watcher/listener, and the sound he strains to 'seize' (586.33-6) is a variant of that trickling woman-water-wind sound which has already conjured up much in this chapter. That Issyan sound, described at 580.19 as 'flispering in the nightleaves flattery' and here as 'wind thin mong them treen' (587.02), is variously reported as 'Hiss!', 'Kiss!', 'Sish!', 'Phiss!', 'Briss!', 'Triss!', 'Trem!', and 'Tiss' (587.03-588.35). Under its influence, the watcher Sackerson fades into the watching soldiers, those regular fixtures of the park's greenery, whispering among the leaves about the famous park sin in language which occasionally (587.22, 588.06-7) reveals the Issy voice in the background and indeed eventually lapses into the idiom of her chimney-borne telegraphic 'Esch so eschess' (588.28).

'If I knew who you are!' (624.27), the wife will lament to HCE at the end; here her daughter's voice, at the book's formal, pre-*Ricorso* conclusion, initiates one last attempt to fix this man once and for all. He is a great tree, an Odyssean returner, a 'hugest commercial emporialist' and *paterfamilias*. Most of all, he assumes the identity earned the day he began the central relationship of his life, just now re-affirmed, by calling his bride-to-be 'Goldilocks'. Since at least 582.29 ('Hokoway, in his hiphigh bearserk!') there have been hints that he is becoming the bear to that fairy-tale figure; now the role is assumed definitively, courtesy of her golden-haired reincarnation, her words mingling with those of the testifying soldiers and echoing those of the disgruntled Kate (141.33-4), who has seen through such things: 'Sish! Honeysuckler, that's what my young lady here . . . she calls him' (587.19-21). And so he is 'Mister Beardall' (587.32) and 'Jimmy, my old brown freer' (588.13), coming forth, with a 'pay bearer' cheque (590.04), from the darkness on this first full day of spring to start again the cycle of which 589.12-590.03 is a final synopsis. Book III, which began with him in bed, closes the same way. Then was shame and a hasty 'Switch out' amid hints of disreputable goings-on; now is 'Dawn' and the honey-suckler in bed with (what more could a honey-seeker ask?) 'the queenbee'. 'Jeebies, ugh, kek, ptah, that was an ill man! Jawboose, puddigood, this is for true a sweetish man!' The purged, resurrected returner who began his long journey when he addressed his beloved as 'Goldilocks' and who now commemorates it with a flower-pattern fan perched above a bearskin rug ought to have been happy to know that his story would come round like this, with himself ending as a honey-sucker, a 'sweetish' man.

TWENTY-TWO

Book IV

BOOK IV takes place, as Clive Hart has shown,[1] 'at six o'clock shark' (558.18) in the morning, the hour of the author's birth.[2] We might accordingly expect to come across signs of some nativity or other, considering that the chapter early on calls for a towel and hot water (594.09-10) and eventually doubles back, by water, to the baptismal incantation of the first page (3.09-10), and in fact such signs are there to be found — notably the 'therrble prongs' of the last page, which as Leo Knuth observes indicate a forceps delivery.[3] As the *Wake* has taught us to expect, Easter (and Book IV is identified with Easter in many ways) looks both backward to death and forward to birth. Like the Biblical flood, the inundation which overwhelms the speaker at the end looks both back to the old covenant and forward to the new one. (Sure enough — turn round to the book's first page, and there (3.14) is the rainbow.)

In general, the chapter looks forward and backward on four main related levels. First, it is the last chapter of the book and prelude to the first; as everyone knows, page 628 continues over to 'riverrun, past Eve and Adam's'. Second, it is conspicuously set on the equinoctial end of winter and beginning of spring[4] : 'But receive me, my frensheets, from the emerald dark winterlong!' (603.08-9) (The bear of III/4, roused out of his hibernation, is 'Arcthuris comeing!' (Arthur plus Arcturus plus Greek *Arctus*, bear — 594.02), when 'clothed of sundust' (601.02) a whitened 'polar bearing, steerner among stars' (602.30).) Third, it signals the final suppression of the night-world, the 'making of Mehs to cuddle up in a coddlepot'. Fourth, it is the chapter in which the sun rises and conclusively triumphs over night.

593.01-600.05: Not without struggle, of course. The light streaking in is a weapon — 'A shaft of shivery in the act, anilancinant' (597.24) — evoking that mantelpiece picture, and achieves final dominion as an eschatalogical conquest, Patrick with his 'firethere the sun in his halo cast' (612.30) vanquishing the druid. Book IV is this text's 'Revelations', apocalyptically dividing light from dark; indeed the news event announced at the beginning is mainly the Millenium, or, as the 'collispendent' of 602.20 calls it, 'Deemsday'. HCE's rising from bed is a pattern for the resurrection of the dead, to be judged by a young, holy figure, come back after long absence (596.03-4), combining Jesus, Michael, Kevin, and Gabriel.

We begin with a medley of morning sounds. Two figures are addressed — HCE and his servant, that inhabitant of lower regions whose job it is to 'agnitest!' (594.02) the fire, the source of the crackling 'friarbird' of 595.30-3, then, since this is his day off, leave: 'Well down, good other!' (598.11)

HCE, on the other hand, is to 'rise'. In one sense the sleeper has been rising towards consciousness from this submarine 'book of the depth' (621.03) 'through dimdom done till light kindling light' (594.06) since about page 500. The journey continues in its sunward direction ('Even unto Heliotropolis' (594.08)), rising above the house and then the landscape until like Peter Pan or Chaucer's Troilus we can look down serenely on the world of men beneath us. 'Wisely for us Old Bruton has withdrawn his theory' (595.18-19) — doubtless as McHugh says a reference to Sir Richard Burton and his hypothesis about the Nile's origin, but also to the best-known of any old Briton's theories, Newton's theory of gravity, associated throughout the *Wake* with the fall which is being repealed. The levitation is acted out on another level: going on their picnic, HCE and ALP will head upward, to the top of Howth, there to 'scand the arising' (623.26).

No wonder, then, that the 'riser' should feel so expansive, even divine, that a hand holding something out to him — probably just his shirt — becomes 'A hand from the cloud . . . holding a chart expanded' (593.18), that he feels as if he's atop Wellington's monument (595.22). By 595.03-5 he sits, Zeus-like, viewing distinctive hill and water placement in the 'langscape' stretching below, having surveyed (595.10-17) all of Ireland's counties. A parallel ascent is occurring on a homier scale: the 'bride of the Bryne' noted at 595.05 signalises both the shore several miles off seen from on high and the Issy who was studying geography in II/2, and into whose room, with its stars on the ceiling, we levitate (finally!) on our way to the heavens (595.05-9).

From there it is a short jump to the room of that young man, called 'Kevin Mary' at 555.16, now waking upstairs. 595.34-596.33 describes this figure as a type of rejuvenated, 'renascenent' HCE, returning now to his proper domain after having been 'kidnapped' to the 'unthowsent and wonst nice' of the dream. (597.12-19 gives us a choice between the two realms.)

The daylight scene to which we are returning in his company is a 'divine' realm of 'brighter and sweetster', retrieved, by the grace of 'Diu!', after a long and 'scarce endurable' period of searching. The effusive guide to this 'supernoctural' realm turns out to be a 'clerk' named 'Time-o'-Thay!' (599.03) who no sooner orients us in time and space than he directs our attention to the mortal world we have just left — 'See you not soo the pfath they pfunded' — and invites us to wax philosophical about an 'Aecquotincts' of that 'socially organic entity' going through its pre-ordained courses below: 'primeval' conditions are as they were; sublunary life continues on its Viconian rounds; through all the bother and obscurity 'the gist of the pantomime' continues.

600.05-607.22: Some items of 'personal place objects' become discernible in the scene unfolded below — elm, stone, flowers,[5] various of the room's furnishings. The most conspicuous feature is a pool, with stream running to it 'from hiarwather' (600.08), its original the bedside basin, being filled (probably by the wife) with water from pipes which, like the fireplace, reach up to the 'hiarwather' of Issy's room, and which carry water whose ultimate source is those Wicklow mountains where according to I/8 the woman's life began, where ALP *was* Issy. For two reasons, then, it makes sense that the awareness of this flowing water should return us to the 'garden of Ireland', scene (600.12-14) of the fall that this female typically induces in men, particularly — 'Sluce! Caughterect!' — the cataract-afflicted father. Similarly, the boulders of the landscape are the sleeper's buttocks (600.26-9), the 'clangalied' of bell-ringings mutating in turn into maidenly voices celebrating Kevin are the pots and pans clanging down below in 'Kathlins . . . kitchin' (601.20-32), and the 'sundust' covering the returned Saint Kevin is just that, golden sunlight (at 580.21 it was silver, but that was a while ago) gilding his body.

The saint in question is Kevin because of his association with Glendalough, home of the best-known lakes in those Wicklow hills whose waters have just been tapped — so the body of still water on which we are looking becomes Kevin's lake there. Thoughts of Glendalough introduce thoughts of the star-crossed Kathleen, the memory of whose unrequited love gives the girls' chorale of 601.18-36 a plaintive tone as they urge him (like the waking bear) to come out of his cave and notice them. Joining with the girls to seek the temporarily obscured or hidden Kevin, the narrator apparently stumbles on our old friend the ass instead, 'afeald in his terroirs' (602.15). The reference and the passage which follow are puzzling,[6] but the search for Kevin seems to have taken us back to the drowsy HCE, lying beneath the bed's 'fore-coroners' like a pauper buried in Potter's Field, reviewing in the mental shorthand of headlines and newsreel images the worst of the dream's events; already the *Wake*'s traumas are becoming, literally, yesterday's news.

Such thoughts are soon overpowered with the breakfast smells arising from below. The departing barrel of Book III, still rolling out to sea with the current (602.11), meets its reflex in a wind-propelled 'Grimstad galleon', sailing into harbour, bearing that breakfast-bringing mail-carrying milk-man, 'Shoon the Puzt'. Thus encouraged to get up (603.07-9), the sleeper discovers that the night's sins of the earlier newspaper account (602.17-27) have become common knowledge (603.16) and that 'summum most atole for it' (603.30). Ostensibly a call for the book's resident bell-toller to ring the church chimes, this summons in fact will bring forth Kevin-Coemghem, on this Doomsday, to 'atole' for the 'crime'.

Kevin's gradual emergence is yet another sign that dawn is breaking, illuminating the 'triptych' of 'supposed windows of the village church' that Joyce ascribed to this chapter[7] (see, e.g., 603.34-6). Our ascending figure is approaching the precincts of light, presided over by a disarmingly Popeye-ish First Cause – 'Oyes! Oyeses! Oyesesyeses!...I yam as I yam' (604.22-3) – calling ('Oyes!') the heavenly tribunal to order, to command the blowing of the last trump. (He is also a tea kettle blowing off steam; five pages later 'Juva' will describe his Jove-like god as 'Old Head of Kettle puffing off the top of the morning'.)[8] Our guide into these celestial regions is Kevin, at 604.27 re-introduced emphatically. The set-piece narrating his 'centripetally' oriented voyage to the centre of 'concentric circles of land, water, land, water, land, hut, land, water, tub'[9] is probably prompted by what *Ulysses* (p. 694) calls the 'waterrings' of the basin water, circling outward from the drips from the faucet whose pipes, again, derive from the 'hiarwather' of Issy's room; hence the insistence on 'river Yssia', 'holy sister water' (605.12-606.01), etc. With its concentric circles, its nine orders of angels and other sacramental and sacerdotal catalogues[10] it is modelled to a great extent after Dante's Paradise,[11] which after all we should be approaching by now.

Partly under the influence of this conceit, the basin/lake becomes the Irish Sea, signalling a magnification which according to the laws of perspective requires that we imagine ourselves many times further up than we were. Simultaneously, Kevin's tub becomes an approaching 'ship of the British and Irish Steam Packet Company'[12] in an account retaining the sacramental overtones of Kevin's ablation: 'Bisships, bevel to rock's rite! Sarver buoy, extinguish!' (606.13) The resulting survey, beginning with the 'three Benns' being sought as landmarks by the ship's navigator, is presented as a nostalgic return to and last look at the scenes and characters of so many stories, especially (as usual) the story of the sin in the park. Having just undergone a baptismal cleansing, we are now able to view 'Old Toffler' – the name combines German and Danish to suggest a shambling, antiquated devil – and his notorious crime with easy condescension, along with the 'old Marino tale' whose moral turns out to be the comforting 'Great sinner, good sonner' (607.01-4). This moral is also the 'motto' of the family whose story is being illuminated, in 'charming details of light in dark' (606.21-2); the recording of HCE's sin ends up here as a stained-glass window or page of an illuminated manuscript.

With which benign resolution, it is time for the dead to rise, in a scene similar to Leopold Bloom's vision of 'every fellow mousing around for his liver and his lights and the rest of his traps' (*Ulysses* 106): 'That my dig pressed in your dag si. Gnug of old Gnig. Ni, gnid mig brawly! I bag your burden. Mees is thees knees. This is Mi.' (607.17-19)

607.23-615.11: Finally, the ascending spirit comes face to face with the 'firethere the sun in his halo cast' (612.30), and HCE greets the rising sun. On both levels the encounter is disorienting, and blinding. In fact for HCE it seems as much assault as encounter, for reasons which the wife later clarifies:

> One time you'd stand fornenst me, fairly laughing, in your bark and tan billows of branches for to fan me coolly. And I'd lie as quiet as a moss. And one time you'd rush upon me, darkly roaring, like a great black shadow and a sheeny stare to perce me rawly. And I'd frozen up and pray for thawe. Three times in all. (626.21-6)

'Three times in all' doubtless refers, as J. V. Kelleher first suggested and Louis Mink confirmed,[13] to the three recorded times when the Liffey froze over. But there is another incident being recounted here, from the history of *Finnegans Wake* itself — the times when the branches of the elm outside the window came barging through, into the room. The first time was at the end of I/2, when the window's glass shattered and the tree's 'bark and tan' branches ushered in the 'billows' of fog which obscured I/3. (For an earlier allusion to that tree's 'laughing', see 31.29-31.) The second time was in II/3, when a roaring northeast gust blew open the windowboards and the tree came rushing in as the wind-borne Norwegian captain, raw and piercing. And there has been a third time, on pages 609.24-612.36, when the wife greets the dawn by opening the windowboards, the tree stands forth royally in its 'all show colour of sorrelwood herbgreen' (611.34), and the sun-light 'which daysends to us from the high' (610.28-9) so bedazzles the man that like 'Bilkilly-Belkelly-Balkally' he is 'for shouting down the shatton on the lamp of Jeeshees' (612.33), for shutting the shutters on the sun, the lamp of Jesus.

Before this event, we are promised the imminent arrival of the sun-king 'Solsking the Frist' (607.28), of the king of heaven calling all souls back home by means of his horn-blowing herald, 'Loftonant-Cornel Blaire' (607.29), and of summer as winter's 'regn of durknass' is 'snowly receassing'. The narrator says goodbye to the strangely 'agreeable' mish-mash of the dream-world, now 'disselving', and gives a lingering glance at some of its inhabitants. The last-named of this crew, the twelve customers, blend into the 'millete-studinous windows' of the village church, suffusing with light. 'Obning shotly', they collectively announce (609.19); there will indeed be an opening, shortly, as the windowboards are flung apart and light triumphs.

As preparation for this Wakean Armageddon, we again meet, as Muta and Juva, the Mutt and Jute who gave us their commentary on that other crucial struggle, Waterloo/Clontarf, at the other end of the book. Their usual main subject, the risen father — here variously manifest as the sun, the steaming kettle, the elm (610.05-6), and Jupiter — is, like them, waiting to see which side will win. Juva informs Muta that this figure has bet 'holf his crown' on each of the antagonists, a comment which allows us to glimpse our old friends Shem and Shaun, two halves of the Claddagh ring's crown, behind the contest. Virtually undifferentiated at first, near the end of their dialogue they mirror the division of the approaching conflict: the 'hordwanderbaffle' which Muta requests is not only a hot water bottle but a baffling hoard of wandering words — that is, the *Wake* itself.

In fact a challenge to the book's dizzying night-time *muta*tions, coming from the re*juve*nation of dawn and Christianity, is a feature of the ensuing debate between 'Pad-drock and bookley' (611.02), spokesmen for, respectively, the rock of reality and the book's nighttime fancies. Considering that 'bookley' is in part Bishop Berkeley, we can discern Dr Johnson, kicking his stone, in 'Paddrock', so that once again a John-son squares off against a whiskey-soaked James-son. 'Bookley' is introduced as 'Bulkily', 'fundementially theosophagusted over the whorse proceedings' (610.01-2) — theologically expressing his disgust for the physical world whose main manifestation is the Waterloo horse-droppings recalled at 609.32-6. (These droppings are then 'Petrificationibus' — petrified to Johnson's stone.) He is 'twyly velleid' (610.14; compare *Ulysses* 48), his vision wrapped in a 'heptachromatic' (611.06) 'photoprismic velamina' (611.13) the better to screen out the 'Outsider' (610.18) world, now crashing and flashing in through the window, and allow him to contemplate the inner vision which 'emprisoms' (127.03) the 'Ding hvad in idself id est' (611.21), a noumenal reality which splices Berkeley to Kant and Freud. It is as predicted at 610.35 a losing battle, what with the sunlit outside breaking in; by 612.34-5 'bookley' is reduced to sticking his head up his arse — hardly what he had in mind when he began his search for 'the true inwardness of reality' (611.21).

The debate in which 'Paddrock' prevails over 'bookley' is among the least paraphrasable things in the *Wake*, partly because Joyce mimetically renders the chaotic effect of dazzling sunlight irrupting on weak vision (and, on the Armageddon level, God appearing to a benighted humanity) with a passage of wildly fractured syntax, partly because every statement, in this final enunciation of principles, is so thoroughly 'puraduxed' (611.19-20). Very generally, the debate is this: the druid says that since sight must involve selective blindness — the colour we think we perceive is really the one part of the spectrum which is not there — in the pursuit of truth we should turn from this self-occultation we miscall vision and seek the image of the full rainbow world by looking inward to that microcosm, our soul. Although his impatience leads Patrick to miss a good deal of the multilayered argument (for one thing, he is humming to himself during much of it — monotone answering polyphony) it does occur to him that, after all, what you miss today you can pick up tomorrow (611.25-6), that in effect we can piece together the rainbow, colour by colour, over time.

One thing at a time: it is the answer that the authors of the Bible might have given to the author of *Finnegans Wake*, with its portmanteau syncretisms, its lust to say everything at once: we understand, I think, why the Archdruid is 'bookley', defender of the book now ending. (Patrick's fire may portend a Shaunian book-burning.) For his part, Patrick is not disturbed that the tree in the window — here as 'Uberking Leary' — should be 'tinged uniformly' in just one colour, green (611.33-612.15). In fact the monochromatic sight inspires him to Ireland's best-known case of someone's making the most of the here and now: he plucks and displays the green shamrock as 'the sound sense sympol in a weedwayed-wold of the firethere the sun in his halo cast' (612.29-30), a sound and sensible symbol in a green and weedy wilderness of the fire which is nonetheless *there*, of the spirit serially revealed in matter. The God for whom he speaks is not an *arcobaleno*, rainbow, but the reverse. 'Great Balenoarch', a no-nonsense sort whose initials G.B. may remind us that in the *Wake* all Irish invasions, whether by Patrick or the notoriously drab British, are the same. Thus does Johnson kick the stone.

Since opening the window on the sun temporarily blinds the rising sleeper, the green-vs.-rainbow debate repeats a familiar pattern of the *Wake*'s ubiquitous glaucoma theme, and indeed there are indications (613.08, 613.17-21) that the waking to light is on another level a descent into blindness. HCE, dazzled by outer brightness back into inner darkness, is despite his condition up and getting dressed. There is a good deal of rousing talk about the things to be done anew in the 'trancefixurashone' (613.09) of the new day, one of them being the drinking of the laxative (613.22-6) which in twenty pages, as the *Wake* turns, will result in HCE's trip to the privy. As for the return to paradise, where we are all to appear washed clean by the 'Annone Wishwashwhose' laundry (614.02-3) — well, this heaven is more Neoplatonic than Christian, is in fact a kind of tiring-room where everyone drops old identities and assumes new ones, becoming a 'new-manmaun' (614.14) in preparation for another go-round below. The same voice that recently brought us up out of sleep (608.33-5) now orders us to 'Forget!' (614.26) — forget the dream now over, the old life left behind. The Viconian 'gazebocroticon' (614.28) which begins its workings once again I take to signify mainly what 'the whole ghesabo' sig-nifies to Leopold Bloom (*Ulysses* 374) — the physical universe, with its laws.

615.12-619.15: Rising is accompanied by the second break-fast of the book, the first having been the late affair which prompted the 'letter' of I/5. Now once again ALP, accompanied with 'cup, platter and pot . . . piping hot' and 'eggs' (615.09-10), addresses her husband in a gossipy apologia mixed with references to the breakfast fare (615.26-7, 615.31, 616.21-4, 617.12, 617.20, 618.07-10), the result being the *Wake*'s final instance of her letter. Although this breakfast/letter apparently extends to the end of the book — the last word, 'the', is French for 'tea', which I/5 taught us is the letter's last sign, and as in I/5 it is accompanied by kisses, there as 'XXXX', here as a series of 'Lps' — the familiar motifs are clustered within these next four pages, to which ALP's farewell (619.17-628.16) is a postscript.

A postscript and also a retraction. Whereas 615.12-619.16 is notably truculent, the 'farewell' that follows is forgiving and resigned, to all appearances an acceptance of the circumstances against which the earlier pages rail. It may be that the earlier passage represents the last traces of ALP's own purgative dream, that her graciousness is made possible by an earlier exorcism of accumulated animosities. Certainly ALP spends most of these four pages conjuring up, abusing, and dismissing her nemesis, who as in I/5 is consubstantial with her husband's buried Shem-past.

She begins (615.12-616.19) with an affectionate salutation and thanks addressed to her husband, probably for the gift (compare 624.21-2), and goes on to a recollection of their meeting and early days together, interspersed with harsh words for the 'Sneakers', 'me craws', 'slimes', 'douters', 'reptiles', and 'snigs' who seem inseparable from these memories. In the next paragraph (616.20-618.19) she focuses on one particular 'coerogenal hun' who becomes increasingly difficult to distinguish from 'that direst of housebonds'; indeed that dearest of husbands has been the source of her direst enemies: he 'would pellow his head off to conjure up a, well, particularly mean stinker like funn make called Foon MacCrawl brothers' (617.10-11). 'Fing! . . . Fing him aging!', she urges, jolting her ageing husband 'to weke' in an action uncomfortably similar to the pummeling of the sacrificial 'Mawgraw' (377.04) of II/3. Waking up, like the Armageddon/reincarnation which parallels it, is a story of suppression as well as exaltation. Asking her husband to rise and greet the

day, ALP is ordering that part of his past which most enliven-
ed the dream to get lost, and at least sometimes (e.g. 617.12-
14) she suspects how indistinguishable the two may be.

In 617.30-618.34 ALP defends herself against her enemy's
charges. She concludes this prelude by affirming that the
'Nollwelshian' scalawag 'has been oxbelled out of crispianity'
(618.34), that although 'Hence we've lived in two worlds',
with 'another he' sleeping 'under the himp of holth', 'The
herewaker of our hamefame is his real namesame who will get
himself up and erect' — the real HCE is now getting up, leaving his false namesake underneath, provided only that 'young
as of old . . . a wee one woos', that Issy, ALP reincarnate,
call to him (619.11-15).

619.16-628.16: ALP's 'P.S.' names this 'wee one' as 'Soldier Rollo's sweetheart', enamoured anew of that atavistic
marauder, the Norman invader (see Mrs Glasheen's gloss on
'Rollo' and 'Rolf Ganger', along with her citations)[14] who
throughout has been identified with the dashing young HCE
now suppressed, and for whom the *Wake*'s females have a
weakness. She is 'fetted up now with nonsery reams', fed up
with the *Wake*'s reams of nonsense (which nonetheless have
'feted' her) and ready to leave the nursery to become a
woman, to 'rain' (627.11) in the mother's stead. If one of
these women (and books — the one just ending; also the old
gown) is a sad story of 'Rags! Worns out', the other is a new
story altogether: 'But she's still her deckhuman amber too.'
'Document number two', apart from being a phrase from
Irish history, describes the *Wake* when in a few pages we will
commence a second reading of it — another document altogether. ALP will be a new human when decked in her new
gown (by her 'wonderdecker' — 620.07), recovering the
young woman she was when she had ('she's' contains both
'she is' and 'she has') the number-two sailor-lover of the
'Soldier Rollo' type described at 202.33-3. This is to say she
will once again be the amber-haired Issy, the blonde young
woman her husband conjured into imagination at their first
meeting long ago, and into reality with the conception of
their daughter.

It follows that in her concluding monologue ALP, mindful
of her recent observation that HCE will get up when 'a wee

one woos', tries to reincarnate that golden-haired apparition mixed up with both her past and her future; as in I/5, her letter is a 'kissmiss coming' (624.06), resurrecting her old lover as the prince's kiss did Snow White. As in *A Midsummer Night's Dream*,[15] the rising sun has gilded the flowing river which, on a level becoming increasingly prominent, she is. So she is justified in referring to 'me goolden wending' (619.24) and, while wending goldenly out to sea, recalling the meeting when she was 'leafy, your goolden' (619.29). (The green gown is also leaves scattered on the river's surface.) She is at her speciality, play-acting, encouraged by the blindness which makes her husband the perfect audience.

It also makes her more tender to him since, as Leopold Bloom seems to suspect (*Ulysses* 182) and Joyce speculated, she finds it mysterious, therefore interesting:

> W drawn to a blind man, to see behind closed eyes (Bluebeard), to give helping hand (woman's) to pity him who cannot see Her beauty, to be thrilled by the sin he did against a goddess or a woman or a queen[16]

So ALP to her husband: 'I'll be your aural eyeness' (623.18), with 'aural eyeness' conveying — in addition to 'royal highness', sound ('oral') and sight ('eyeness') — Latin *aurum*, the 'goolden' 'goldylocks' of the first meeting. Returning that favour, she completes the cast of the fairy tale: 'Come! Give me your great bearspaw, padder avilky' (621.20-1). Thus is *Ursa Major*, the bear who terrorised the boys of II/3 as the Russian General and who has been stalking through the narrative ever since, now gently brought back, not to reality exactly, but to the play-acting with which these two began their history together. The poignance of ALP's concluding monologue is mainly, I think, due to this woman's awareness of how much of that history has been a matter of play-acting, and to her determination to keep it up despite the approach of reality and mortality. Issy, ALP, eventually Kate (and, doubtless, a chastened author) coexist in suspension, lamenting the 'leaves'[17] of the book, their depleted number a sign that the story is about to end.

The outline of this last nine-page paragraph is clear enough. Having got her husband up, ALP helps dress him while de-

scribing the picnic trip to the top of Howth that they have
planned for this day, the result being that as usual the text
incorporates both actions, both a man being made ready to
go out and a couple taking a walk, making an ascent, and
looking down on among other things the scene where that
other couple are still talking. It may be that the first of these
two levels is entirely fictive, a word-pantomime similar to
Edgar's beguilement of the blind Gloucester. (Why, after all,
should a blind man want to climb a hill? Not for the view.)
Roland McHugh believes that HCE remains 'motionless in
bed' until the end,[18] and on one level this may well be true:
ALP boasts that 'I could lead you there and I still by you
in bed' (622.19-20), and seems to hint that something of
the sort is going on when she tells her husband, 'Rise up
now and aruse!' (619.28-9)

If the end (and thus the beginning) of *Finnegans Wake* is
a ruse, it is a persuasive one. It begins as ALP finishes dressing her husband and painting a glorious picture of how he
looks, like the 'exsogerraider' he was when young. He is, she
lies, hard to distinguish from his younger self: 'You make
me think of a wonderdecker I once.' Beginning at 620.10,
she then urges her husband to come with her on the long-
planned picnic.

The departure has other, graver, dimensions: the thought
of it leads her into surveying the establishment they are
leaving (620.11-621.06) in a mood continuous with her later
'I'll slip away before they're up. They'll never see. Nor know.
Nor miss me' (627.35-6), and culminates in the haunting lines
'It's Phoenix, dear . . . Since the lausafire has lost and the
book of the depth is. Closed' (621.01-3). As the book has
long schooled us to expect, this resurrection is also an interment, this waking a wake: HCE is urged to shed his burden-
some 'rucksunck' (621.06-7), to — borrowing Molly Bloom's
(*Ulysses* 751) image for regeneration — burn off his 'old
fletch' (621.33; 621.24-7), to join in repudiating that decrepit
old Adam, 'MacGarath' etc. (622.04-8), 'before in the timpul
they ring the earthly bells' (621.33-4). Joining him in darkness, ALP promises 'to close me eyes. So not to see' (621.29),
to be with him 'in thadark' (622.15), the result a deathbed-like
sequence of flashbacks from their past lives, real or imagined

(621.29-32, 622.16-19) culminating (622.23-623.03) with the *Wake*'s last recall of the calendar picture, that ambiguous testimony to HCE's eminence.

Thus summoned up, this image, with its publican standing before an open door, fades into a vision of the earl of Howth Castle (and Environs) standing before his ever-open door — and so they are almost at the destination. Next is the ascent to the top (623.20-6) from where, like the Blooms at the end of *Ulysses*, they can view the vista beneath them and the wife recalls an earlier visit during her maidenhood when a friend advised her the time had come to get married (623.26-7). She took that advice, and much of what follows surveys her husband's courtship of her and its consequences. The letter in the bottle that she is watching to see 'cast ashore' below doubles as a memory of her arriving sailor-lover, 'After rounding his world of ancient days', coming 'With a bob, bob, bottledby'; below is the 'bankaloan cottage' where she 'made me hoom' with her man; the contrast between their perch of the moment and their plot of ground below configures the contrast between her husband's aspirations ('Tilltop bigmaster, Scale the summit!') and achievement ('All your graundplotting and the little it brought!').

'Howsomendeavour', she sums up, 'you done me fine' — all in all they have made out as well as could be expected. Contemplating the fury and folly of the past and the 'bitter ending' coming on, she exerts her Scheherezadian powers ('I will tell you all sorts of makeup things, strangerous. And show you to every single storyplace we pass.' (625.05-6)) to reconcile him, and herself, to age and finally death. She tells him stories of past exploits — of the days, for example, when his now-vanished teeth were powerful enough to eat lobsters in their shells — and diverts him with improvisatory pantomime even while urging him on (625.21-2) to the end which is now just two leaves away. (Speaking for the book, she promises, truthfully, that 'I'll begin again in a jiffey' (625.32-3).) My, but he was something to behold in those days! A blast of north wind comes through the window (626.04), like the 'rebellious northers' earlier blowing up Issy's skirts (437.04-6), like *the race of the saywint up*' the '*ambushure*' of the Liffey (201.19-20), like any number of other sea-wind invasions of female precincts, and the HCE called to memory is a version of her seagoing lover sweeping in from the north, 'the pantymammy's Vulking Corsergoth' staging 'The invision of Indelond' (626.27-8).

But that was in the past, when she was the 'princeable girl'. 'Like almost now', she comments, and the 'almost' is enough of a concession to signal her final resignation to time and tide. She gives up attempting (e.g. 626.03) to mimic the daughter now growing into her former place, and with the relinquishment her voice modulates to Kate's. Paralleling the river's rush into the sea's bitter waters, she sees herself 'among' the company of 'the seahags' — her people, she now says — joining in a savage ritual resembling, and perhaps meant to recall, that of the mediaeval women who during the height of the witchcraft trials 'thronged in multitudes toward the sea, and often, as the blue waters opened to their view . . . chanted a wild hymn of welcome, and rushed with passion into the waves', immolating themselves.[19]

With the arrival of the book's last leaf and the departure of the gown's last leaf,[20] she lies naked and amazed under the imagined/remembered onrush of her cold father/lover: 'If I seen him bearing down on me now under whitespread wings like he'd come from Arkangels, I sink I'd down down over his feet, humbly dumbly, only to washup.' 'Bearing' sounds the 'Goldilocks' story; 'Arkangels', far to the north-east, is the source of the icy polar wind sweeping her away, plus the Russian bear/general over whom there was such a pother. But as McHugh says, the vision unquestionably contains as well Noah's dove, bringing promise of refuge from this flood, and the dove of the Annunciation.

The reflection on *Finnegans Wake*, now losing its last leaf, is similarly double-edged. Doubtless we ought to hear the author here scattering and drowning his book, like Prospero at the end of Shakespeare's swan song (see *Ulysses* 212). But there is another literary tradition at work here as well, the tradition of the *envoi*, sending the completed book out on the waters of circulation like a letter in a bottle, and wishing like King Hamlet's ghost that its readers may 'memo-mormee!'[21]

There is I think in this last appeal an echo of the infant

Joyce remembered by his brother:

> Stories were told ... of his habit, at a still earlier age
> [than four], of coming at dessert time down the stairs
> from the nursery one step at a time, with the nursemaid
> in attendance, and calling out from the top of the house
> until he reached the dining-room door, 'Here's me! Here's
> me!'[22]

Thus, on the verge of extinction, the same cry as at the
beginning of life: 'Me! Me! More me!'[23] And the end is also
a beginning, of a life and of a book. The flood of page 628
will be followed immediately by the rainbow of page 3,
the waters of drowning are also the waters of birth, and our
crafty old maestro is cranking up to run his 'hornemoonium'
once again.

Books III and IV round out the seven-stage sequence
which structures the whole book. Under the inquisition
Shaun has paid 'himself off in kind remembrances', summoning up his past like the Joyce who when convalescing
after his eye attacks 'saw before his mind's eye a cinema
of disagreeable events of the past',[24] killing 'his hungery self
in anger as a young man' as he conjures and exorcises Shem.
With that, we are ready for the recirculating flood of Stage 7
— that flood which carries ALP out of the book and us back
to the ocean voyage with which it begins again.

Notes

INTRODUCTION: 'MIMESIS', pp. 1-8
1. Ellmann, 564.
2. Power, 107. Power's reminiscence is full of similar passages. Compare August Suter's account: 'I was working on Joyce's bust, and he explained to me that he had just been working over a scene in which someone was pouring beer into a glass and that the noise — "glou glou" — was like that of sacrificial wine upon the altar. The Holy Father himself, Joyce said, would have to smile. He was faithful to his sensations and associations — they were realities to him, and I did not get the impression that he wanted to parody or ridicule; his sole intention was to present accurately the real effects of noise or similar phenomenon, especially in the quietness of mental absorption' (Suter, 196). The passage Joyce was working on must have been 345.16-26.
3. McHugh (1981), 28.
4. Compare Hart (*Structure* 1982), 147.
5. Ellmann, 382.
6. This last term has been contributed in Dorrit Cohn's authoritative study of the practice, *Transparent Minds*. Also see Kenner (1978), 18.
7. Beerbohm, 137.
8. Benstock (1982), 120.

ONE: 'PLACE', pp. 9-36
1. Ellmann, 16.
2. Letter to the author from Mrs Keenan, 31 May 1982.
3. Letter to the author from Mrs Keenan, 31 May 1982.
4. Mink (1978), 507.
5. Letter to the author from Mrs Keenan, 31 May 1982. My thanks as well to Mr Peter Costello, who has ascertained and documented several of the facts in this last paragraph.
6. See also Gordon ('Secret', 1981), 451-2 for speculation that the Blooms' house may also feature a sound-conducting chimney.
7. Glasheen (1977), 221.
8. 'G.O.M.', 143-4.

9. Burrell (1980), 95-8.
10. See Benstock (1969), 7-8 and Aubert, 116 for other evidence that HCE's sin involves masturbation.
11. Ruth von Phul gives a slightly different version: Von Phul (1957), 31. See also Grace Eckley in Begnal and Senn, 234.
12. 'Cranly wore a very dirty yellow straw hat of the shape of an inverted bucket.' — Joyce (1963), 113.
13. Senn, ('Queries' 1966), 47.
14. McHugh (1981), 8.
15. *Larousse*, 566.
16. Hayman (1958), 165.
17. Joyce (1959), 72.
18. Joyce (1966), Vol. I, 52.
19. Norris, 45.
20. Mercanton (1967), 20.
21. Rose and O'Hanlon ('Constructing' 1980), 7. The authors point out the following line in Joyce's notes: 'E lends clothes to Δ'.
22. McHugh (1981), 64.
23. Joyce (1966), Vol. I, 269; see also Glasheen (1977), 270.
24. Ellmann, 268.
25. P. W. Joyce, 344.
26. Benstock (1965), 273; see picture on p. 165.
27. Yates, 191.

TWO: 'TIME', pp. 37-43

1. Gordon (1981), 157-61.
2. Bayley, Vol. I, 94.
3. Halper (1983), 29-46. Clive Hart, who resists pinning the book down to one date, nonetheless argues that it 'begins and ends at the vernal equinox' (Hart (*Structure*, 1962), 73). Like Halper, Mrs Glasheen notes the echo of 'ram' in 'Tristram' and concludes that the book begins in Aries, but her month of choice is April (Glasheen (1965), 8).
4. See my *James Joyce's Metamorphoses*, 160.
5. Mink (1978), 313.
6. As I have pointed out elsewhere (*James Joyce's Metamorphoses*, 159, 192) the summation of HCE's career at 589.12-590.03 comes, numerically, to fifty-six. Two entries in Joyce's notesheets also seem to support this number: 'M aged 56 years' (Connolly, 82) and 'biography begin in middle at 28' (Hayman (1978), 31).
7. Budgen (1967), 294; see also Halper (197), 273-80.
8. Ellmann, 593.
9. Hayman (1963), 200.
10. Joyce (1966), Vol. I, 214.
11. McHugh (1976), 72.
12. Mercanton (1968), 40.

THREE: 'MALES', pp. 44-62

1. McCarthy, 109.
2. Ian MacArthur notes that HCE's white horse 'symbolizes his back-side': MacArthur (1977), 44.
3. Edward A. Kopper remarks that HCE is 'getting heavier from two much food and drink': Begnal and Senn, 119.
4. Norris in Henke and Unkeless, 207.
5. Jarrell, 275.
6. Begnal and Senn, 119.
7. Epstein, 73-106; compare as well Mark L. Troy's observation that at times we can 'discern the distinctive image of Osiris seated upon Set' (Troy, 40) — that is, a Shaun type atop a Shem type.
8. Devlin, 31-50.
9. This point has been partially anticipated by Clive Hart, who in suggesting an identification between Sackerson and the Norwegian captain of II/3 also demonstrates that both figures share certain Shem features: Hart (*Structure*, 1962), 125.
10. This correct spelling has been discovered by Pádraic Ó Laoi (1982), 33.
11. McHugh notes that HCE 'has a competitor in Magrath', though he takes the competition to be one of business rivalry: McHugh (1976), 127.
12. The connection between McGrath and Shem seems to have occurred to Halper: see 'Twelve O'Clock in *Finnegans Wake*' in Halper (1983), 25.
13. Solomon, 16.
14. Herring (1977), 44-5.

FOUR: 'FEMALES', pp. 63-90

1. Hart (*Structure* 1962), 60.
2. Mink (1978), 382; see also Connolly, 95.
3. See Mink 382 (1978) for a list of this motif's occurrences.
4. Mink (1978), 382.
5. Ellmann, 564.
6. Ellmann, 561.
7. Begnal and Eckley, 43.
8. Cheng, 184.
9. Glasheen (1977), 182.
10. Glasheen (1977), 169; see also Eckley (1971), 177-8.
11. Peter Costello has found that Mrs Keyes is first listed as proprietor in 1894, and was still owner in 1918. She was almost certainly related to the Alexander Keyes of *Ulysses* (Letter to the author, 16 March 1984)
12. Nutt, 134-5.
13. Unsigned translation in *Transactions*, Vol. II, 7.
14. For an intriguing array of Cinderella lore incorporated into Issy's characterisation, see the chapters 'The Fair Shulamite' and 'Cinder-

ella' in Volume II of Bayley's *The Lost Language of Symbolism*, a book which Joyce evidently knew well, as David Hayman has suggested (Hayman, 1958, 139). It connects the legendary Cinderella with Isis, Cordelia, and the names 'Lucia', 'Isabel', and 'Sin', details her traditional blonde hair, her dress 'of all colours', and, in one version, the seven maidens accompanying her, and records the following chant associated with her: 'Darkness behind me, light on my way,/Carry me, carry me, home to-day.' (Compare *Finnegans Wake*, 628.08-9.)

15. Mink (1978) 190, 540.
16. Joyce (1966), Vol. II, 237.
17. Gordon (1982), *passim*.
18. Ellmann, 550.
19. Norris (1976), 45; see also Sheldon Brivic, who in his essay 'Joycean Psychology' (Peterson, 108) calls attention to a passage in one of Joyce's notebooks describing Shem as 'observing a coitus'.
20. Graham, 11.
21. Hart, ('Explications' 1962), 8.
22. Graham, Part II, 9-10.
23. Norris (1976), 46.
24. Glasheen (1977), 207-8.
25. Bayley, Vol. II, 177.
26. For Issy's association with Christmas carols, see Mabel P. Worthington in Senn (1972), 171.
27. Thompson, 4.
28. Kelleher, 13-14.
29. Glasheen (1966), 7.
30. Benstock (1966), 61.

FIVE: 'DREAMER(S)', pp. 91-105

1. Kenner (1956), 265-75; see also Ellmann, 22.
2. Jolas, 159.
3. Heckard, 468-71.
4. Dr Garvin has confirmed this account to me in a letter dated 24 April 1984. The hoax story itself has a similar pedigree: O'Nolan told Niall Montgomery, who told John Kelleher, who mentioned it in a review and sent details to Margaret Heckard, who wrote it up for the *James Joyce Quarterly*.
5. O'Connor, 89.
6. Jolas, 160. This information is confirmed by Peter Costello, who in a letter dated 16 March 1984 reports that according to records one Robert Broadbent was the proprietor from the middle of the century up until 1892.
7. Kenner makes this point in a later study: Kenner (1983), 23-4.
8. See Atherton (1974), 22.
9. Letter from Peter Costello, 16 March 1984.
10. Mink (1978), 453.

11. Ellmann, 696.
12. The following repeats, with many additions, the analysis of these seven stages given in my *James Joyce's Metamorphoses*, pages 162-5.
13. Bury, 274.
14. Joyce (1966), Vol. II, 233.
15. Joyce (1966), Vol. I, 248.
16. Halper (1970), 44.
17. Joyce (1966), Vol. I, 216.
18. Joyce (1975), 326.
19. Ellmann, 581.
20. Ellmann, 588.

SIX: BOOK I, CHAPTER 1, pp. 106-121
1. Rose and O'Hanlon (1982), 307.
2. Glasheen (1966), 9.
3. Eckley (1977), 37.
4. 295.10-12: 'When I'm dreaming back like that I begins to see we're only all telescopes.' Rose and O'Hanlon have traced the 'telescopes' of this sentence to the following passage from Yeats's *A Vision*, noted by Joyce in one of his workbooks: 'If . . . I dream in images . . . I may find him [Yeats's father] represented by a stool or the eyepiece of a telescope.' Rose and O'Hanlon (1979), 42.
5. Joyce (1966), Vol. III, 386.
6. Glasheen (1965), 7.
7. I must here differ with Jacques Aubert, who thinks the echo of Baudelaire in 'Baddelaries' is a red herring: Aubert (1968), 111.
8. See Jacquet, *passim*.
9. For a survey of the French elements in this chapter, see Aubert.
10. O'Connor, 99. In an unpublished 1923 letter to his father on display in the Joyce Museum at Sandycove, Joyce describes his apartment as 'near the Eiffel Tower'.
11. Nat Halper confirms the light atop the Eiffel Tower (Halper (1975), 68) and *Ulysses* 379 gives Howth one red light.
12. See Troy (1976), 33 for a reproduction of the Egyptian funeral scene referred to here.
13. Begnal and Senn, 114.
14. Atherton (1974), 30-1.
15. Graham, et al., Part II, 102.
16. Unsigned interview with John Joyce, Jolas, 160. Peter Costello (letter to the author, 16 March 1984) reports that the backyard of the Mullingar could accommodate a small bowling green.
17. Aubert (1968), 19.
18. Graham *et al*, Part I, 3.
19. Campbell and Robinson (40) point out that Wellington served in India before Waterloo.
20. Graham *et al*., Part I, 3.
21. Hayman (1963), 50.

22. Hayman (1963), 111-12.
23. Adams, 201.
24. Adams, 201.
25. Henseler, 64.
26. Bury, 79.
27. Halper ('Stuttering', 1975), 7.
28. Connolly, 82.
29. Hayman (1963), 58-9.
30. Mink, 514.
31. See, for instance, Gomme, II, 215.
32. Joyce (1975), 322.

SEVEN: BOOK I, CHAPTER 2, pp. 122-128
1. Breon Mitchell, 'Marginalia from Conversations with Joyce', in Hart & Senn, 81.
2. Ellmann, 546-7.
3. Rose (1976), 56.
4. Begnal and Senn, 30.
5. In 'A Structural Theory of *Finnegans Wake* Revisited', (McHugh (1976), 95), Roland McHugh says that the Cad is 'more probably' Sackerson than the Shem-Shaun amalgam he had originally proposed.
6. Bury, 79.
7. Halper ('Nod', 1975), 5.
8. Rose and O'Hanlon point out that Joyce's notes identify one of them, Hosty, with Shaun: Rose and O'Hanlon (1982), 39.
9. Gardner, 21.
10. Glasheen ('Molly', 1967), 56-7.

EIGHT: BOOK I, CHAPTER 3, pp. 129-136
1. Boldereff, 181.
2. Staples (1964), 3.
3. Joyce (1959), 104.
4. Halper ('Bakers', 1967), 13.
5. McHugh ('Semisigns', 1979), 62.
6. Mitchell, 27.
7. McHugh (*Sigla* 1976), 48.
8. Mink (1978), 535.
9. Senn (1960), 8.
10. Campbell and Robinson, 80.

NINE: BOOK I, CHAPTER 4, pp. 137-143
1. Moore, 43.
2. Rose and O'Hanlon (1982), 56.
3. Glasheen ('Secret Language', 1969), 1-2.
4. Joyce (1966), Vol. I, 230.

TEN: BOOK I, CHAPTER 5, pp. 144-150
1. Begnal and Senn, 57.
2. Kopper (1965), 9.
3. Glasheen (1977), 34, 192.
4. Joyce (1959), 234.

ELEVEN: BOOK I, CHAPTER 6, pp. 151-158
1. Hart ('Explications', 1962), 5.
2. Hart ('Explications', 1962), 9.
3. Hart ('Explications, Addenda'), 4.
4. Begnal and Senn, 57.
5. Begnal and Senn, 67.
6. Cowan (1973), 74.
7. Von Phul (1966), 84.
8. McHugh (1976), 18.
9. Von Phul (1966), 85.
10. Bosinelli (1976), 23.

TWELVE: BOOK I, CHAPTER 7, pp. 159-164
1. Knuth ('Riddle', 1972), 80.
2. Knuth ('Riddle', 1972), 82.
3. Hart (*Structure*, 1962), 90-1.
4. Von Phul (1959), 14.
5. Ó hEithir (1977), 160.

THIRTEEN: BOOK I, CHAPTER 8, pp. 165-169
1. Begnal and Eckley, 202.
2. McHugh (1976), 66.
3. Joyce (1966), Vol. II, 232.
4. Ogden, 86.

FOURTEEN: BOOK II, CHAPTER 1, pp. 170-182
1. Rose and O'Hanlon ('Constructing', 1980), 8-11.
2. Joyce (1966), Vol. I, 295.
3. See Matthew Hodgart in Begnal and Senn, 85.
4. Glasheen (*Third Census* 1963), xlviii.
5. McCarthy, 122; Armstrong, 56.
6. P. W. Joyce, 244.
7. Joyce (1965), 295.
8. Hylton, 615.
9. Senn ('Klitty', 1962), 2-7.
10. Rose and O'Hanlon (*Understanding Finnegans Wake*, 138) render 240.08-9 as 'No more will he sit on a stool all day with a tome of Aquinas covering the lump between his thighs', a picture which takes us back to the Waterloo scene of I/1.

11. Campbell and Robinson, 152.
12. Mercanton (1968), 40.
13. Rose and O'Hanlon (*Understanding Finnegans Wake*, 142) take 'Twice is he gone to quest of her, thrice is she now to him', seventeen lines down the page (250.27-8), as indicating that these three questions are spoken by the girls rather than by Glugg, and that Glugg's third 'quest' occurs later, unrecorded, during 'a gap in the story'. I would argue that the passage in question is Glugg's third series of three questions but only his second 'quest', since the drama of exile-and-return-in-quest-of-Issy does not begin until after the first series of guesses at 225.22-7. See also Solomon, 23 and McCarthy, 148.

FIFTEEN: BOOK II, CHAPTER 2, pp. 183-193
 1. Solomon, 105.
 2. Knuth ('Bathymetric', 1972), *passim*.
 3. Campbell and Robinson, 184.
 4. Brivic (1983), 11, 27; *see also* Shari Benstock in Henke and Unkeless, 194.
 5. Joyce (1975), 181.
 6. Brivic, 17.
 7. Thompson, 4.
 8. See Hart (*Structure*), 248-9, Rose and O'Hanlon (1982), 161-2.

SIXTEEN: BOOK II, CHAPTER 3, pp. 194-213
 1. Solomon, 34.
 2. Ellmann, 23.
 3. Glasheen (1977), 211.
 4. Ellmann, 398.
 5. Ellmann, 398.
 6. Luigi Schenoni points out as well that 'Taff' is Amara for 'buttocks': Schenoni (1976), 36.
 7. Hayman ('Dramatic', 1958), 169, 172.
 8. David Hayman (Hayman, 'Dramatic Motion', 1958) gives a detailed reading of this line.
 9. Campbell and Robinson, 233.
10. McHugh (1970), *passim*.
11. Ó hEithir (1977), 598.
12. Rose and O'Hanlon, ('Finn Maccool', 1980), *passim*.
13. Senn (1960), 19.

SEVENTEEN: BOOK II, CHAPTER 4, pp. 214-219
 1. Cowan (1971), 21.
 2. McHugh (*Sigla* 1976), 104.
 3. Joyce (1966), Vol. I, 205. Peter Costello believes this to be Edmund

Curtis, author of *The History of Ireland*, whose wife ran off with Liam O'Flaherty.
4. MacArthur (1977), 4.
5. Gordon (1981), 170-6.
6. Hayman (1963), 212.

EIGHTEEN: BOOK III, CHAPTER 1, pp. 220-226
1. Bushrai and Benstock (1982), 98. Compare *Ulysses* 496, where Bloom grows 'asses' ears' when degraded and pilloried.
2. For other pertinent discussion of the ass's identity, see Von Phul (1957), *passim* and Hart (*Structure*, 1962), 80.
3. Dalton (1963), 5.
4. Campbell and Robinson, 258.
5. Joyce (1966), Vol. II, 51.
6. Higginson, 454.
7. Gordon (1981), 7.
8. Scarry, 161.

NINETEEN: BOOK III, CHAPTER 2, pp. 227-235
1. Mink (1978), 376-7, 499-500.
2. Mink (1978), 274.
3. According to McHugh's *Annotations*, 'The valiantine vaux of Venerable Val Vousdem' (439.17-8) splices the name of a novel about a ventriloquist with the name of a music hall entertainer.
4. Tindall, 242.
5. Stuart Gilbert in Beckett, *et al.*, 68.
6. Joyce (1975), 334.
7. Gilbert in Beckett, 72.
8. Mrs Glasheen suggests (Glasheen, 'Hoang Ho', 1975) that 457.07-8 may contain an allusion to the Hoang Ho, the Chinese river famous for its disastrous floods; compare 627.31.
9. Epstein, 155.
10. Edward A. Kopper Jr. has shown that 'Dave' is in part the patron saint of Wales, thus a typical Welshman: Kopper (1969), 42.
11. Joyce (1966), Vol. I, 263-4.

TWENTY: BOOK III, CHAPTER 3, pp. 236-253
1. Rose and O'Hanlon (1982), 243.
2. Joyce (1966), Vol. I, 214.
3. Solomon, 74.
4. See Rose (1982), *passim*.
5. Also discussed in *James Joyce's Metamorphoses*: Gordon (1981), 9-10.
6. Glasheen (1977), 182.
7. Ellmann, 92.

8. Hugh B. Staples in Begnal and Senn, 189.
9. Bury, 504.
10. Atherton (1971), 9.
11. Rose and O'Hanlon (1982), 259.
12. Joyce (1959), 203.
13. Knuth (1971), 58.

TWENTY-ONE: BOOK III, CHAPTER 4, pp. 254-262
1. Benstock (1965), 81.
2. Mink (1968), 469; Hart (*Structure*, 1962), 72.

TWENTY-TWO: BOOK IV, pp. 263-278
1. Hart (*Structure*, 1962), 73.
2. Ellmann, 593, 642.
3. Knuth (1975), 104.
4. McHugh (1976), 107.
5. Rose and O'Hanlon (1982), 295.
6. I do not understand the reason for Clive Hart's assertion that 'the donkey and Shaun are merged' in this passage: Hart (*Structure*, 1962), 135.
7. Glasheen (1977), lxviii.
8. Rose and O'Hanlon (1982), 302.
9. Evans, 6.
10. Dalton, in Dalton and Hart, 109-37.
11. Evans, 6.
12. Rose and O'Hanlon (1982), 300.
13. Kelleher, 15; Mink (1978), 382.
14. McHugh (1976), 110.
15. *A Midsummer Night's Dream*, III.ii.391-3:
     Even till the eastern gate, all fiery red
     Opening on Neptune with fair blessed beams
     Turns into yellow gold his salt green streams.
16. Connolly, 101.
17. Knuth (1975), 104.
18. McHugh (1976), 106.
19. Lecky, Vol. II, 55. Lecky quotes a verse from this hymn which recalls ALP's 'Carry me along, taddy': '*Allu Mari mi portati/Se voleti che mi sanati*'.
20. Mercanton (1967), 30.
21. Knuth (1975), 103.
22. Joyce, Stanislaus, 6-7.
23. Knuth (1975), 103 notes these words and attributes them to ALP. They will shortly be picked up by the 'mishe mishe' of 3.09, as the 'thou . . . thee' in 'thousendsthee' will be repeated as 'tauftauf'.
24. Ellmann, 566.

Bibliography

Adams, Robert, *Common Sense and Beyond*, New York 1967

Armstrong, Alison, 'Shem the Penman as Glugg as the Wolf-Man', *A Wake Newslitter* X/4 (August 1973), 51-7.

Atherton, J. S., *The Books at the Wake*, New York 1974

Atherton, J. S., 'Lodge's The Survival of Man in *FW*', *A Wake Newslitter* VIII/1 (February 1971), 8-10

Aubert, Jacques, 'Notes on the French Element in *Finnegans Wake*', *James Joyce Quarterly* V/1 (Winter 1968), 110-24

Bayley, Harold, *The Lost Language of Symbolism*, London 1951

Beckett, Samuel, *Our Exagmination Round His Factification For Incamination of Work in Progress*, New York 1972

Beerbohm, Max, *Zuleika Dobson*, New York 1966

Begnal, Michael H. and Grace Eckley, *Narrator and Character in Finnegans Wake*, London 1975

Begnal, Michael H. and Fritz Senn, *A Conceptual Guide to Finnegans Wake*, London 1974

Benstock, Bernard, 'Every Telling Has a Taling: A reading of the Narrative of *Finnegans Wake*', *Modern Fiction Studies* XV (Spring 1969), 3-25

Benstock, Bernard, *Joyce-Again's Wake*, Seattle 1965

Benstock, Bernard, 'Lucia', *A Wake Newslitter*, III/3 (1966), 61

Benstock, Bernard, *The Seventh of Joyce*, Bloomington 1982

Boldereff, Frances M., *Reading Finnegans Wake*, Woodward, Pennsylvania, 1959

Bosinelli, Rosa Maria, 'The Relevance of Italian in *FW* with Reference to I/1-8', *A Wake Newslitter* XIII/2 (April 1976), 19-32

Brivic, Sheldon, 'The Mind Factory: Kabbalah in *Finnegans Wake*', *James Joyce Quarterly* XXI/1 (Fall 1983), 7-30

Budgen, Frank, *James Joyce and the Making of Ulysses*, Bloomington and London 1967

Burrell, Harry, 'The Illustrator in the *Wake*: Aubrey Beardsley', *A Wake Newslitter* XVII/6 (December 1980), 95-8

Bushrai, Suheil Badi and Bernard Benstock, eds., *James Joyce: An International Perspective*, Gerards Cross, England, 1982

Bury, John B., *The Life of St. Patrick*, London 1905

Campbell, Joseph and Henry Morton Robinson, *A Skeleton Key to Finnegans Wake*, New York 1964

Cheng, Vincent John, *Shakespeare and Joyce: A Study of Finnegans Wake*, London 1984

Christiani, Dounia Bunis, *Scandinavian Elements of Finnegans Wake*, Evanston 1965

Cohn, Dorrit, *Transparent Minds*, Princeton 1978

Connolly, Thomas E., *Scribbledehobble: The Ur-Workbook for Finnegans Wake*, Evanston 1961

Cowan, Thomas A., 'Jeff Earwicker', *A Wake Newslitter* X/5 (October 1973), 69-75

Cowan, Thomas A., 'What Shall I Call A Research Project On the Four Evangelists', *A Wake Newslitter* VIII/2 (April 1971), 19-24

Dalton, Jack, 'Re Article by Thornton Wilder (Litter No. 6)', *A Wake Newslitter* No. 10 (February 1963), 4-6

Dalton, Jack and Clive Hart, *Twelve and a Tilly: Essays on the Occasion of the 25th Anniversary of Finnegans Wake*, London 1966

Devlin, Kimberly, 'Self and Other in *Finnegans Wake*: A Framework for Analyzing Versions of Shem and Shaun', *James Joyce Quarterly* XXI/1 (Fall 1983), 31-50

Eckley, Grace, 'Between Peas Like Ourselves: The Folklore of the Prankquean', *James Joyce Quarterly* IX/2 (Winter 1971), 177-88

Eckley, Grace, 'The Wellington Career in *Finnegans Wake*', *Éire* XII/3 (1977), 23-40

Ellmann, Richard, *James Joyce*, New York 1982

Epstein, E. L., *A Starchamber Quiry*, New York 1982

Evans, Simon, 'The Ultimate Ysland of Yreland', *A Wake Newslitter, Occasional Paper No. 2*, 6

Gardner, Helen, *The Composition of the Four Quartets*, New York 1978

Glasheen, Adaline, '*Finnegans Wake* and the Secret Languages of Ireland', *A Wake Newslitter* No. 10 (February 1963), 1-3

Glasheen, Adaline, 'Hoang Ho', *A Wake Newslitter* II/5 (October 1975), 94

Glasheen, Adaline, 'Molly and FW', *A Wake Newslitter* IV/2 (April 1967), 56-7

Glasheen, Adaline, 'The Opening Paragraphs (concluded)', *A Wake Newslitter*, III/1 (February 1966), 6-14

Glasheen, Adaline, 'The Opening Paragraphs, Contd.', *A Wake Newslitter* II/6 (1965), 17-22

Glasheen, Adaline, *A Third Census of Finnegans Wake*, Berkeley 1977

'G.O.M.', review of Ioannes Swicker, *Fontes Historiae Religionis Celticae* in *Béaloideas* VII/1 (1937), 143-4

Gomme, Alice, *The Traditional Games of England, Scotland, and Ireland*, New York 1964

Gordon, John, *James Joyce's Metamorphoses*, Dublin 1981

Gordon, John, *Notes on Issy*, Colchester, 1982

Gordon, John, 'The Secret of Boylan's Bottom Drawer', *James Joyce Quarterly* XVIII/4 (Summer 1981), 450-8.

Graham, Philip L., Philip B. Sullivan, and G. F. Richter, 'Mind Your

Hats Goan In!: Notes on the Museyroom Episode of *Finnegans Wake*', *Analyst* XXI (July 1962), 1-21

Halper, Nathan, 'The Bakers and Butchers', *A Wake Newslitter* IV/1 (February 1967), 13-14

Halper, Nathan, 'Baubletop and Burning Bush (5.02)', *A Wake Newslitter* II/4 (August 1975), 68-70

Halper, Nathan, 'A Kidscad', *A Wake Newslitter* VII/3 (June 1970), 43-6

Halper, Nathan, 'Leap Year', *A Wake Newslitter* XII/3 (1975), 273-80

Halper, Nathan, 'Of the Stuttering Hand', *A Wake Newslitter* XI/6 (December 1974), 7-9

Halper, Nathan, 'A Nod to Hemingway', *A Wake Newslitter* XII/1 (February 1975), 5

Halper, Nathan, *Studies in Joyce*, Ann Arbor 1983

Hart, Clive, 'Explications — FGCC: Addendum (No. 3)', *A Wake Newslitter* No. 5 (September 1962), 4-9

Hart, Clive, 'Explications — for the greeter glossary of code', *A Wake Newslitter* No. 1 (March 1962), 3-10

Hart, Clive, 'explications — for the greeter glossary of code, Addenda to No. 1', *A Wake Newslitter*, No. 2 (April 1962), 1-5

Hart, Clive, *Structure and Motif in Finnegans Wake*, London 1962

Hart, Clive and Fritz Senn, *A Wake Digest*, Sydney 1968

Hayman, David, 'Dramatic Motion in *Finnegans Wake*', *Texas Studies in English* XXXVIII (1958), 155-76

Hayman, David, *A First-Draft Version of Finnegans Wake*, Austin 1963

Hayman, David, *James Joyce: Finnegans Wake: A Facsimile of Buffalo Notebooks VI B.9 — VI B.12*, London 1978

Heckard, Margaret, 'The Literary Reverberations of a Fake Interview with John Stanislaus Joyce', *James Joyce Quarterly* XIII/4 (Summer 1976), 468-71

Henke, Suzette and Elaine Unkeless, *Women in Joyce*, London 1982

Henseler, Donna, '"Harpsdichord", The Formal Principle of HCE, ALP, and the Cad', *James Joyce Quarterly* VI (Fall 1968), 53-68

Herring, Philip, *Joyce's Notes and Early Drafts for Ulysses: Selections from the Buffalo Collection*, Charlottesville 1977

Higginson, Fred, 'Notes on the Text of *Finnegans Wake*', *Journal of English and Germanic Philology* LV (July 1956), 451-6

Hylton, William H., ed., *The Rodale Herb Book*, Emmaus, Pa. 1974

Jacquet, Claude, *Joyce et Rabelais: aspects de la création verbale dans Finnegans Wake*, Paris 1972

Jarrell, Mackie, 'Swiftiana in *FW*', *ELH* 26, II (June 1959), 271-94

Jolas, Maria, *A James Joyce Yearbook*, Paris 1949

Joyce, James, *The Critical Writings of James Joyce*, ed. Ellsworth Mason and Richard Ellmann, New York 1959

Joyce, James, *Dubliners*, New York 1967

Joyce, James, *Letters of James Joyce*, vol. I, ed. Stuart Gilbert, New York 1965

Joyce, James, *Letters of James Joyce*, vols II and III, ed. Richard Ellmann, New York 1966

Joyce, James, *A Portrait of the Artist as a Young Man*, New York 1968

Joyce, James, *Selected Letters*, ed. Richard Ellmann, New York 1975

Joyce, James, *Stephen Hero*, New York 1963

Joyce, James, *Ulysses*, New York 1961

Joyce, Stanislaus, *My Brother's Keeper*, London 1958

Joyce, P. W., *English as We Speak It In Ireland*, Dublin 1912

Kelleher, John, 'Notes on *Finnegans Wake*', *Analyst* XII (April 1957), 9-15

Kenner, Hugh, *Dublin's Joyce*, Boston 1956

Kenner, Hugh, *A Colder Eye*, New York 1983

Knuth, Leo, 'A Bathymetric Reading of Joyce's *Ulysses*, Chapter X', *James Joyce Quarterly* IX/4 (Summer 1972), 405-22

Knuth, Leo, 'The Last Leaf', *A Wake Newslitter* XII/6 (December, 1975), 103-7

Knuth, Leo, 'More Dutch in *Finnegans Wake*', *A Wake Newslitter* VIII/4 (August 1971), 54-62

Knuth, Leo, 'Shem's Riddle of the Universe', *A Wake Newslitter* IX/5 (October 1972), 78-9

Kopper, Edward A., Jr., 'Saint Olaf in *Finnegans Wake*', *A Wake Newslitter*, VI/3 (June 1969), 35-9

Kopper, Edward A., Jr., 'Some Additional Christian Allusions in the *Wake*', *Analyst* No. 24 (March 1965), 5-22

The Larousse Encyclopedia of Animal Life, New York 1967

Lecky, William E. H., *A History of European Morals From Constantine to Charlemagne*, New York 1919

MacArthur, Ian, 'A Note on the Horse', *A Wake Newslitter* XIV/3 (June 1977), 44

MacArthur, Ian, 'The Self Archetype' in *FW*, *A Wake Newslitter* XIV/1 (February 1977), 3-5

McCarthy, Patrick A., *The Riddles of Finnegans Wake*, London 1981

McHugh, Roland, *Annotations to Finnegans Wake*, London 1980

McHugh, Roland, *The Finnegans Wake Experience*, Berkeley 1981

McHugh, Roland, 'The Pelagian Heresy', *A Wake Newslitter* VII/2 (April 1970), 28-9

McHugh, Roland, 'Semisigns of His Zooteach' (IV), *A Wake Newslitter* XVI/4 (August 1979), 62

McHugh, Roland, *The Sigla of Finnegans Wake*, Austin 1976

McHugh, Roland, 'A Structural Theory of *Finnegans Wake*', *A Wake Newslitter* V/6 (December 1968), 83-7

Mercanton, Jacques, 'L'Esthétique de Joyce', *Études de lettres* XIII (October 1968), 20-46

Mercanton, Jacques, *Les Heures de James Joyce*, Lausanne 1967

Mink, Louis O., *A Finnegans Wake Gazetteer*, London 1978

Mink, Louis O., 'Woeful Dane Bottom', *A Wake Newslitter* XVII/2 (April 1980), 27

Mitchell, Breon, 'On the Verge of the Gutter: More French Slang in the *Wake*', *A Wake Newslitter* VI/1 (February 1969), 27-9

Moore, Thomas, *Moore's Irish Melodies*, Cork 1972

Norris, Margot, *The Decentered Universe of Finnegans Wake*, Baltimore 1976

Nutt, Alfred, '*Cinderella* and Britain', *Folklore* IV, 133-41

O'Connor, Ulick, *The Joyce We Knew*, Cork 1967

Ogden, C. K., 'Notes in Basic English on the *Anna Livia Plurabelle* Record', *Psyche* XII (April 1932), 86-95

Ó hEithir, Breandán and John M. Dillon, *A Classical Lexicon For Finnegans Wake*, Berkeley 1977

Ó hEithir, Breandán, *A Gaelic Lexicon for Finnegans Wake and Glossary for Joyce's Other Works*, Berkeley 1967

Ó Laoi, Pádraic, *Nora Barnacle Joyce: A Portrait*, Galway 1982

Peterson, Richard F., Alan M. Cohn, and Edmund L. Epstein, *Work in Progress: Joyce Centenary Essays*, Carbondale 1982

Power, Arthur, *Conversations with James Joyce*, Chicago 1974

Rose, Danis, *Chapters of Coming Forth by Day*, Colchester, England 1982

Rose, Danis, 'His Occupational Agomen', *A Wake Newslitter* XIII/3 (June 1976), 56

Rose, Danis and John O'Hanlon, 'Constructing *Finnegans Wake:* Three Indexes', *A Wake Newslitter* XVII/1 (February 1980), 3-15

Rose, Danis and John O'Hanlon, 'Finn Maccool and the Final Weeks of Work in Progress', *A Wake Newslitter*, XVII/5 (October 1980), 69-87

Rose, Danis and John O'Hanlon, 'Specific Use of Yeats' *A Vision* in *Finnegans Wake*', *A Wake Newsletter* XVI/3 (June 1979), 35-44

Rose, Danis and John O'Hanlon, *Understanding Finnegans Wake*, New York 1982

Scarry, John, '*Finnegans Wake* III.i: A Portrait of John McCormack', *Irish University Review* III/2 (Autumn 1973), 155-62

Schenoni, Luigi, 'Further Notes on Amaro in *FW*', *A Wake Newslitter* XIII/2 (April 1976), 32-6

Senn, Fritz, 'Every Klitty of a Scolderymeid: Sexual-Political Analogies', *A Wake Newslitter*, No. 3 (June 1962), 1-7

Senn, Fritz, 'His Pillowscone Sharpened', *A Wake Newslitter* IX/6 (December 1972), 109-10

Senn, Fritz, ed., *New Light on Joyce*, Bloomington 1972

Senn, Fritz, 'Queries', *A Wake Newslitter* III/2 (April 1966), 47

Senn, Fritz, 'Some Zurich Allusions in *Finnegans Wake*', *Analyst* IX (1960), 1-23

Solomon, Margaret, *Eternal Geomater: The Sexual Universe of Finnegans Wake*, London 1969

Staples, Hugh B., 'Some Notes on the One Hundred and Eleven Epithets of HCE', *A Wake Newslitter* I/6 (December 1964), 3-6

Suter, August, 'Some Reminiscences of James Joyce', *James Joyce Quarterly*, VII/3 (Summer 1970), 191-8

Thompson, Diane and Paul, 'A Geometry Problem in *Finnegans Wake*', *Analyst* XII (1961), 2-4

Tindall, William York, *A Reader's Guide to Finnegans Wake*, New York 1969

Troy, Mark L., *Mummeries of Resurrection*, Uppsala 1976

Unsigned, translator of 'The Festivities at the House of Conan of Ceanne-Sleibhe', *Transactions of the Ossianic Society for the Year 1854*, New York 1972, Vol. II, 7

Von Phul, Ruth, 'Five Explications', *A Wake Newslitter* III/4 (August 1966), 84-5

Von Phul, Ruth, 'Who Sleeps at *Finnegans Wake*', *James Joyce Review* I/2 (February 1957), 27-38

Yates, Frances, *Giordano Bruno and the Hermetic Tradition*, Chicago 1964

Index